Make It Morning

Jodi Bainter

First published by Dog Ear Publishing
4010 W. 86th Street, Ste H
Indianapolis, IN 46268
www.dogearpublishing.net

dog ear
PUBLISHING

ISBN: 978-1-4575-1497-5

This book is printed on acid-free paper.

Printed in the United States of America

In Loving Memory of
Ronald J. Bainter, 1938 – 2011

In 2009, Pop was diagnosed with terminal brain cancer.
He lost his battle with cancer in August of 2011.

Pop, you were Jake's light...
And your spirit shines on in him.

We miss you every day.

Acknowledgements:

We are endlessly grateful for the love, prayers, tears, wisdom and never ending support our family offered us during those difficult years. Thank you Mom and Mike, Dad, Grammie, Todd and Sandy, Matt, Stephanie, Corey and Tammy. There is no way we would have survived this journey without you by our side. To Jake's sweet cousins, Gage, Luke, Katie and Colin thank you for loving Jake during his most difficult days. We love you dearly.

To our loyal and faithful friends and those we met along the way, thank you for offering us a safe place to cry, a safe place to reconcile our circumstances, and a safe place to heal. Our time on earth is fleeting and you reminded us of the generosity of the human spirit. We are forever grateful.

To Brett: I am so happy you chose me to share this life.
We are blessed to reach this place.
I love you, always.

Authors Note:

In order to maintain authenticity, journal entries have not been edited for grammar or punctuation.

CHAPTER 1

April 9, 2004

I try to remember Thursday, April 8th. What did we have for dinner that night? Did I kiss Jacob before he went to sleep? Did God know what Friday would hold for our family? I try to remember what it was like to see Jacob run up the stairs on his own two feet, his sweet baby face smiling. I wonder what I thought were burdens before the events of April 9, 2004.

I went through the days before the accident over and over in my head, trying to piece together the memories of that week. Nothing, I just cannot remember. You see, you can't go back. Life can change in a blink of an eye, that quickly. In a single moment of the unexplainable, the unbelievable, the unimaginable, everything can change.

I wonder if I was paying attention. Did Brett and I appreciate all the blessings our life together had given us? These are the questions you ask yourself. You can't help but to ask. When crisis strikes these questions race through your head, you have to seek answers, but most of all you have to learn from them. This is why I share our story.

It is interesting, because I do remember Friday morning. It was Friday, April 9th, and when I left for work that day Brett and Jacob, who was three at the time, were outside. Jacob was riding his bike up and down the driveway. He got his new green bike for Christmas, and although it still had training wheels he prided himself on speed. It would take everything he had in his little body to race up and down the driveway, all the while smiling from ear to ear. Brett works from home, so he would often be moving boxes and merchandise in the garage, which is what he was doing on this particular morning.

They were waiting for Jennifer Lief, our nanny, to arrive. Jennifer watched Jacob after preschool three days a week and on Fridays she watched him all day. I kissed Brett and Jacob goodbye, as I do every morning, and waved as I backed out of the driveway. Our morning ritual was the same one we had done hundreds of times. There was no reason to think that day would be any different. There was no reason for me to pause and savor the moment of watching Jake ride his bike. No reason to squeeze Brett extra-tight. My only focus was to get out the door and be on my way to work.

Jennifer arrived around 9:30 a.m. She and Jacob headed over to a friend's house for a play date. I will admit to being a little nervous whenever Jennifer and Jacob had plans to go somewhere other than our house. There is no doubt that Brett and I trusted Jennifer implicitly, however a mom's concern is always present—all the more so when your child is in the care of another. You see, for the three short years Jacob had been on this earth, he had spent many days with the nanny. Brett and I both worked full time and had no choice but to entrust him to the care of another. To be honest, probably one of my biggest fears was that somehow Jacob would be hurt or injured when out of my sight. The irony is who would have ever imagined the accident I feared would happen in our own backyard? I often had the conversation with my mother that no matter whose watchful eye your child is under—yours or another's—accidents can happen in an instant. You cannot shelter your children; you have to allow them to live, explore life, and not fear the unexpected. So, having thought this many times over the years, you can imagine the wave of emotions that flooded over me when I learned of the accident.

Brett was working in his office, a normal workday. Jennifer and Jacob returned from their play date around 1:30 in the afternoon. As they pulled into the driveway, they could see our neighbors Jessica and Hayleigh playing in their front yard. We had lived next to the Blair family for eight years. Our children had grown up together, and they bounced back and forth between homes as if they had dual residency. Jacob played with the Blair girls every day. So, of course, on this Friday they decided to play outside a little while longer. Why not? It was a beautiful spring afternoon. It was Good Friday, and there was a buzz in the air in preparation for the holiday weekend.

Jacob and the girls spent most of the rest of the afternoon riding their bikes. In between bike riding; they ran back and forth between the two yards, laughing and having a carefree afternoon. Jennifer joined the girls' mother, Crystal, and both sat on the front porch watching the children play. After a while, Crystal and her husband, Rob, went to their backyard to work on some yard projects. The girls joined them, so Jennifer and Jacob retreated to our house. Jake decided to bike a little longer, so Jen found a chair in the driveway and watched Jake as he raced up and down. His energy was boundless.

As Brett and I tried to retrace the events of that day, he told me that the thought had run through his mind to hold off on mowing the lawn. The kids were playing, and he was in no hurry. But then he would think, "It's a holiday weekend; if I can have the lawn mowed when Jodi gets home from work, we can enjoy the evening and weekend." So, even though his intuition had nudged him to stop, he brushed it aside, as many of us do, and he pressed on. For no other reason than to get his chores done so he could spend quality time with us.

The day had been pretty quiet in my world. In fact, the office was almost empty; most of my co-workers were off that day or had left early for the holiday weekend. Things were slow; with the exception of a short lunch break, I had spent most of the day working at my desk. The time was really a blur to me until I actually saw the time of the call to 911 documented on a medical bill.

I would later learn that Jennifer made the call at 15:20:16. I am not sure what time I received the call at my office, but I believe it was sometime before 4 p.m. A co-worker and I were standing in my office when one of our secretaries popped her head in to tell me Brett was on the phone and that it was an emergency.

When I lifted the receiver, the first thing I could hear was sirens ringing loudly in the background. I could also hear a lot of commotion and voices. Brett was breathing hard, it sounded like his mouth was directly against my ear. He could barely catch his breath. "Brett, what is going on?" I kept saying. "Brett, what has happened?" Finally, he said, "Honey, I have hurt him really bad, I have done the worst thing possible. Honey … Honey … Honey, oh God, I have hurt him so bad." I kept asking him what happened, and he just kept repeating the same thing over and over. Finally, during a conversation that seemed like hours but was probably less than five minutes, he said, "Jodi, I ran over Jake with the riding lawn mower." I think I kept saying, "No, Brett, tell me you didn't, please tell me you didn't." I was staring out the window of my fourth-floor office watching people walk in and out as they always do. My world was being rocked, the floor felt like it was being ripped out from under me, and people just kept sauntering in and out. He then said, "Honey, I have to go, just come, please come quickly." He hung up.

My heart was racing; I could feel the blood pumping through my veins. I was shaking and could not collect my thoughts. Everything was spinning. I am now told that I was shouting, over and over,

"Where is my purse?" and "I have to go," and "Oh, my God." I remember moving my feet quickly as if to release some of the anxiety. My hands were visibly shaking, when it occurred to me, go where? Where was Jacob? "Ran over," what does that mean, exactly? How badly was he hurt? I knew none of this. I knew only that my precious little boy was hurt so badly as to require an ambulance. Subconsciously, I didn't need details to confirm; "I'd heard it in the sheer terror of my husband's voice."

I collected my thoughts for a moment and called home. The phone just rang and rang until the answering machine picked up the call. I hung up and called our neighbor. Rob answered the phone. I asked him what was happening. He told me that the ambulance had just left with Jacob. He said Jacob was doing OK; he was losing a lot of blood but had not slipped into shock. He was completely coherent. I was numb. My precious son and husband were experiencing the most terrifying moment of our lives, and all I could do was stand there. I just stood there staring out the window, watching the footsteps of other people. Everything was in slow motion. This was impossible. Did I just receive that call from Brett? Is this really happening?

As Rob and I were talking, I could hear Brett wailing in the background. I asked to speak to him, but he would not come to the phone. I think at this point Rob had handed the phone to Crystal, his wife and my dear friend. "Crystal," I said, "please tell Brett I love him." I was gasping for breath. "Tell him this was not his fault, tell him I love him." I was begging her to make sure he knew how much I loved him. My heart was being ripped out of my chest. I was so far away, and they needed me so much. Crystal told me another ambulance had just arrived to take Brett to the hospital.

Later I would learn that a lawn mower blade rotates at 200 miles per hour. The idea of this blade making contact with our son's body is really unimaginable.

Something changed in Brett that day as a result of the trauma. When I told Crystal I had to understand what went on after the accident and to put the pieces together for me, she decided the best way would be to make a tape recording. She talked me through the whole afternoon.

At the end of the tape, she stops the recording. Then after a pause, the message begins again. "I have shared all I remember about that day," she says, "but there is one thing I have never told you. It is the memory that keeps me up at night and will probably never leave my soul. Because I watched your husband experience something no father should ever experience."

4

She went on to say that once the ambulance drove away with Jacob, Brett fell to his knees. He just dropped to the ground, his head in his hand. In his agony, he began vomiting. He was crumpled in a pile in the front yard, retching and crying.

By the time Crystal approached him; he had gotten up and walked to the front porch. He was leaning against the front porch, staring straight ahead. He couldn't even respond to her presence. His eyes had glazed over. I can only guess that is the beauty of the human brain, It had rushed to his protection, and in its wave of restoration it left a six-foot shell, completely absent, numb, and disconnected. On that day, we lost something beyond the physical injuries to Jake: Brett lost a piece of his spirit.

The sheer horror of the event, I am convinced, had penetrated Brett's soul. All logic was suspended; his emotions and heart were shattered. I was fortunate, in not being there that afternoon, not hearing the screams or the silence that followed. I will admit I have re-created the image in my mind, and it haunts me. Before Crystal and I hung up the phone that day, she told me to go to Orlando Regional Medical Center (ORMC). She and Rob and the girls were on their way, she said, and they would take care of Brett and Jake until I could get there.

******

As I pieced together later from Brett and Crystal's account, Jacob had been riding his bike up and down the driveway; it was about 3:10 p.m. Brett passed the driveway heading toward the side of the garage on the riding lawn mower. He waved to Jacob as he passed; they did a thumbs up like buddies, Jacob on his bike, Brett on the lawn mower. Jennifer, was sitting at the front of the garage. Minutes earlier, she and Jacob had been searching the yard for bugs and other critters. Suddenly, Jacob hopped off his bike and ran to the side of the garage. Just as Jennifer stood up to see where he was sneaking off to, she heard the screams and she heard the impact, the sound of the lawn mower hitting an object.

At the exact moment that Jacob ran up behind the lawn mower, Brett had shifted into reverse. He looked over his shoulder, but Jacob was too small to see. Later, after talking to him in the hospital, we would learn that he had wanted to tell Brett something. This thought would haunt Brett and me for a long time. The image of Jacob running up behind the lawn mower, hoping to get Brett's attention over the sound of the lawn mower—the innocence of his inability to understand the potential danger—is more than we can bear. We can

5

only imagine his fear as the lawn mower reversed and he knew he could not escape.

Brett said when he felt the impact, his heart sank. He could not fathom what he had struck. He thought it was maybe the house, maybe a stick, but what could it be? Was there something he over-looked?

When he turned around, he could see Jacob's blond hair sticking out from under the lawn mower. He could see that our son was trapped. He could hear the lawn mower continuing to rage, its noise loud. Brett's instinctive response was to jump from the mower. When he did, the mower's engine stopped. Jacob was too far under the mower to be pulled out. With the strength of an army, Brett reached under the mower cover and tilted the mower on its side.

He told me through his tears that he scooped Jacob into his arms and began running. The blades had struck Jake's right leg and foot. The power at which those blades rotate makes it hard to believe that his leg wasn't severed. As Brett lifted Jacob, Jennifer rounded the corner. She took one look, turned around, and ran into the house to call 911.

Brett's screams began to echo through the neighborhood. He was screaming "Crystal".... "Crystal"....Crystal and Rob were working in their backyard when they heard the screams. Crystal later told me that when she heard Brett's screams she knew something awful had happened. We are thankful for all the years of training Crystal had received in her medical career. That day, her skills, quick thinking, and love for our family, I think, saved our son. Crystal and Rob took off running. From Brett's screams, they thought he was in the back-yard, so they jumped the chain link fence that divides our two yards. They continued to run in the direction where his screams were orig-inating. As they rounded the corner, Brett had already run to the front yard. He turned to face Crystal. Sheer terror in his eyes, our son in his arms, bleeding, Brett gently placed him in Crystal's arms. He handed over his son knowing Crystal was capable. Knowing at that moment he needed help, he needed someone who could take the lead. He had just pulled his son from the blades of a riding lawn mower, having had the sound mind to lift the lawn mower and carry him to safety.

Crystal ran to her house with Jacob in her arms. They tell me he was not screaming; he was crying softly, trying to catch his breath. Crystal cradled Jacob in her lap on the floor of her kitchen. The time was passing quickly, but I am sure to Crystal it seemed like hours. Jen-nifer had followed Crystal to the kitchen, having already called 911.

Crystal sent Jennifer for towels and scissors. She wrapped Jacob's leg and foot in a towel, wrapping them tightly to control the bleeding. She used the scissors to cut off Jacob's shorts; it was then that she lowered him to the towel to visually access the injury. The blade had cut through his upper thigh, through muscle, tissue, bone, having no mercy on his little leg. His toes were gone; bone and tissue were showing.

******

After the frantic call from Brett and the follow-up call to Crystal, I stood in my office. Co-workers began to gather outside my door. Apparently they heard my screams and came down to see what was happening. They stood there, faces filled with shock and horror; their minds, I am sure, were racing, wondering what to say. At that time they didn't know what had happened. They knew only that I had received an emergency call from Brett and that the situation, whatever it was, was bad.

Trisha Warne, my leader at the time, walked through the crowd and stood in front of me. She asked me what was going on. I couldn't cry, I could hardly speak, and I felt completely numb. I told her what Brett had told me. I remember her face distinctly: wide-eyed, jaw dropped, pure shock. I still had no idea of the extent of Jacob's injuries. All I knew was that he was hurt badly. I needed to get to the hospital. Trisha helped me gather my things; she gave me a reassuring hug reminding me to be brave and, walked me to the door.

After a few minutes, I think everyone was talking and I was standing there. I couldn't even hear what they were saying. It was decided that I was in no condition to drive and that my friend Michael Black would drive me to the hospital. Michael was a colleague who doesn't even work in our building. He happened to be there that day attending a meeting. He was on his way out but had walked by our area of the floor to say hello when he saw the commotion around my office. His keys were in his hand, and he was on his way out the door to go downtown. He immediately volunteered to take me. I followed him down the hall, out the elevator, and to the car. I don't think I said much. My mind and heart were racing. The fear of the unknown was tugging at my being.

Michael began driving; it was about a 15 to 20-minute drive on a good day, and this was 4 p.m. on Good Friday. The traffic was horrendous on Interstate 4, which was the only logical route to travel. Michael focused on the road, silently offering me support. I focused on what to do.

I began making phone calls. The first was to my in-laws. As I dialed their number waiting for an answer, I could feel my heart in my throat. I was so thirsty. I wanted something to drink so badly. I could feel my body sweating. The palms of my hands were so wet; I had trouble dialing the number. I heard my father-in-law's voice, and the tears started to roll down my cheeks. I said to him "R.B., there has been an accident … its Jacob." He groaned, "Oh God, what's happened?" I heard Grammie pick up the other phone. I now had them both on the line. How do I tell them? The pain was unbearable. I asked them to listen closely, that I could answer questions later. "Brett accidentally ran over Jacob with the riding lawn mower." Brett's dad immediately said, "Oh, no—oh, my boy—where is he?" I told them they needed to get to ORMC as soon as possible and that Jacob was taken away in the ambulance alone. Brett had slipped into shock, so they had called another ambulance. He was on his way to the hospital as well, but he was in no condition to make decisions.

All I could think about was our little man, there by himself, scared and hurting. We needed to get there as soon as possible.

At the time, I had no idea of the condition that Brett had slipped into. While we were driving to the hospital, Jacob was in highly capable hands, the best care Orlando has to offer. But my poor sweet husband was struggling, slipping into a very dark place that would take years to pull him out.

I remember just looking out the window; it was a beautiful sunny day. Commuters were driving by, making plans on their phones. Everything was blurry, and I felt like I was being sucked into a tunnel. I just could not believe what was happening.

My next call was to my mom. As I dialed her number in Michigan, I kept thinking there was nothing she could do, so why worry her. But, instinctually, I needed Mom to know. Michael Bergen, my stepfather, answered the phone. It was a fluke that he was home from work early that day. Mom was still at work, but he told me that as soon as we got off the phone he would call her. At that point I couldn't tell him any details about Jacob, but I told him it was bad. I really cannot remember the conversation, but I remember him saying, "I love you, stay strong … everything will be OK." Then we hung up. Mike called my mom at work. The first time I spoke to her after that, she was standing in front of me at 1 a.m. in the intensive care waiting room at ORMC. I later learned she had caught the 6 p.m. flight out of Flint, Michigan.

After speaking with Michael, I returned to staring out the window. We were in really congested traffic. I kept thinking, are you kidding me? I cannot believe my family is in a full crisis and I am sitting on I-4. I think I was rocking back and forth. I just could not digest the range of emotions; the unknown was eating away at me as I sat there. Bless my friend Michael, eyes on the road, just giving me my space to sort this out. What a blessing he was that day. God misses nothing.

Suddenly it occurred to me to call the hospital. I dialed 411, and they spouted out a number to Orlando Regional Medical Center. This will be great, I thought: I will be bounced around from person to person trying to track down my son. Although, frankly, any type of distraction at that point would have been good.

To my surprise, an operator answered immediately. I told her I was trying to reach someone who could give me an update on my son, who had been brought to the emergency room within the last 30 minutes. The next person to pick up the phone identified herself as an emergency room nurse; her name regrettably slips my memory. I identified myself, explaining to her that I was on my way. I told her how concerned I was that Jacob was there by himself and that I was trying to get there as quickly as I could.

In my flurry, the only thing I wanted to know at that moment was if Jake was going to die. Were his injuries life-threatening? Oh God, I needed to know.

She never answered those questions directly. She did say, "Mrs. Bainter, I am standing right next to Jacob as we speak." She went on to say something like, "He has sustained some traumatic injuries to his right leg; however his vitals are stable at the moment." I couldn't believe it—she was there, holding his little hand. I was so thirsty. I needed something to drink. My mouth felt so dry as I spoke.

She continued on to say, "Please, Mrs. Bainter, it is important you get here safely. Take your time, we have everything under control. Your safety is critical at this moment. Your family needs you." As I was taking all this in, she said, "Your husband has arrived, and we are tending to him. He is having a difficult time but is going to be OK, again, please travel safely."

It is probably good I never knew the true extent of Jake's injuries at the time of that call. Apparently, Jake had lost a lot of blood. They were having a hard time stabilizing him, and indeed this was a life-saving exercise.

I hung up the phone with the ER nurse, and the next 10 minutes we sat in silence. My family was in crisis. I needed to collect myself; I needed to be strong and prepare for what I was about to face. This would be a defining moment in my life, and I could not let my boys down.

As Michael pulled into the Porte Cochere at the emergency room entrance, I said my goodbyes by the time the car rolled to a stop and I jumped out. I took a deep breath and walked through the emergency room doors.

CHAPTER 2

The beginning

Within minutes of my arrival, a group of people came through the swinging doors to greet me in the lobby. I try to recollect who they were; I think it was the emergency room administrator, a couple of paramedics, the social worker and a nurse. They were all waiting for me to arrive. We made a quick right turn down the hall, and straight ahead were the double doors to the emergency room area. As we neared the doors, I could hear Brett. As I walked through the double doors, Brett was right in front of me. He was strapped on a gurney in the hallway. He was facing away from the entrance and could not see me. He was wailing, "What have I done, I've hurt him so bad." He just kept saying that over and over. Between words, he was moaning in pain, crying out in sheer agony.

I stopped at the head of the gurney and paused. What was I about to face? The strength and pillar of our family was broken. His moans were unlike anything I had ever heard. It was gut-wrenching. He was just lying there helpless, arms strapped down, staring at the ceiling, in his own world. I put my hand on his shoulder and slowly walked beside him. He sobbed harder when he felt my touch. I turned to look at him, and I couldn't believe what I saw. His eyes were red, his face pale, ghost white. Still in his work boots, he was covered in dirt, grass, and blood. He looked as if he hadn't shaved in days, and it had been only 24 hours. I leaned over him and put my arms around him. "I love you," I said. All he could say was, "I'm sorry, I'm so sorry." I just held him; there was no need for apologies. I knew Brett loved his son more than life itself. "Sorry" was not necessary. He had done nothing wrong. I told him I loved him over and over again.

Our world was being rocked to the core, and the pain was like nothing I had ever felt, an ache so deep that it takes your breath away. I was rattled by what I had already seen, and afraid of what I would see next. I was almost immobilized. How would we survive this?

I was so thirsty.

Brett asked me to go see Jacob. I had been standing there only a few minutes while the nurse and paramedics were waiting to take me to see him. I asked them to help Brett. Help calm him down, maybe move him out of the hall, and allow him some dignity. I begged for someone to help him. Little did I know, there was nothing that could be done. The damage was way too deep. How can you mend wounds of the soul that are not visible to the naked eye? They tended to his medical needs, blood pressure, vomiting—all the side effects of shock, but his heart—that would take time. The tears just kept coming; the cries of agony went on for days. At that moment in the emergency room, as painful as it was to see Brett in that condition, there was nothing anyone could do. The only relief for Brett would be the recovery of our son.

As I walked into the emergency room to see Jacob for the first time, I felt strong. I had no choice; I knew Brett needed me to be strong. I composed myself and walked to the gurney where Jacob was lying. There were doctors and nurses running all around; everyone seemed busy. I could see him lying there in the middle of the commotion, so little that he hardly covered the gurney. He was just a baby. When I walked up to him, I could see him before he could see me. His face was still covered in freshly cut grass. It was in his hair, his eyelashes, on his lips. He had a neck brace that made it difficult for him to look anywhere but up. I leaned in over the top of him. I looked in his eyes, his lip curled. He didn't make a sound at first; he just had tears running down his cheeks. He was crying but so silently and so softly.

He said, "Mommy am I bleeding? Do you know what happened to me?" I told him that I knew what had happened and that I had just seen Daddy and that he loves you very much. Jake was completely coherent, but the pain medication was making him groggy. I could tell he was trying to communicate with me but just couldn't find the words. I put my hand on his head and told him to close his eyes, Mommy's here.

He was lying on his back; the neck brace was securing his head, neck, and back. They had a board hooked up to his left arm where they had administered an IV. Both arms were lying flat on his sides. His right leg was bound with many layers of bandage and elevated high above his body. He was wrapped in blankets to keep his body temperature stabilized from all the blood loss.

Mi Mi was laid across his body. She was his old and trusted friend, his thumb-sucking companion. He had gotten "lamby" when he was born. Years earlier she was a soft fluffy lamb that had a sweet head with a pink nose and black eyes. Her body was a blanket that was sealed at the bottom with blue satin. Through the years, she had been loved. The satin was gone; the stitching, split and worn, had been mended many times with a needle and thread. The stuffing in her head and ears, gone, her little black eyes and pink nose were faded. But her comfort for our son was stronger than ever. He was never really able to say her name when he was little, so lamby turned into Mi Mi. She, too, was covered in grass and dirt, not from the accident but from the love she offered her special friend on this difficult day.

I stepped away from his bed and tried to gain my composure. I was aware of the nurses and doctors gathered in the room working around me. In my mind I was screaming, "Help," but I stood there silently. I didn't even know what to ask.

The first doctor I met I remember well. He was the young man who happened to be on duty that day. He explained to me that they were in the process of paging a pediatric orthopedic trauma surgeon from Arnold Palmer Hospital for Children (APH), who later that night would perform the first of many debridement operations on Jacob's leg and foot. They assured me he was not in immediate danger, but he had lost a lot of blood and was susceptible to infection so they needed to address it immediately. After the brief consultation, I knew Jake was in good hands and resting. I needed to let Brett know what was happening to ease his mind that Jake was going to be OK.

When I left the room, I went back out in the general emergency room area. Brett's parents were walking through the swinging doors. The fear ran down my spine when I saw Pop's face, I could tell he was terrified. Brett was positioned in the same place where I left him. The paramedics who had responded to the scene were gathered around him, still working to calm him down. When he saw his mom and dad, the wails began again. The sound of his cries were unbearable, it was just so overwhelming. I remember Brett's mom holding his hand and crying with him. I knew that as a mom, she was feeling such heartbreak for her son. There was nothing we could do.

I updated Brett's parents with what I knew, which was very little. I didn't really fully understand Jacob's injuries at that point, and I was so scared the doctors were going to tell me they would need to amputate. How could I make that kind of decision on my own? Not much time had passed when the nurse came to retrieve me. I asked Crystal to come with me. She is a radiologist at APH, and she knew her way around the hospital. More importantly, she knew the surgeons I was about to meet. She was such a godsend; she provided me comfort, helped me think things through. She also knew what questions to ask, and she represented Jake's interest.

It was determined that Jacob would need to be transported to the APH trauma unit. The children's hospital was less than a block away. He would need immediate attention, which would entail debridement of the wound. Lawn mower accidents are extremely dangerous, and the dirty blades are a breeding ground for bacteria. Debridement would remove the contaminated tissue.

I went back into Jacob's room. He was lying there, his eyes wide open and completely alert. He wasn't in pain at that time, just scared. They had begun to administer morphine upon his arrival to alleviate the excruciating pain. Jacob asked me what we were going to do. I told him to sleep if he could, go back to sleep; it would make him feel so much better. I sat there for a long while holding his hand, kissing his head, fighting back the tears. He kept drifting in and out of sleep. To this day, he remembers the accident and the ambulance ride, but much of his time in the hospital is a blur.

I stood in his room next to the gurney for what seemed like hours waiting to prepare him for transport. So much was happening in the room, so many other people were coming and going, but I felt like it was just Jacob and me. I was torn because I knew Brett and Jake both needed me, but at the time I knew Brett would want me to sit by Jake's side. It all seemed surreal.

While I was in the emergency room with Jacob, friends were beginning to gather in the lobby. In fact, I vaguely remember seeing our neighbors in the emergency room and another friend who lived across the lake. Later when I asked Crystal how everyone knew of the accident in such a short period of time, she simply said they had heard Brett's screams for help. They gathered in the waiting room, helplessly, their hearts broken. What could they possibly say? This was bad. This was really bad.

After we had made the decision to transport Jacob to APH, I went out to inform the rest of the family. By then they had taken Brett from his gurney and wheeled him into a private room. He was in a wheelchair now, no longer crying but numb. He was just staring into space. Still in his boots and bloodstained shorts, he had slipped away from us, retreated to a place in his mind where I think he could cope. He would stay this way for days, months and years. The chaplain held my hand; she knew what I was thinking. How can I do this without Brett? How can Brett get through this? The pain was daunting.

I sat down on the sofa, and we moved some chairs around to make room for everyone. R.B., Brett's father, sat in the chair next to me. We tried to call Brett's brother Corey, who had not yet been notified. When Corey answered, I said, Corey we need you to come to Arnold Palmer Hospital for Children; there has been an accident. I couldn't get any more words out; Pop took the phone and told him what happened: that Jacob had been accidentally run over with the lawn mower. As he said it, I felt myself cringe. I didn't want Brett to hear that. But Brett didn't budge. He was completely numb, just staring straight ahead. Sadly, that phrase would be said over and over again for weeks and years to come. I cannot imagine Brett's pain every time he heard those words. But I commend his strength to move on. He is a strong man who proved his strength as a son, father, and husband that day. He survived.

Medical staff began to come in and out of the room, along with social workers, administrative staff, and the chaplain. The paramedics even came by to tell me how brave Jacob had been and how worried they were about Brett.

When I returned to Jacob's room, it was time to go to APH. I sort of lost track of everyone as I was consumed with Jake. They loaded Jacob in the back of the ambulance and informed me I would unfortunately need to ride in the front. I climbed in skirt, heels, pantyhose, and all! We rode over in silence. The paramedic who drove the ambulance respected my privacy and my need for silence. No small talk, no nothing, although when we arrived, he turned and said, "Good luck, it will probably be a long night, take care." With that, we wheeled into APH.

Jake was getting uncomfortable by then. He wanted the neck brace removed, and the pain meds were beginning to make him nauseous. I was standing next to him, his little eyes looking at me, begging me for help. He wasn't talking, but he didn't need to, I could see the fear and pain in his eyes. I later learned that Brett walked to APH with his mom, dad, brother, and the chaplain. When Brett walked into the room; thankfully it was pretty dark; I wanted to protect Jacob from seeing his daddy in such a tragic state. It was all confusing; who was I protecting from whom? I know today it didn't matter—there was nothing I could do about any of this—but my "mom mode" had kicked into high gear, and I was unbelievably aware of the situation for everyone. I am happy that neither Brett nor Jake would remember any of this.

Brett's lip was quivering as he got closer, and he couldn't help but sob. He turned away in an attempt to collect himself. When he turned back, Jake said, "Hi, Daddy." Brett said back, "Hi, buddy. Daddy's here." Brett stood there, fighting back his tears; I'm sure he wanted to shout at the world in agony. But he composed himself, and there he stood.

We worked hard on distracting Jake. The nurses got bubbles and other toys to try to take his mind off what was happening, but it wasn't really working. In the meantime, the X-ray technician was moving him around, trying to get the slides they needed before surgery. He wasn't crying too much; he was so pumped full of morphine that for the moment the pain was invisible. Although, he still didn't like us moving him around. By this time, he was getting crabby and asking me to do something. We never talked about why he was there or what was happening; he just kept asking me to make him feel better.

I vaguely remember filling out paperwork. We were signing consents allowing the surgeons to conduct the debridement. I was agreeing to handing our son off to surgeons we had never met. I was agreeing to trust that they would clean the dirt, the bacteria, and the grass—the remnants of the accident—from his little leg. I was going to trust that they would put him properly under anesthesia on top of all the medication he had already been given and return him to us safely. We had no choice. It all happened so quickly, there was no time for questions but even if there were, what would I ask? I didn't even fully understand the magnitude of the injury, and, at the time, neither did they. I could only pray that Dr. Mark Birnbaum had studied in college and had slept well the night before. I hoped he wasn't distracted with other things, that he had mentors, teachers, peers, and experience that prepared him, and will guide his hand through our son's surgery. There was a lot happening during this time. The nursing staff was in and out. All were so gracious and compassionate. I remember them doing everything they could to make us comfortable and most importantly to make this as easy on Jake as possible.

Outside of this room, I had no idea what was happening. I am guessing it was dinnertime as our family began to gather in the ICU waiting room, a situation probably very different from their Friday dinner plans. Our friends and acquaintances were probably home preparing for a holiday weekend, not having any idea of where we were and what was happening. This night for them was like any other; for us, it changed everything. It is eerie how that happens; it felt like the world had stopped. It was hard to even conceptualize that people were driving home from work, grocery shopping and leaving for vacation.

Prior to the surgery, we had the opportunity to meet Dr. Birnbaum, and he attempted to explain the severity of Jake's injury. He told us some facts that we had not yet learned. Jacob had received severe trauma to his right leg, and most of the toes on his right foot had been amputated. He said that there was gross contamination of dirt and grass to the affected area all the way down to the bone and that it would need to be addressed immediately. Lack of attention could expose him to infection and other complications, so they needed to operate as soon as possible.

Eventually, I was able to obtain the hospital notes for that first night. They reported that the patient's mother was informed of the gravity and severe nature of this injury and that Jacob would likely require multiple procedures done to his right knee and that it will never be as functional as his uninjured left knee.

At the time we had no idea the degree in which his knee had been affected. There was no way we could understand. In our simple, layman minds, we could imagine the damage a lawn mower could do, but the details of the injury were just too complex for someone unfamiliar with the anatomy of a child's knee to comprehend. I now know how important the femur is to the knee joint, but at the time, I had no idea.

Time became untraceable. When you are in a hospital, the bright lights cause you to lose your balance between day and night. By this time I had simply stopped looking at my watch. My mind was in such overload; I either never processed what I saw or just couldn't remember. Eventually it no longer mattered. We would not be leaving the hospital anytime soon, so time seemed to be irrelevant.

Jake had gotten so groggy, although he still was in severe discomfort. He was relentless in asking to have the neck brace taken off, but the nurses didn't want to remove it until he went into surgery. Another point of contention for Jake was the location in which they put the IV board. He was a serious thumb sucker, and his one source of comfort was hindered by the medical equipment. I could feel my blood pressure rise and fall with his every request. I just wanted him to be as comfortable as possible. The tension in those initial hours was almost numbing.

Eventually, it was time; the nurses opened the big glass doors and said the surgical team was ready. I was relieved for a moment; it was like when my mom would take Jake when he was a newborn— moments of relief letting someone else tend to the needs. The relief this time was only momentary, though, when I remembered why I was sending him off. I felt like I was about to vomit. The intensity continued to mount.

I told Jake we would follow him and found myself spouting lies that I would never in my right mind tell. I told him that we would be in the room through the surgery and that we would be there when he woke up. He was satisfied. He believed and trusted us, I fought back my tears as I vowed to not leave his side. He was so tired at that point that I think he had sort of drifted into his own world. I told him to sleep, dream of all the things he loves, and when he wakes Mommy and Daddy would be there. My knees were weak.

It is painful for me to even reflect on how I felt as they took him away. He was hooked to so many tubes and equipment that he could barely get his hand to his face to put his thumb in his mouth. As they wheeled him away, he was silent, thumb in his mouth and Mi Mi at his side. I closed my eyes and held Brett's hand. My mind had been spinning ever since the call arrived at work hours earlier. Now for just a moment I sat down next to Brett, and we were silent. The room was cold, the lights had been dimmed, Brett was gone; he had mentally checked out. Even though we were together, I was alone, and I was scared.

We would spend the next 18 days in a hospital where we had spent very little time prior to this day. Even though the hospital was located 10 minutes from our house, our exposure to what went on there was limited. If you had asked me before this day what they did there, I would have said they mostly deliver babies. Today, I say they save children, they give families hope, and they work daily to give children comfort. Oh, and in addition to all that, they give families the miraculous gift of life by delivering babies!

I went from high-voltage adrenaline to the feeling of bottoming out. I was absolutely exhausted. A day that began like any other had changed in a matter of hours, and I no longer even remembered how the morning began. I kept thinking surely this cannot be as bad as it feels. But as I looked at Crystal, her eyes were red from crying. I saw fear in the face of Brett's parents. We were all speechless. I mean, what do you say? Brett, as I've said, was gone. His eyes were blank, his soul broken. Things were blurred. This was real.

The hospital was cold. But I was sweating. I could feel my hands were damp. I was clammy and disheveled. Brett was still just sitting there with pieces of grass and bloodstains covering his socks and boots. He stood out against the crisp, sterile walls of the hospital. Passersby must have wondered what brought the two of us here. Just standing in the hall, me in my suit, Brett in his lawn gear, only a tragedy would bring us in this condition. That is what happens; you see families huddled in the hallways and waiting rooms. You wonder what brought them there.

It was decided that Brett and I would ride home with Crystal and get some clothes and other necessities while Jake was in surgery. We would go quickly and throw a bag together, not knowing the next time we would be able to get away. I am not sure who made the decision, but it seemed like a good plan. Brett and I were walking, instinctually putting one foot in front of the other. Our bodies were begging to sit down and figure out what had happened, but our feet kept moving. We knew we had very little time and we needed to be back when he woke up. Little did we know that the initial surgery would take hours.

We drove home in silence. Crystal has a pickup truck, so we sat side by side, all three of us lined up, me in the middle. We stared straight ahead. I can only imagine what Crystal was thinking. I know her heart was breaking. I imagine she was thinking about her own daughters and in her own mind was conceptualizing what we were going through.

Brett started talking. He said things like, "Crystal, can you feed and water Dash?" Poor Dash, he would spend the next three weeks without us. From that night on, I had sort of forgotten about him, but dogs are loyal. He didn't hold us accountable when we finally returned home. He loved us all the same.

Brett was short and concise. He would ask a question, Crystal would answer, then silence. Nobody talked about what had just happened or what was next. We just rode along, looking out the window, each of us processing what was going on. At that time I was beginning a mental inventory of what to pack. I tried not to think about where Jake was; it was almost more than a heart can bear. I knew that to sit and think about what was happening in that operating room would be toxic, and I needed to be strong, I needed to hold it together for us. There would be plenty of days and nights for worry and reflection. For now, this moment was about preparation.

Following the departure of the ambulances from our home, there was a mandatory search and recovery mission by the police department. They sent an officer and search dog to excavate the accident location. It is my understanding that it was standard protocol to recover the amputated appendages when possible. So in reality, this was a toe search. Another memory I wish I could forget.

Mark Martin, a close friend and neighbor, had already recruited his son Christopher to help finish mowing the yard and clean the mower. They quickly finished the job Brett had started earlier that day, so when we arrived home everything was complete and put away. I didn't really think of it at the time, but later after we were home I often thought about how lucky we are to have friends who were so thoughtful and proactive to keep us from facing another painful situation. Had we come home to a half-mowed lawn and a lawn mower sitting on its tail end, I am not sure how Brett would have responded. Thankfully, from that day forward Christopher has tended to our lawn, grooming it every week. Brett has not sat on a riding lawn mower since that day.

By the time we got to the house, it was dusk. It was very eerie pulling into our driveway. We walked to the house, and Crystal followed to see if we needed any help. Brett opened the door; everything was as we had left it that morning. Jake's toys were scattered, his bed unmade. I think about this now, and how it would have felt had we lost Jake that day. All the reminders of a three-year-old boy were still scattered around the house. The silence was nauseating … everything was still. It didn't even seem like our home. I felt as if we were trespassing, collecting belongings for a friend whose child was in the hospital. The reality of the circumstances was just too big to comprehend.

We moved through the house slowly. I was opening drawers and adding things to my bag. The house was still, but of course my heart was manic. I quickly packed some clothes, in my head, I was repeating things like, "socks, will I need socks? Will it be cold? Pack socks, it could be cold. " Then I would jump back to, "Oh my God, oh my God—OK, focus—hurry." We packed in what seemed like minutes. I said nothing to Brett. He was moving in slow motion. He was on autopilot. He was in the bathroom; I could see him packing his doc kit: Visine, glasses, toothpaste, all the basic necessities. We knew we would not be home for a while. It was not as if we forgot something that we couldn't return, but we piled random items into our overnight bags as if we were never coming back.

We had no idea how long we would be at the hospital. I remember one of the nurses saying weeks, but I don't think at that point "weeks" had registered in my head. I knew one thing: Grab what I needed, because I would not be returning home again until Jake was with me, no matter how long.

We drove ourselves back to the hospital in silence. It was a beautiful evening; the sun had set. The roads were bustling with traffic. Most families were preparing for a holiday weekend. We were silent.

I remember looking at the people in other cars. A woman driving next to me was on her cell phone, chatting, laughing. I remember wondering where she was going. I wanted to go with her. It is strange when something horrific is happening in your life, and you look around and nobody knows. I wanted to drive with lights flashing and a sign that said, "We just had a tragedy, our son has been run over by a lawn mower, he is in surgery now." I guess I just kept wondering how people could be happy. But no one knew the horror we were facing. I think of that now, when I pass other people on the road when I am having a brilliant day and the sun is shining. Did the person in the car next to me just learn about a death in their family, just have a fight with a loved one? Did that person's child just get injured in an unexpected accident? We all live with pain and suffering, but unless the pain is visible, others may never know.

When we returned we parked in the parking garage, I vaguely remembered where to go. We walked into the hospital. I can't imagine what we looked like; Brett was still grass-stained and dirty. We walked past people, but they were a blur. We went straight to the third floor, the pediatric Intensive Care Unit (ICU) waiting room. Brett's parents were still there, waiting for us along with other friends and my sister Stephanie Bergen. I can't remember if there was talking. You could feel the agony in the room. I think there were other families waiting on their children. The waiting room was for families of pediatric patients in surgery. It is a narrow room with chairs that line both sides. There is a small TV on the wall, but no one was watching. Mostly we just stared at the walls and floor, waiting. Preparing our minds for how we will handle this situation we have been delivered. We knew he was in good hands. We knew that we were fortunate to have a children's hospital in our backyard, but we just had no idea what we were facing.

When I sat down, I finally had a moment to simply pause. Jake was still in surgery and my mind starting drifting back to the months leading up to this day. An incredible peace came over me, because I knew that God had been preparing me. I did not know yet what that would mean, but I knew we were not alone.

CHAPTER 3

Summer 2003

Divine appointment

It was the summer when I started to notice something stirring in my heart. At the time, I had no idea of the magnitude or scope of the impact. I had no idea it would completely turn my life upside down, transforming both Brett and me from the inside out. But I knew something was happening.

I had been a sales director of Florida Tourist Sales at the Walt Disney World Resort for about five years. I wasn't quite sure why I had the good fortune of landing this great job, but I didn't ask questions. I had a team of salespeople who focused on selling Disney tickets through the travel trade. We had worked together for years, and not only did we have great professional relationships but these individuals had also become my close network of friends. As is the case with most professionals, many days it seemed I spent more time in the company of my co-workers than I did with my own family.

We had been happily sharing a nanny for just about three years. Every morning, the routine was the same. I would bring Jake on the 40-minute drive to work and drop him off at a friend's house in Celebration, Florida, just minutes from my office. I would load Jake up with all his supplies, and he would spend the day with Miss Pam Swoger and the other kids. This was Jake's crew. Miss Pam had been babysitting for the kids since they were three months old, and Isabella Rosa, Miss Pam's daughter, loved them like siblings.

Things started to change in the summer of 2003. First, Miss Pam notified us that she would be moving back to New York in August. Of course, this sends any mom into a tailspin—the whole idea of finding a new nanny who can be trusted and can care for your most precious possession is painstaking. So quickly I put in motion the wheels of what we would do in the fall. Jake had finally reached an age where he could begin attending preschool. We had sort of contemplated a nearby school for when he began kindergarten but had not considered any type of preschool program.

Our first meeting at Pine Castle Christian Academy (PCCA) was pretty intimidating. Neither Brett nor I had been brought up with a strong Christian foundation, and the idea of worship and God's word were definitely out of our comfort zone. Not that we didn't believe there was a greater power; we just didn't practice or exhibit this in our home or, for that matter, our lives. After a brief interview, we kind of muddled through our Christian beliefs and answered a series of questions. Then we took a tour of the campus. I remember feeling good. Intuitively, I knew this was right. I couldn't put my finger on the magic; I just knew this was the right place for our son at that moment in our lives.

Later, I would learn how purposefully God places us where we need to be. But at the time, I just thought I was enrolling Jake in a Christian academy.

Soon, Jake was signed up and would have new beginnings. Our new babysitter, Miss Jen, joined us in August and Jake started preschool shortly thereafter. And so it went, Jake went to preschool Monday, Tuesday, and Thursday, and Miss Jen watched him on the alternate days. It was a fairly smooth transition, minus Jake being wrapped around my legs for the first few weeks of preschool drop-off.

Somehow during this transition, things started to feel different to me. I knew we had begun a new season in our lives, but I just couldn't put my finger on what felt so different. It wasn't long before Jake was coming home singing Bible songs and really beginning for the first time to talk about God in our house. This was a welcomed addition, and Brett and I were pleased with our decision. I would think, isn't this sweet, Jake is learning about God. But it was all so surface, I didn't understand it was about knowing God, trusting him, and turning to him. I had no idea that within eight months I would be on my knees begging him.

During this same time, things were changing at work. I was definitely at a high, working on all cylinders and really enjoying the role I had worked so hard to achieve. Life was good. In fact, sometimes I didn't want to say out loud how good life was, so as not to jinx this little slice of heaven.

Over the summer, I had started to build an uncanny friendship. There was a company that serviced the plants of our entire six-floor building. Every Friday, "the plant man," as we called him, would pop his head into my office and ask if it was OK to water the plants. I would say sure, oftentimes barely looking up from my desk, and he would go about his business. He was an Asian man, probably in his early sixties. He had a strong accent that sometimes I found hard to understand, but the kindness in his eyes was almost hypnotizing. He was very petite, and, I could tell, a simple man of material needs. He was very quiet and worked quickly. Sometimes I would even forget he was in the room. I would just continue on in my conference calls or whatever the task at hand, so focused on work, in some ways I forgot the human element of welcoming this person into my office.

Over time, he would quietly ask me about my day, or maybe comment on a photograph in my office. Sometimes he would give me tips on keeping my plants green or just take a minute to wish me a good weekend.

At first when he would talk to me, I probably acted startled, as consumed as I was with my own agenda.

Once he took the initiative to break the silence, I found him to be captivating. Slowly, I started to stop what I was doing when he would come into my office. I would turn to him and give him my undivided attention. After he would walk out, I would frequently catch myself pausing, thinking about him. I wonder where he lives or what he does when he is not here. He was such a kind and humble presence, different from anyone I had known. He had certainly captured my curiosity.

I cannot pinpoint the time frame, but sometime between July and November, we began to develop a friendship. He was no longer "the plant man"; he was Roger, my friend who showed up sometime between 10 a.m. and noon each Friday.

He was always smiling brightly, his face beaming, when he would walk into my office, and he would say, "Hello, my friend." He made me feel like I was the only person in the building he had greeted that day. I knew this was just who he was and that everyone got this special greeting. But still, it felt special when it was directed at me.

What really caught my attention first was how he said good-bye. When Roger would leave my office, he would usually hug me or take my hand and say, "God bless you." For a person who believed in God but had limited understanding of "God's word" in the Bible, this was incredibly uncomfortable. First, what would people think when they see me and "the plant man," hugging and, second, I just could not find the words to say it back. I would find myself saying things like, "You, too!" or "OK, thanks." Oh, and this was classic, sometimes I would say, "Oh, Roger, that's sweet, thanks." What was I thinking? Well, I wasn't. But what I do know is that Roger was unlocking a part of me that was always there and had just never fully explored. I was learning that all the sales statistics and work-related tasks were important but it was the personal connections that matter in life.

After awhile, I wanted to say in return, "God bless you too, Roger," but I just couldn't. It didn't feel authentic, it felt so awkward, and it just felt like words. Now I know that when you feel a relationship with God, and you pass on the sentiment of "God bless you," the words are not empty; they are from the foundation of this everlasting love. It is so powerful. I do believe that when Roger passed those words on, he was praying that the Holy Spirit would move in me.

After our initial getting-to-know-you dance of small talk on Fridays, we really started to connect. In fact, I would find myself arranging my schedule so that when Roger showed up, I could close the door and spend uninterrupted minutes with him. He started to fill my soul and make me think about myself and life as I had never done before. He shared stories about his daughter and wife, and I shared stories about Brett and Jake. I told him about challenging work situations, and he would give me wisdom. Then he began to share scripture. Nothing overwhelming, he would simply plant a seed that would leave me processing the rest of the day. In time, I would begin to tell him about my life dilemmas, and he would be such a friend in helping me think through whatever crossroad I was facing.

I remember juggling motherhood, my career, and my marriage, and I was feeling the pressure from all angles. My time on Fridays with Roger was always brief; I mean, I was there for my job, not my personal therapy session. He started to come with very purposeful messages. He would say: Listen to what I am going to tell you. And then he would tell me about compromise, tolerance, obedience, grace and mercy. Whatever the topic, he would feed it to me quickly and concisely, like my own personal spiritual advisor. I would savor every word and try to ask questions. Roger would wave me off and say, "OK, more next week."

I was so intrigued; I began to tell Brett about our conversations. Roger had this uncanny ability to sense what was happening in my life and be able to quickly give me insight and wisdom. Eventually, Roger became a topic of our dinner conversations. I started to say things to Brett like, "Do you think God really puts angels in our lives?" I would tell him the uncanny stories and conversations Roger and I would have. Brett was equally intrigued, and he would just smile and shake his head and say, "I don't know, but my advice is to listen."

One time Brett and I were having a huge argument. This particular day, Roger showed up and the first thing he asked about was Brett. He said he was thinking about us and how important it is for us to keep our marriage strong. He had no idea what was transpiring in my life that day, but he said for some reason he wanted to talk to me about compromise. He was telling me how important it was to be tolerant and to work on my marriage that it needed to be strong for whatever God had planned for us. On a crazy level, I felt like he was right, but how could this be? I chose to stop asking "Why?" and start asking, "What can I learn?".

So in those months between August and December of 2003, I was beginning to change. I wanted to learn more about our God. What did he intend for me? Simultaneously, Jake began to tell us stories from the Bible that he had learned at school that week. He would ask that we say grace before dinner, and at bedtime he started to say prayers for those he loved. The heart of our whole family was softening as we began this pursuit for a relationship with God.

In November 2003, Roger left a note on my desk. We had missed each other during his visit that day, and he wanted me to know he had been by. I was touched that he took the time to leave me a message just so I knew he was thinking of me. The note said this:

Father of Infinite Mercy and Comfort
Teach me that sorrow is only but a minute but the joy is forever

Help me, kind father, to have such faith that I will feel it in the sad moments of my life as well as the happy ones

Fill me with the faith that will hold me up on the tossing waters of life

The faith that knows and feels that my every prayer is answered one way or another

Give me the faith that will make me as happy as I am now as uplifted and thankful

Thank you god for the blessing

I don't think I really fully understood or reflected on those words until much later. Looking back now, I am confident that Roger and I shared a divine appointment that summer. Little did I know how his words would resonate and provide me encouragement in the days and weeks ahead.

CHAPTER 4

Settling in

"**J**odi"—Brett, was staring at me. "Did you bring a blanket?"

"What?" He had startled me; suddenly I was back to the reality of what was happening. Brett was standing in front of me with his tired and bloodshot eyes. "Did you bring a blanket?" He looked so helpless and broken. For a moment I had gone back to a place of hope, and it almost took my breath away when I looked back at Brett and realized where we were. I pulled a fleece blanket out of my bag. I stood up and wrapped it around his shoulders. He moved back and sat down, almost in a mechanical fashion. Looking at Brett, knowing our son was in surgery, I knew how desperately we needed God's help. I was suddenly very grateful that he had reached out to me before this day.

We waited for the phone to ring. We sat in silence, cold and exhausted, praying that this first round of surgery would bring good news.

I learned my first lesson of the "hospital routine" that night. There is a phone in the waiting room. When it rings, you pick it up and the nurse on the other end will ask for the family of the patient. Whoever was sitting next to the phone would answer. Then this stranger would look around the room at all the anxious parents and say a child's name. It is a completely unnerving process. Each of us hoping the call is for us, that the surgery is over, and that our child is waiting for us in recovery.

Depending on the duration of the surgery, sometimes the nurse calls during the operation to give you an update. No matter the process, you can hear all the people in the room catch their breath when the phone rings. Sometimes the surgeons come directly to the waiting room after the surgery. They will pop their head in the room and ask you to follow them to the hall, if the room is full; they have a small room at the end of the waiting room where they can meet with you in privacy.

On the first night, time was ticking by slowly, almost standing still. Dr. Birnbaum, the on-call pediatric orthopedic specialist, and Dr. David Miller, the on-call pediatric surgeon, finally joined us in the waiting room. They immediately eased our fears by letting us know that Jacob was resting well. Dr. Miller began. He told us that Jacob had several lacerations to his side and hip. The tip of his hip bone had actually chipped off, but it did not seem to need repair. Even today, I can run my hand across his hip feeling the small indention left by the missing bone and remember that conversation with Dr. Miller.

In addition, his liver was bruised and swollen. Dr. Miller assured us that this was nothing serious at this point but that it would need to be monitored. They had X-rayed his entire body, and the only damage and broken bones were his right leg. They had administered two blood transfusions, one when he arrived and one during surgery.

Dr. Birnbaum had completed the first of four debridement and wound irrigations. This process involved "flushing" the wounds, the soft tissue, and the bone. It was determined that Jake's kneecap was gone; the blade had sliced directly through his right thigh. It had cut away bone, muscle, and soft tissue, having no mercy on what remained. The damage was not beyond repair, but it was so severe that the necessary reconstruction could not even be identified at that time. In addition, the lawn mower had amputated his second, third, and fourth toes. It nearly amputated his great toe and his little toe, catching those two toes enough to graze their tops and remove the toenail and tissue but leave the structure of the toe intact. This was actually not an insignificant blessing, for had he lost all his toes balance would become much more difficult.

The hospital notes following Jake's first procedure read as follows: "Prognosis: Very guarded. He sustained a severe open injury to his right knee. There was substantial damage to the growth plate and due to his young age this will likely affect the growth of his right leg. He will be scheduled for a repeat irrigation and debridement on this Sunday. At that point we will reassess the wound. In the interim, we will keep him on triple antibiotic coverage." The notes didn't mention that Jacob began a morphine drip that was administered almost steady for the next three weeks.

The haze had begun. The meds, the pain, the confusion—darkness had moved into our lives. Nothing we had ever done before had prepared us for this. It was almost too much to process.

That first night, my mom, Brett, and I slept in chairs in the ICU waiting room. There was no talking and not even a lot of sleeping, just silence and prayer. You never really know when you are going to find yourself in this type of situation. It is the strangest feeling to look around at the unfamiliar walls; hear the sounds and feel the chill in the air. The atmosphere made our situation all the more surreal.

The thing I learned about hospitals is they never go to sleep. The lights stay on, the TV runs, the elevator continues up and down all night long. I would get up to walk the halls, and nurses would be having a conversation as if it were the middle of the afternoon. You pass people in the hallway at 3 a.m., and they smile and carry on. It felt like another planet, a place I had never been. As hard as I tried, I could not translate the feeling into something familiar. In the middle of the night, the nurse would step into the waiting room; Mom and I would immediately awaken. She would tell me Jake was awake and looking for me. My heart felt like a rocket as I raced to his room.

The pediatric ICU at APH is on the third floor. You get off the elevator and make a right. The hallway is lined with windows on the left, and on the right are two waiting rooms. The first is for families whose child is in surgery. This is the room we waited in during Jake's first surgery. Following our ICU stay, we spent a fair share of days in that room staring at the phone, waiting for the call looking for the parents of Jacob Bainter.

During the daytime hours when there are a lot of scheduled surgeries, the first waiting room can become pretty busy. I found it very awkward. You look around, and everyone is quiet and respectful. You wonder what brought each family to the hospital that day. Some of the children were having their tonsils out, some to mend broken bones. Others have been hurt in an accident or born with a congenital disorder. The list goes on and on. The anticipation to hold your child again is thick and felt by everyone in the room.

No matter the circumstances, the waiting is daunting. I think they should have a wall of honor. The parents could sign, saying things like, "I read People magazine three times while waiting but never read a word." "It is very cold in here but the nurses' station has blankets," or "My respect and compassion to those who came before me and my love to those who follow." Or, my favorite would be "Came, saw, conquered and with all due respect to the amazing staff of APH, I hope we never have to come back!"

That room for me was like a rite of passage in my life journey. When I walk by today, or even when I visit another hospital, I want to poke my head into the waiting room and gather the parents in waiting in a circle like at an AA meeting. I could begin, "Hi, I'm Jodi; I am the mom of a little boy who was critically injured. A few years ago, I sat in these same chairs just like you." But since that would probably be awkward, instead I just glance in, I pause and pray. If I catch an eye, I give them a knowing glance.

The second waiting room has an imprint on my heart. I can close my eyes and feel the room. The room is just further down the hall. You enter through double doors, which are propped open except for the wee hours of the night—and even then they are closed only to give the people sleeping in the chairs relief from the stark hallway lights.

The room is narrow from left to right. Chairs line both walls. These chairs are an upgrade from the day patient waiting room. They are miniature recliners, kind of like flying first class on an international flight: The chair offers the ability to stretch out in a horizontal position, but to consider the chair comfortable would be generous. Although, as I have experienced firsthand, when your body reaches a certain tolerance level with little or no sleep, even a concrete platform would feel like a Serta mattress.

This ICU waiting room was where families "settled in". They sort of staked out their area, claiming chairs for sleeping and tables to store their overnight bags and other necessities. There are no rules posted or directions handed out when you enter, but fortunately for us, our introduction to ICU went something like this.

We had spent our first night in chairs of the day patient waiting room. Side by side, Mom, Brett, and I tried to get some sleep. The room was empty except for us. When Jake came out of surgery, they transferred him to the pediatric ICU.

On day two, we moved down the hall. When we woke up Saturday morning, we gathered our bags like nomads and drifted one door down. The doors were closed, and the morning shift nurse had arrived.

I cracked the door just enough to let a streak of light shine through so as not to startle the sleeping families. I quickly apologized for disturbing them. Then I heard a man say, "You're fine, come on in." He was sitting in the dark, drinking his coffee. He encouraged me to come in and join them.

There were three other families who had used the room for their overnight accommodations. They were in street clothes wrapped in random blankets on loan from the hospital. It reminded me of camping, when everyone rolls out of their tents, hair messy, teeth not brushed, still dressed from the night before. I could hear the Mr. Coffee brewing in the corner.

We wandered in as everyone began to stir. I shared some moments in that room that will be embedded in my heart forever. In the center of the room was the famous phone. This was the phone that granted you access in and out of ICU. When you picked up the phone, it would immediately ring the nurses' station. They would buzz the door to unlock and let you in. This also worked in the reverse fashion. The phone would ring, and whoever was close by would answer. Soon we knew each child and each family by name, so someone would turn to me and say "Jodi, Jake is looking for you."

The thing about the ICU is that you cannot be in the room 24 hours a day like the other floors. So when Jake was sleeping, I would wait in the ICU waiting room. When he was awake, I was by his side. Sometimes we would both fall asleep, and the nurses just let me stay close.

The man who had welcomed us in was Dwayne. He was the father of an eight-year-old boy who had been admitted two days before Jake. In the time they had been there, Dwayne had already learned the ropes. He was so kind, and when he saw we were completely disoriented, he quickly came to our rescue.

We soon learned his son, Cullen, was in far worse shape than our Jake. A recycling truck had backed over him, and the accident left him in critical condition. His injuries were catastrophic. In the coming years we had the opportunity to see Cullen on a variety of occasions. He, too, persevered through tragedy and despite his original prognosis was doing well.

Dwayne told us to get ourselves together, meaning a quick hair comb and teeth brush in the neighboring ladies room because the doctors would soon be making their rounds. It did not take me long to learn this is one of the most important times of the day. The doctors often keep moving because they are on a time schedule, and if you miss the doctor during rounds, you may not see him or her again that day.

The ICU is laid out in a way that the nurses' station is positioned in the center and the patient rooms circle the station. The glass doors on the patient rooms allow the nursing staff to see the kids at all times.

Jake was heavily sedated on pain medications, and fortunately this kept him sleeping through most of the night. I cannot explain how helpless I felt. He was just a baby swallowed in the hospital bed, connected to cords and tubes, his right leg immobilized in layers of metal and bandages. When he talked, which was very little, he would whisper. His eyes told me everything. I could see pain and fear, and he was begging me to make it better. I am not sure I will ever again feel such agony in my heart.

The trauma of the last 24 hours coupled with the pain medications had left him groggy and confused. He would hold his hand out, then pull my hand to his face and pull me close. He would put his thumb in his mouth and with his remaining fingers he would wrap them around my fingers. After hours of leaning over the side of the bed, one hand wrapped in his little fingers and other rubbing his head, I finally just crawled into the bed right next to him. The bed was very narrow, kid size, so I lay straight on my side so as not to tip and snuggled close. That night when I was able to be in the room, I spent the evening whispering in his ear, Mommy's here, you are going to be OK.

I had no idea we were at the bottom of the mountain, and as the pain meds wore off and the scope of his injuries became clearer, I realized those words would seem empty. Mommy was here and he was going to be OK, but I could not stop the pain. The only one who could climb this mountain was Jake.

At 3 p.m. the day before, Brett's mind had checked out. He had a five o'clock shadow, and his eyes were bloodshot from tears and no sleep. He just stared straight ahead, unresponsive. I felt torn about leaving him behind, but I knew Jake needed me and if Brett could express himself he would have wanted me to focus on Jake. I anticipated Brett's mom and dad would be back at the hospital early and that they would help my mom look after Brett. He had been admitted on Friday and released. After a rocky night, he was readmitted to ORMC Saturday afternoon. He required an IV for hydration and he was provided some sleeping sedatives. Brett's parents and my mom reserved us a room at the Ronald McDonald House. Upon release late Saturday afternoon Brett went straight to the Ronald McDonald house and went to bed.

The rest of Saturday is very hazy. I settled into Jake's room and really never left. He slept most of the day. Friends and family began to arrive.

The vigil had begun.

CHAPTER 5

Easter Sunday; reality sets in

The Easter baskets started to arrive early Sunday morning. I had completely forgotten it was Easter Sunday. Jake was awake but groggy. Pop was trying to divert his attention from what was really happening, so as he unpacked the Easter baskets, he would take the surprises out one by one and show Jake what the Easter Bunny had left. Jake didn't respond; he would just stare, thumb in his mouth. If Pop would stop and put the basket down, Jake would take his thumb out and whisper, "Keep going, Pop." So Pop carried on, showing him all the treasures buried in the shreds of plastic green grass.

I remember the waiting room was full of friends and family who had come by to check on us. The word was spreading about what had happened Friday, and so many people came to the hospital to see us and offer us comfort. The mood was somber. I could see the heart-break of those who loved us and their concern over little Jake.

I sort of milled through the crowd saying hi but I can't remember any conversations in particular. Seeing everyone in their Sunday church clothes, knowing they would be spending the afternoon celebrating the holidays, just seemed peculiar.

The reality of Jake's injuries became clear during morning rounds on Sunday. It started with a visit from Dr. Birnbaum, who told us in greater detail the scope of Jake's injuries and the course of action over the upcoming days and weeks. We knew he would be going back in for surgery either that day or the following day. Managing infection was the immediate concern as they began to consider reconstruction efforts.

After our time with Dr. Birnbaum, he introduced us to Dr. Rai B. Gupta, the pediatric plastic surgeon who had been called in to consult on Jake's case. The reconstruction for Jake's knee and thigh was extensive; it would require several skin grafts and repurposing his calf muscle as tissue to rebuild his thigh. Thinking back on those days in the hospital, they were filled with so many IVs, pain medications, and dressing changes that each day sometimes would be a blur of one treatment to the next. But there are some moments that were so powerful they are crystallized in my mind forever. Our first meeting with Dr. Gupta is one of those moments.

He was a very gentle, unassuming guy with a soft-spoken nature. He introduced himself as the pediatric plastic surgeon. I was still sort of confused on why we would need a plastic surgeon, but in quick order Dr. Gupta made it clear. He moved our conversation to the hallway out of Jake's scope of hearing. He told us he would be taking part in the reconstruction of Jake's leg in the upcoming surgeries that week. He explained to us the procedures would include removing skin grafts from his left thigh and transplanting them to his right leg. Further, Dr. Gupta would be using the muscle from Jake's calf, creating a flap that would be folded up to his knee and thigh, providing tissue and substance to the vacant spot ripped open by the lawn mower. There was some concern he may need to also use muscle from Jake's shoulder if there was not enough left on his calf, but that decision would be made during surgery.

Brett and I were doing our best to listen and understand the details of the procedures and the anatomy of Jake's small leg. Before the day was over, we would once again write our initials on a release form authorizing Dr. Gupta to carry out the procedures.

As Dr. Gupta was explaining the procedures, he opened a file folder. As I looked at the first image, I felt a wave of nausea. The pictures had been taken in the ER the night before. The images at first were hard to even identify. I saw only flesh, blood and bone. Dr. Gupta started to explain, "This is where Jake's knee was, you will see a little fragment of bone is left where his kneecap once was". As he talked, he had a little pointer he was using to highlight the areas he would be working on. The sounds became fuzzy, and everything beyond the photos blurred. I couldn't believe I was looking at our son's leg. It was complete destruction—the perfect and beautiful leg God had created had been torn apart.

I now knew what Jake's leg looked like underneath the bandage—bone and flesh open and raw. I wanted to throw up. There were no choices here, as if a bomb had exploded, not just shattering Jake's little leg but at the same time sending pieces of our souls in a million directions. The weight of this responsibility already felt unbearable.

34

I was thinking and feeling so many emotions. I couldn't stop focusing on how painful this was going to be for Jake. How many surgeries it would take to put him back together. My mind hadn't even begun to process the implications of walking, running, or function. I could think of only the suffering. I just wanted to reverse the clocks. I didn't want to have to walk this journey. I wanted to quit, maybe just pick up my purse and walk out of the hospital. I just didn't know if we were strong enough. What would I say when I looked into those big blue eyes of his? Where was God? We needed him now.

Looking back, I think he may have been right there with me that day. Standing behind me, his arms slipped through mine, propping me up, encouraging me to take a step. For the first time since we had walked through the doors of the emergency room, this was real. The photos were real, and what would need to happen to reconstruct Jake's leg was real.

Dr. Gupta showed us a series of about five photos. Some might say that was too harsh to show a parent at such a volatile time. For me, it took a moment to catch my breath, but I think it grounded us in what would lie ahead. It was like a bucket of ice poured over my head sort of jolting me into consciousness and into action.

When he finished talking, we were still standing outside of Jake's room. I could see him and Pop through the glass door. I stood there, feeling this unbelievable sense of tunnel vision. The sound was gone, I could hear nothing. All I could see was our son lying in the bed, completely reliant on us as parents.

I turned and walked to the end of the hallway. I could feel the tears welling in my eyes and the lump in my throat. I wanted to gasp for air. To the right was a set of double doors that led into the hallway, the ICU waiting room on the left. As I reached the double doors, they swung open and I could see crowds of people. They were all familiar faces; they were my family and friends. There were so many visitors that they had spilled over from the waiting room into the hallway. I remember seeing bows and bags, they brought food and gifts— anything to show us their love. I stood there looking out at everyone.

Rather than walk into the arms of so many who loved me, I needed to be alone. I turned left and continued down the hall and kept walking until I found a private hallway. With my back to the wall, I slowly slid down until I was sitting on the floor. I put my head in my hands, and closed my eyes and cried.

I cried deep moaning cries, trying to release the aching in the core of my soul. Jake was just a baby, and this was so unfair.

CHAPTER 6

Bugs11

T
he weekend of Jacob's accident we began to receive calls, too many to count and certainly too many to return. As you can imagine, our families and friends were devastated by the news. On Sunday night a friend contacted us and told us about a website called thestatus.com, where families struggling with medical situations could communicate with friends and family via a website/blog. We had already located the computer room at the Ronald McDonald House, so Monday morning we set up a website and began our communication, sharing Jake's journey with our friends and family.

After Brett's brother Corey set up the registration, Brett and I sat down and entered in the patient name: Bainter and password: Bugs11. Mom helped come up with a password which was a combination of Jake's interest in insects and his birthday, May 11th.

We had no idea at the time that the password would be keyed in more than 150,000 times over the following four years. We had no idea our story would touch so many in such a profound way. The days we spent at APH were just the beginning.

This blog became an archive of our most difficult days and private moments, and also a celebration of accomplishing the impossibilities of life. The website was a view into the trials of a father and son, a husband and wife, a family finding their way and putting the pieces back together.

Brett and I sat at the computer late into the evening on Tuesday writing a background so when people visited the site they would know what had happened. That night, Brett found the courage to make the first journal entry. I have left the journal entries as they were written to maintain the authenticity of the moment.

Tuesday, April 13, 2004 12:45 PM (journal entry) Brett

At 11 a.m. Jacob went back into surgery. Three doctors will be reviewing the wounds. First, a device (Broviac) will be surgically placed into Jacob's chest for the sole purpose of providing antibiotics and offer comfort to Jacob. This will eliminate the tubes and needles in his arms. Second, the primary surgeon will be reconstructing bone on Jake's femur for growth purposes. Third, the plastic surgeon will analyze the tissue and muscle damage to initiate the mending process. The muscle and tissue replacement will not happen today. Hopefully, the wound is clear of infection and we can move forward later this week for another surgery to start the muscle and tissue replacement.

Look for further updates shortly. Love, Brett

Until April 9, 2004, we had all spent very little time in a hospital. I have learned it is like living in a bubble. Through the windows you can still see grass, sunlight, and life passing, but strangely it seems like a foreign land. We immediately lost track of days, time, and really anything beyond the four walls of Jake's room. Although seeing the nurses and doctors come and go, tanned, carrying a Big Gulp or a McDonald's bag—were signs that life outside of APH still existed.

Upon our arrival to this new world, our days were dictated by watching the clock for medicine time and keeping Jake comfortable between surgeries. When Jake would close his eyes, sometimes I would just sit and stare at the wall. I would be much more comfortable if I had laid down with my blanket and pillow, but I was just too exhausted to move. So I would just sit there. Often I would doze off, but it wouldn't be long before I heard my name softly and desperately: "Mommy."

On Tuesday, Jake went in for his third surgery in four days. When he came to recovery, we were moved from the ICU to a critical care floor. We were grateful for no sign of infection, and Jake was once again resting. When we saw the surgeons briefly after the surgery, they told us they had scheduled the next surgery for Friday, when they would begin the bone reconstruction, muscle transplant, and skin graft.

Thankfully, the vigil of friends and family continued to grow. The hallway leading to the critical care floor became a campground for our loved ones. When I would walk out of Jacob's room in the morning, straight ahead I could see Pop, Grammie, and my mom, waiting patiently for someone to wake.

We started with a couple of chairs in this waiting area, and eventually the nurses notified custodial of the need for additional chairs to line the hallway and accommodate our visitors. So many of our friends became fixtures for our morning ritual, they would show up with Dunkin' Donuts and sit quietly in the hall. Brett's friends in particular were such a source of constant encouragement. Those men showed up every morning, week after week, and sat in the hallway with Brett, often in silence, always in friendship. They would get the update from our parents or the website and sometimes I would never even talk to them, but when I glanced out the door I was comforted by their familiar faces. They had families of their own, but in this crisis they made my family a priority. Tommy Kelley, Rich Davis, Clay Worden, Tom McFadden, Steve Roche and Kenny Hanks, we will be forever grateful.

My mom had been with us since the night of the accident and was flying home that weekend. I knew she would return soon but I was heartbroken to see her leave, as she had been an incredible support for both of us. Thankfully, both of my brothers flew in that week with a new supply of love and support.

Thursday, April 15, 2004 2:56 PM (journal entry) Jodi

I really don't have much new to report. But, I wanted to send a message.

As I read all of the guest book entries, I cannot help but have tears streaming down my face. But, through my tears I am smiling because I am so touched by each message. In a sometimes volatile world where hate and sorrow happen daily and people move faster than the day will allow, I am reminded of the kindness of the human spirit. How people can put their needs aside and rally around those in need. And today, I am thankful the prayers are for Jacob and our family.

I hope you all find inspiration from our story. Hug your families and don't forget to tell the people closest to you that you love them every day! Things can change in an instant and life is simply too precious to take it for granted.

Tonight when Brett leaned over to kiss Jake good night, he gave him a big thumbs up, and Jake did the same. He followed by giving Brett the, "I love you" sign that he learned from Mr. Mark Ritchhart, Dean of students at Jacob's school. And Brett did the same!

We are blessed. Love, Jodi

CHAPTER 7

The reconstruction

On Friday, April 16, we gave our little man a big kiss, and he was off to surgery. Before Brett and I walked away, the three surgeons who were going to be operating on him shared some final thoughts. We knew he was in good hands, not only the hands of these highly talented surgeons but more importantly God's hands.

After about five hours in surgery, Jacob was back in his room. The doctors completed much of the reconstructive process of the knee joint, which included inserting bone cement to reconstruct the lost femur. In addition, Dr. Gupta began the tissue reconstruction process using a muscle flap from his calf. We were grateful there was not a need to borrow muscle tissue from his shoulder.

He would rest for a few days before they completed the skin graft to his knee and toes. The intent was to leave the joint area open to heal for a few days (that helps to ward off infection) before applying the skin graft. At that time, Jake had several pins in his leg connected to a halo that kept his leg immobile and straight. Unfortunately, he was very uncomfortable. The bone fixator (halo) is the length of his leg. Two bars come all the way up to his waist, so it was difficult to keep him comfortable. It was very constricting and for a little guy, really hard to understand why he had this thing on his leg. All he knew is that he was in pain.

Jake had spent over a week in bed, and he was beginning to get a pretty good rash on his bottom. We had to keep moving his positions, and adding the external fixator made this more difficult. Not only were his body and leg so tender that we could barely move him without pain, but the fixator was so bulky there were not many comfortable positions other than lying on his back.

By that time thousands of people had visited Jake's website. Many of them we had never met. Some had heard of our story through a friend or possibly church group; others through a prayer chain or work. And strangely, though we may not have met or would not recognize one another in passing, I felt as though I was reuniting with old friends. I felt so fortunate to share our most personal experience, and we were humbled by the outpouring of love and prayers.

Writing became such therapy and helped me get through those days. Looking back now as I blend these journal entries into our story, I know I could not have gotten through those days without the love and encouragement of so many people.

That Saturday, Jake underwent another five-hour surgery. We continued to fill him with pain medicine just trying to keep him comfortable. He would say, "Mommy, it hurts so bad, please rub my boo-boo." So I would gently rub my hand on the many layers of bandage. He would say, "Mommy, that's so much better," and drift back to sleep. It is amazing the comfort a mom can bring. I felt so lucky to be his mom.

The days and surgeries were blurring together. We had gotten into a routine of preparing for surgery, sending him off and working with the staff to manage his pain when he was in recovery. That was it. There were not really good days; it was mostly just a struggle to get through the day.

On Saturday, Brett took the night shift, and I remember I was able to get eight hours of sleep. Brett, however, said it was a long night. Jacob slept well but would wake up about every hour and say, "Daddy," and Brett would answer, "Yes, little man," and Jacob would reply, "Just checkin'!" Just about the time Brett would get back to sleep, Jacob would check back in. I often put myself in his position. He was so frightened and just trying to survive. My heart aches to think of those days.

Around the seven-day mark, the bedsores were beginning to be a problem. To make matters worse, Jake's leg would drain through the bandages. Since his leg was elevated, it would run down the back of his thigh and settle underneath his bottom.

Sunday night when I got up to help reposition him through the night, I reached down along his hips and my hands were soaked. I was horrified. His leg had been draining continuously and completely soaked his bedding. I could feel my stomach turn and the tears well up in my eyes. Jake looked at me and said, "Mom, what's wrong?" He was so sedated and numb; he didn't even realize the damp waste he was lying in. I felt like someone was ripping out my heart. I wanted to scoop him up and cradle him in my arms, but he was hooked to wires and his fixator was just too awkward. More importantly, he was in such pain that just a jostle sent him through the roof. If he had his way, he would rather stay in the wet bed.

Since it was the middle of the night, we did our best to lift him up enough to simply elevate him over the bed. Three of us held him and the other nurse pulled the sheets out from under him and replaced them with clean sheets. He cried through the whole thing, begging me to stop. "Please, Mommy, please, just leave it ... Mommy, it hurts so bad ... please, Mommy, stop!!!" Over and over he said this until we were able to place him back in his position. Beads of sweat were rolling down my forehead. I was holding his head, kissing his forehead, and kept whispering, "It's going to be OK, buddy. They are almost done, just be brave, it's OK, my love."

When we were able to lay him back in the bed, he had pulled me so close I was hunched over the side of the bed and we were cheek to cheek. Mi Mi was wrapped around his hand, and my hand wrapped on top of Mi Mi. I could feel his tears as they continued to roll down his cheek as he drifted off to sleep. I stayed in that position for hours. I just couldn't move. My legs were numb, but his grip was so tight on my hand I didn't have the heart to move him.

The next morning we learned that Dr. Birnbaum ordered a new bed for Jake. We explained to him that we were going to transfer him to a wheelchair for the first time so we could change his mattress. After hearing this Jacob looked at me and said, "Mommy, I don't want to do this today!" I didn't blame him!

Around 3 p.m., the time came that he had been dreading all afternoon. We transferred him into a wheelchair, which allowed him to take his first trip outside into the fresh air in over a week. It also allowed the nurses to change out his bed.

Jake was running low on energy. The lack of food was catching up with him. All day we had tried to get him to eat. Pop tried chocolate ice cream, doughnuts, popcorn, but no luck. He just had no appetite. He was sipping a Boost, but it just wasn't enough. I was fearful that a feeding tube was inevitable. Finally as the day ended, Jake was resting comfortably. It had been a difficult week, and we had no idea what lay ahead. We were only two surgeries into the reconstruction, even though it felt as if we had been at the hospital for a month. We were working hard to manage the physical impacts of the accident, but I couldn't help but constantly wonder about the emotional impact. Although I could not pinpoint how he felt, I knew one thing: he was a fighter, and a feisty one at that. When the resident orthopedic surgeon walked in for rounds, Jacob took one look and said, "Don't touch me!" I knew he was of sound mind and up for the fight!

Jake and I had come upon a rhythm in finding him comfort. He would like me to gently rub the bandages on his leg. While I am not sure he could physically feel the sensation of my rubbing the bandages, I think it soothed his heart. So I spent many days rubbing, but that evening he made me chuckle. His lips had gotten really chapped, I guess from the lack of nutrition and all the medicine. So, they were very sore.

I was sitting beside his bed rubbing his leg and he looked at me and said, "Mommy, will you rub my lips?" I took my finger and sort of gently brushed his lips back in forth with one hand. "Mommy, can you keep rubbing my leg, too?" So with the other hand, I gently rubbed his leg. When the nurse came in she chuckled because by then my arms were getting tired. His eyes were heavy, but if I would slow down or stop, they would pop open. "Keep rubbing, Mommy." Finally as my arms began to shake, he drifted off to sleep. Even though my arms were heavy and my eyes were tired, I would have sat there rubbing all night. It was amazing all the pain he was in and how he found comfort in the simplest things. I considered it such a privilege to be the one who can provide that moment of calm and peace. I was so grateful God picked me for the job.

CHAPTER 8

Suffering

Ten days into Jake's recovery, we began to realize what a toll it was taking on his little body. He was so pale and weak. Looking back, I really had not gotten my mind around what was happening, but it was clear that Jake was just struggling to get through each day.

On a daily basis, the activities coordinator would come by. She would poke her head into Jake's room and ask if he was interested in Play-Doh or maybe sand art. Jake was so sick, he would just stare at her when she opened the door. He was so weak and strung out on medications; I can only imagine how he felt. He was just a baby. I still wonder what was going through his mind. Since he had no point of reference, maybe he thought all little boys go through this type of trauma. He was so sad and just begging for it to go away.

He continued to struggle with bedsores; his rash seemed to be getting worse, and he was out of energy. The impact of his injury and the consecutive surgeries were extremely draining. Eventually, it was getting dangerous, so Dr. Birnbaum told Jake he needed to eat something by the end of the day. If he didn't, the doctors had ordered a feeding tube be inserted. Jake just cried. He said, "Mommy, what's that? What's a feeding tube? I don't want one, but I can't eat—my tummy hurts too badly." It was just too much. He was exhausted, and his body was working overtime to fight off infection and heal.

At 6 p.m. they decided that we couldn't wait any longer and that it would be best to insert the feeding tube. As sad as we were to see him have to go through this, we knew it was for the best. I decided after a long day to let Brett take the lead on that one. Although Jacob was really upset, I could hear his screams all the way down the hall. Brett was able to calm him down, and he adjusted to the tube quickly. The feeding tube ran through his nose and directly into his stomach.

They immediately began pumping high-protein and high-calorie drinks into his body. Within five hours I could already see the color returning to his face.

Hospital care is sort of like a house of cards. You fix one problem, and frequently something else begins to fall apart. Once the feeding tube began to work, he was complaining about a tummy ache. His stomach had gotten so small; it hurt to fill it with food. Once we worked through the tummy ache, he was finally ready to fall asleep.

I was feeling weary. I had not stopped since I received the call 10 days earlier. My heart was on a roller coaster, and my emotions were frazzled. It felt like we would take two steps forward and three steps back. After the difficult decision to go forward with the feeding tube, I was reminded of our purpose. Jacob needed Brett and me to make tough decisions, to hold his hand through the ouches, to smile even when we wanted to cry. He needed us to push him forward even when he wanted to stop. I just wasn't sure if I had the courage to do what needed to be done.

Tuesday, April 20, 2004 9:36 AM (journal entry) Jodi

We made it through another night. I dread the nights the most. Jacob is always uncomfortable and seems to want me to sit by his bed and hold his hand all night. He struggles to find a comfortable spot. The fixator on his leg has a tendency to poke into his stomach. He is sweating a lot mostly from anxiety so his hair is always wet. The worry alone can make for a very long night.

Jacob keeps having bad dreams and it will startle him out of a sound sleep. Well, last night around 3:00 a.m., he woke up startled from a dream and he accidentally pulled his feeding tube out half way. Well, of course it scared me mostly because I knew they would have to put it back in. He was so upset and worried that it was bleeding. Once I was able to calm him down, they had to re-thread the tube. It is truly heart wrenching to see him go through un-necessary pain. He has already suffered so much, I pray every day that God will ease his pain. He is just a baby.

I am at the Ronald McDonald house this morning, as I walked over here I could feel the sun on my face. The night is over and today we are one day closer to healing.   Love, Jodi

17 And may the Lord our God show us his approval and make our efforts successful. Yes, make our efforts successful!
– Psalm 90:17 (New Living Translation)

That Wednesday morning Jake was once again wheeled away for another surgery. After 3½ hours, the doctors came to see us. They had told us the surgery had been a great success. Our plastic surgeon was able to graft skin onto his right leg and toes. They decided to do the toes as well; apparently they heal quicker with a graft.

They had told us they used a pretty good portion of the skin on his left thigh for the graft. From what we understood, there were several layers of stitches and staples holding the skin in place. They used a mesh lining over the top of the graft on the left leg, which secures the skin and allows new tissue to form.

Both surgeons were pleased to inform us there was still no sign of infection. The body seemed to be accepting the muscle flap and begin to heal as planned. If they had identified any sign of infection or "bad tissue," they would not have gone forward with the skin graft. While he was under anesthesia, they also adjusted his right foot into a better position. It had begun to droop and without resetting could have caused bigger problems later on. They set his foot flat and secure in an orthopedic boot.

Brett and I always had a pit in our stomachs waiting for him to return to his room. The minutes seem like hours when you are waiting to see your child again. When the nurses returned him to the room, he was sound asleep. The nurses just continued to carry on about how amazing he was and how strong he was. They told us stories, throughout our ordeal, about his peaceful demeanor and cooperative disposition. Even though he was just a baby, he was handling this tragedy with such maturity and courage. We would tell him what is going to happen, and sometimes he cried but never long. He just wanted his boo-boo to be better.

Jake's next surgery was scheduled for that Friday. The plan was for our plastic surgeon to clean the wounds and change the dressings on both legs and remove some of the staples. The reason they did this as an operation is that the wounds were simply too painful to apply new dressings without anesthesia. If his leg was healing as planned, we were hopeful to be able to go home. The grafts take about four weeks to heal, and they were anticipating the bone fixator on for another ten days.

I knew it was going to be a difficult week for him. We had already been digging deep to overlook his pain and tears and make him do what we knew was required to get him healed. Things that we take for granted like bathing, rolling over, and sitting up became major events for Jacob. Each one was painful and time-consuming. Generally, even though Jake would beg us not to move him, he would cooperate in the end.

45

Brett and I went back and forth between the hospital and the Ronald McDonald House for our daily shower. Every morning I would traipse through the lobby in my pajamas with my toiletry bag, and the guest service staff would say "Good morning, Mrs. Bainter." I would walk out the doors and feel the sun on my skin and a breeze on my face. I would feel tears roll down my cheeks, thinking of Jake lying in the hospital room.

Jake's room seemed to get smaller and smaller as the gifts continued to arrive. In the moments that he felt good, we looked at every single card, letter, gift, and toy that he had received. It was such good therapy for him. We had turned his room into a makeshift easel, hanging all the handmade cards and gifts around the room. The love for him was plentiful.

On Friday, Jake went for another surgery. His leg was responding well to the graft and healing nicely. No sign of infection. They redressed the wounds as well as the donor site. They also removed the stitches and staples from the graft site and his hip.

The next step was to begin heat lamp treatments. We would put his leg (donor site) under a heat lamp for three to four hours a day, to begin to heal the skin grafts. Jake's scar (from the skin donor site) took up most of his left thigh. There was a mesh cover over the graft locations that eventually fell off once his scar healed completely.

That Friday around 5 a.m. we had another incident. I was sleeping in a cot right next to his hospital bed, so I jumped up immediately when he started to call me. He had once again inadvertently pulled his feeding tube, except this time it came all the way out. It wasn't a problem because they had stopped the food at midnight in preparation for his next surgery, but it just scared him. The classic part of the story is when I asked him what happened, he said, "I accidentally pulled my feeding tube out." He was holding it up to his nose, and he said, "I have been trying to put it back in so I can keep getting my food." As tears rolled down my cheek, I just hugged him thinking what a responsible thing to do. He was already maturing beyond his (almost) four years of age.

CHAPTER 9

Praying to go home

On Saturday, April 24th, the doctors were finally eager to begin a transition plan to get Jake well enough to go home. They started with removing Jake from a morphine drip and switching to oral pain medicine. At the time I had no idea what we were dealing with, but the morphine weaning process is tough and transitioning to a new type of pain management was another obstacle for Jake. He felt so sick to his stomach and now he needed to take oral (liquid) pain medicine. Also with the IV pump, the relief was almost instantaneous; now when he would take the oral medicine, it was generally another 30 minutes before he felt relief. When Dr. Birnbaum asked Jake how he was feeling, Jake just held up the morphine tube and said, "Get that nurse—I need some medicine in here now." I guess he got his answer.

Managing pain was probably the most challenging feat of Jake's journey. He was in unbearable pain for most of his stay at APH and begging me to fix it. When your child delivers commands like "Get the nurse—I need some medicine now," you know that things have gotten out of control. The quest was to release him from the hospital as soon as possible, but, once again, the suffering would be felt by Jake as we weaned him off IV meds. I felt that constant pit in my stomach with no help in sight.

I now understand that bone pain can be excruciating. And I don't blame him for demanding his pain medication. I am sometimes grateful he was so young that he won't be able to remember those days. For me, it will be embedded in my mind forever.

I asked God every day to give Brett and me strength to face another day. I am not sure what greater pain there is than seeing your child in the kind of agony Jake was experiencing. Interestingly, how God can give you peace when you need it most, I remember going to sleep exhausted, and when Jake would call me in the morning, I would wake up thinking, OK, I can do this another day.

When we found out we were finally going home. We had our first flicker of hope that we were beginning to get Jake's pain under control. We were alternating meds (by mouth), so the only time we really struggled is when the last dose was wearing off. It would usually take about 40 minutes for the next dose to set in.

Prior to leaving our orthopedic surgeon came to the room and informed us that we needed to change Jacob's dressing before he could be released. The most painful part of the entire dressing change was his toes. Jacob looked at his leg and toes but was very quiet. He didn't ask any questions. His questions would come in time.

When the surgeons walked in on our release day, they told us how nice it was to meet our family. We thanked them, and when they shook our hands we were silent. Brett and I had tears in our eyes, and from the expression on their faces no words were necessary. They understood. After 17 days, we would soon return home. So what happens next? We had so many unanswered questions. How do we bathe him, where does he sleep, how would I do the dressing changes, how do we move him around, how does the wheelchair fit in the house? So much had changed since we started our day on Friday, April 9th.

CHAPTER 10

No place like home

It was so great to be home again. While Jacob had not said the words, he was definitely going through an adjustment. At bedtime we tried to resume our normal nighttime routine. The first night home we figured out how to maneuver the wheelchair upstairs, we got him into his bed, and I crawled in next to him to read some books. Just before he fell asleep, he said, "Mommy, please don't leave me, I am really scared." I said, "Jacob, this is your bedroom that we love, there is nothing to be scared of." He said, "But Mommy, I can't walk with this fixator," then he was silent.

Our first morning home, Jacob woke up and said, "Mommy, I am awake, can you put me in my wheelchair?" I had to fight back the tears. It was sweet, he just wanted to get downstairs and he knew the only way to get there was with help. No more jumping out of bed and running down the stairs. Although I knew it was temporary, his newly disabled state was just too much to accept. While I was making breakfast, I kept thinking of the families whose children are dependent on wheelchairs for their entire lives. They will never get to run down the stairs in the morning. I found myself thanking God for our blessings, no matter the circumstances.

That week we had our first visit from the home nurse. I learned that I would need to "flush" Jacob's Broviac (catheter) every day. Dr. Birnbaum had made the decision to leave the catheter should they need to administer additional antibiotics once he returned home. The nurse brought all the supplies to show me how, and Jacob was a pretty good help. He listened closely when she trained me, and he said, "Mom, if you forget, I can help you." Between the two of us, I knew we would be able to figure it out!

After the nurse left, my dad and I were standing in the kitchen when Jacob called for us to come and look at him. To our surprise he was wheeling himself across the living room floor in his wheelchair. He quickly figured out he could transport himself. My dad said, "This is just another sign that nothing is going to slow this boy down."

Jacob consumed 100 percent of my time. Providing comfort, pacifying his frustration, enriching his day with entertaining activities, handling the constant medicine battle every four hours, and tending to his care were a full-time job and then some.

I was so incredibly grateful when the hot meals began to arrive. Our family from PCCA had jumped into action when they heard we would be returning home. Every day for the following six weeks, a familiar face would show up around dinnertime blessing us with a warm meal, oftentimes a new toy for Jake and a prayer for our family. I had never felt so loved.

When my brother Matt Bishop arrived, we settled into our nightly routine, and sadly his first night in town turned out to be one of our worst nights yet. He didn't arrive at our house until after 11 p.m. When he first got to the house, we had about 30 minutes to catch up while Jake was sleeping.

Sometime around midnight Jake woke up, and the night went downhill from there. Jake was so restless and just could not get comfortable. Finally we brought him down from his bedroom and tried the living room. For hours he continued to flip-flop from the couch to his wheelchair, which at times he found the most comfortable.

He just cried and moaned in pain. I remember looking at the clock, and it was sometime after 6 a.m. I knew the sun would rise soon, and we had not gotten an ounce of sleep. I was so tired from the 17-day hospital stay, and yet there I was at 6 a.m. sitting alongside Jake's wheelchair and rubbing his leg. My body was moving on its own. I was no longer in control; it was complete autopilot. I think I discovered the seventh sense, the mother sense that operates your body, even when you cannot, to comfort your child.

I was so grateful for my brother that night. He sat there with me, both of us with bloodshot eyes from tears and lack of sleep. We cried, we laughed, and sometimes we just sat in silence. Mostly, we both ached inside for Jake. In our entire lifetimes we had not experienced what he was going through, and we were unable to help him through it. Matt and I have reflected many times about that particular night and to this day it can bring tears to our eyes remembering what Jake went through.

We later learned that Jake was having extreme withdrawals as a result of the morphine he had received during his hospital stay. He was dealing with the incredible complications of being weaned from an addictive drug like morphine, and it was all-consuming. It was incredibly stressful for us to watch. I learned so many lessons in our journey, and understanding the implications of medicine ranks up there as a top ten.

As the days wore on, Matt was my saving grace. Brett had spent most of the days since we had been home in bed. He had disappeared. The house was small, Jake's crying in agony was frequent, and Brett just couldn't bear to watch. I would crack the door to ask him to come down for dinner, and he would wander downstairs in his flannel pajama bottoms, sit at the table, eat, and go back upstairs. My heart still continued to break for Brett. As I watched Jacob improving I saw Brett slipping. He was in so much pain, and I just didn't know how to help him. I asked friends and family to lift him in prayer. He was an amazing dad; I wanted to see this burden lifted and for him to not miss another day.

Now almost a week into our "return to normal," we made some management decisions. We needed to implement some new sleeping arrangements. We purchased an air mattress for Jake, and we put a little TV/VCR in his room (unfortunately the iPad was still only a vision of Steve Jobs). In the hospital they played the TV all night; apparently the distraction is a pain control techniques. I think that's why his days were manageable. We kept his mind off the pain. But at night when he was lying there, it was difficult to think about anything else. In fact often we would start in his bed, move to his wheelchair for half the night, and then to the couch. Wherever he was, he wanted me sleeping next to him, so I made the rotation as well.

We were up to eight heat lamp treatments a day. Sometimes we would be almost done, and he would beg to not do any more. Then he would say, "Mom, I am ready to do my last heat treatment, then I will be done for today." It was so responsible for someone who was not quite four years old. He knew what he needed to do to get better.

We were sad to see Uncle Matt go home, but we managed to maximize every minute. Jacob loves his Uncle Matt dearly, and that weekend his presence provided healing for Jake's spirit.

Despite everything we had faced, no matter the conditions of the night, Jacob always woke up happy. One of his first morning rituals was to ask me to open his shades and allow the sun to shine in. I think it helped him mentally prepare to face another day.

CHAPTER 11

Will the pain ever end?

Jacob was very uneasy about his first doctor visit subsequent to his hospital stay. He kept questioning me about the purpose of the visit. He was really concerned that we were going back to his room at the hospital. I felt bad because I knew he was going to have his dressings changed, but I didn't want to give him too much information ahead of time. I knew it would just have created more anxiety.

With a lollipop in each hand, Jacob allowed Dr. Gupta to remove the bandages on his right leg. He cried throughout, but I think they were tears of anxiety and fear, not really pain.

I sat right next to Jacob, lifting the fixator for Dr. Gupta and helping him rewrap the bandage. If I looked away, Jacob would shout, "Mom, keep watching, watch what he is doing!" I don't really think Jacob was in pain. I just think his wounds looked so bad, he maybe thought it hurt. The sight of his fresh skin graft and the external fixator was pretty disturbing.

I felt faint every time we removed his bandages, and I could feel my heart thumping and my hands sweating as the conflicting words came out of my mouth, "Honey, it looks great, you will be healed in no time."

The skin grafts looked like a big shark bite. Very misshapen and covered with pink raw skin. The site was very gory, and at the time I had a hard time comprehending how it would heal. His thigh had a big indention where he had lost muscle and tissue. We were always happy to know that there were no signs of infection and that the grafts were healing as planned.

We had only been home from the hospital a week when we had a little setback. Jacob's left leg was starting to get really itchy as it healed. While he was sleeping, he was scratching his leg around the bandage. When his crying woke me up, there was blood all over his leg; he had scratched down into the bandage and right into his donor site. He was out of his mind in pain and pretty inconsolable. That night he begged me, "Mom, just make it go away. Make it stop hurting. I want this to be over." I just continued to hold him and comfort him and reminded him how far he had already come. I tried to endorse his feelings and told him I can't imagine how much that must have hurt and I was sorry it had happened, but we just needed to work through and try not to let it happen again. Eventually, in his exhaustion, he fell asleep in my arms. I glanced at the clock: 4:12 a.m. We had almost survived another night.

Thursday, May 06, 2004 3:50 PM (journal entry) Jodi

I knew today was the first dressing change with the home nurse, so I woke up with that sinking feeling in my stomach. When the nurse showed up Jacob was immediately concerned. I didn't tell him ahead of time because I didn't want to cause him extra worry. We decided to change his dressing right there in his wheel chair, we thought that would provide him the most comfort. So away we went unwrapping bandages.

He was so upset he wasn't throwing a fit but simply pleading with me to not go forward with change. It is hard as a parent to force your child to do something that you would never want to experience yourself. Especially when your natural instinct is to provide comfort. We have all done it at one time or another, whether it's the first day of kindergarten or a dressing change like Jacobs, the guilt is the same.

As we unwrapped the bandages, he continued to beg us to stop. "Please mommy, please no more." I just stayed focus on the task at hand, whispering words of comfort, "it's OK buddy, mommy is here."

The fear of the unknown, at the same time the fear of what we did know, were such contradictory emotions and overwhelming. The nurse and I changed his bandages one by one. Sort of like a team, as if we had done this before. My dad (grandpa) was the prep nurse, he handed us gauze, prepared the ointment pads and threw away the soiled pads. At the end, he did the most important prep nurse job, gave mommy (his daughter) a big hug while I had a good cry!

It took us about 40 minutes in all. To me, the wound looked worse than ever. The skin looked grayish which is apparently normal due to the healing process and all the ointment. It was bleeding in several locations, again normal is what they tell me. One of the reasons I think the dressing change is so stressful is because Jake is so tense (understandably so). I was holding his leg by the fixator so the nurse could wrap the bandages but when I let go, his leg was still up in the air. He was holding it there himself, something I can't even do in a good aerobics class. I hated to see him do that, because he was flexing all those muscles that have been cut, torn, sewed, etc, the poor guy just could not relax. Eventually he reached the point of exhaustion and let us finish without fighting. My heart was aching.

These moments are a swift reminder of the severity of Jacob's injury. Sometimes when a day goes by and he is out of pain and enjoying himself we can forget the devastation of his injuries. When I see his leg it is a terrible dose of reality.

I have said this before, my mind knows what must be done and that things could be worse. But, my heart continues to break. My hearts asks why? How much can he take? I just wish I had answers.

When the dressing change was over today, he looked at me and said "mommy, please don't do that ever again." I gave him a kiss on his forehead, knowing that Monday, the next change is right around the corner.

Today is one of those days that I write through the tears. However, I will tell you, I can hear him laughing downstairs with Grandpa Bishop and Pop. He has already moved on, the brilliance of a child is contagious so, I too will feel better soon. His laugh is the best remedy.

In fact, this morning he asked me to sing him the "You are my sunshine" song. When I sing that song to him his eyes light up, I think he likes being my sunshine!

Well, its 3:30 p.m. and the rule in my house growing up was not to be sad for long. We were allowed to feel sorry for ourselves for a couple days and then it was time to open the shades, let the sunlight in and move on to something productive.

So, I am done for today.

By the way, Brett left for a meeting just as the nurse arrived. He called me about an hour ago to find out how everything went. As I told him I couldn't fight back the tears. He said, "Stay strong for us, you can do it." I said "OK!" Even though he is struggling every day, he believes in us—and I believe in us too.

Kiss your friends and families tonight. Be thankful. Love, Jodi

PS. On Friday, Jake was sitting on the couch and out of the blue he said "Mom, why don't you go jump on the air mattress?" I sort of laughed and said "What? Why would I do that?" He said "Just go jump on it, I think it would be fun. He paused and said "Go jump and let me know if it is fun." This struck me as funny in one respect and of course sad in another. He really thought that air mattress jumping must be fun and since he couldn't do it himself he was willing to send in a pinch hitter even to experience it by default. So I went and did a few jumps. When I returned downstairs I assured him it was fun, he smiled and said, "I thought it would be."

Saturday, May 08, 2004 12:48 PM (journal entry) Jodi

Last night, Jake woke up and threw a BIG fit. He was scratching again and although he didn't go into his donor site, he got sooooo frustrated that it itched so bad he started throwing himself around. Pillows, sippys, blankets and even Mi Mi were thrown around the room. The bed was bare and he was exhausted.

After a 60 minute battle I was able to get some medicine down him and he finally let me cuddle up next to him and soothe him back to sleep. Poor daddy, he was running up and down the stairs fetching things like juice, medicine a wash cloth. We must have been quite a sight. In the end, I must say it was only 60 minutes and we were done, allowing everyone to have a restful sleep. In fact, I was sound asleep on my air mattress when I heard "mommy ... mommy, my leg feels good this morning." So, we started our day with smiles and dimples. Thank you God for that!

I did have to laugh last night. Before we decided to mix his medicine with liquid, I had crushed the pill and put it on a miniature cupcake then frosted the cupcake. I thought what a perfect trick. The only catch, it was bedtime so Jake was suspicious. When I came out and said "Jacob, look what mommy has, a chocolate cupcake." I said, "I thought you would like a treat before bed." I went on to say "Doesn't it look yummy?" Well, he wasn't falling for it, he said "Mom, why don't you eat that one and get me a different one." Now, how he would know I have no idea, but he certainly is smarter than the average bear. So, I went back to the kitchen to re-strategize! My second plan was a success. Yeah for MOM!

Grammie and Pop are here to play for a little while this afternoon. Jacob is having a good day. He loves when Grammie and Pop are here because he gets everything he wants. In fact, its lunchtime but downstairs I hear talk of brownies and powdered donuts!

I asked Jacob at bedtime if he had any special prayers he wanted to say. He said, "Yes, I want the whole world to pray for me so my leg will be better." What a wonderful prayer. Love to all. Jodi

CHAPTER 12

Happy Birthday Jake

Tuesday, May 11, 2004 10:20 PM (journal entry) Jodi – Precious Pop

Today Jake turned four; we have been home for about two weeks. When he woke up this morning, the first thing he asked was, "Where's Pop?"

Thankfully he scooched down the stairs and straight to the couch, looked out the window and Pop's blue truck was already in the driveway. Pop was sitting there patiently waiting to see some movement in the house. As soon as the front door flew open he jumped out of his truck and came jogging up the sidewalk, happy birthday buddy, both of them smiling from ear to ear!! They proceeded to have a cupcake for breakfast and a trip down to the lake for a little fishing. Jacob received an awesome message from his entire pre-school class singing Happy Birthday and the mailbox was overflowing with gifts and cards. I am so grateful for May 11— it was a day of reprieve.

Unfortunately, no day is without Doctors so, at 2:00pm we began our adventure to Dr. Birnbaums office. Jacob was extremely uptight about the visit. He was so apprehensive after all that he has been through. In fact, before we left he said, "Mom, I have an idea, why don't we go to the dentist instead." Now if you are opting for the dentist over the doctor you know it's got to be bad.

Dr. Birnbaum x-rayed Jake's right leg and the x-ray looked good. The following week we return to Dr. Gupta (plastic surgeon) and get his OK for a cast. The cast will be on for a short time, enough to allow the tendons to continue to mend and to straighten the leg for a while.

When we left Dr. Birnbaum's office I decided it was time for some fun. I went to the party store and bought sparklers, party poppers, squirt guns, party hats, blowers, balloons and other festive party activities and Jacob, Brett, Miss Crystal, Hayleigh and Jessica (the girls next door) and we had a little party on the back deck. The highlight was Jacob shooting everyone with his Spiderman Web Blaster, which shoots silly string! Aunt Steph brought over a huge chocolate chip cookie cake. We had a lot of fun, just what the doctor ordered. Festivities to all! Love, Jodi

On that day, I had no idea what the future would hold, but regardless what it was, we had certainly discovered what was important in life. My heart was full, and my life was blessed. The sparkle in our son's eyes, the comfort of our home, the love of my husband, Pop who never lets us down, and our dear families are the things I was reminded to value most.

At last the mesh fell off of Jacob's donor site. Hiding under that yellow meshes were three really pink patches of skin (strips about 1 inch wide and 3 inch long, each less than a millimeter apart). They were really pink and looked sore, but dry and healing around the edges. With that, we received the nod to discontinue heat lamp treatments. Pop performed a goodbye ceremony to the "yucky" heat lamp and put it back in the shed.

The bedtime saga continued. On average, it took Jacob an hour and a half to fall asleep. He just could not get comfortable. We would try different pillows, blankets, juice, and new sleeping positions.

When our nurse arrived that week for Jake's dressing change, he was upset immediately. He was on the air mattress and of course decided he didn't want to get in his wheelchair. I just kept reminding myself, he is four years old. As usual, he begged me not to go forward with the change. In fact, at one point he said, "Mommy, I am going to give you one option." Guess what my option was: "Put me back on my air mattress and do not change my dressing." He repeated, "Mommy, that's your option." I tried reason, to explain why we had to do it, and then as usual we just had to go for it.

With each bandage I would see that his leg did not look much different from Monday or last week for that matter, although there was less bleeding and drainage. The wounds just looked so raw and moist. He had an incision scar that ran down the back of his calf, where they pulled the muscle flap. The skin across his thigh was tight and lying right on the muscle so it was really defined.

His toes looked so sore covered in stitches and dried blood. The top of his big toe was gone—no toenail or remainder of the perfect toe he had just weeks ago. It was complete devastation.

We would go to work rewrapping the wounds, and when we were all done, we were always exhausted. Our nurse left, and Jake drifted off to sleep.

The upcoming week, Sandy Bishop, my sister-in-law, and Katie Bishop, my niece, were coming to stay with us for a week while Brett was away for work (he was doing his best to keep life moving). His job as regional director for Ducks Unlimited had entered a busy season, and frequent travel was not uncommon. Since I was not entirely ready to be on my own, I was thankful that Sandy and Katie were coming down. Before they left home, Katie asked Sandy, "Is this the day we leave to go take care of Jacob?" She was only five years old at the time but already so connected to Jake, almost like a sibling. In fact, she has been protecting and looking out for him ever since. I was just grateful I would not have to face the upcoming days alone.

Well, so much for my optimism. That night was a roller coaster. Jacob had one of his worst fits yet. Each time he is stronger and more determined and certainly more frustrated than the last. We were having a great evening. He and Katie were such pals, and they were so excited to see each other. Around 8:30 p.m., I decided it was bedtime. No problem, I took Jake up as I always do, and he was being very cooperative. However, when we got in bed, he started the flipping from side to side trying to find a comfortable sleeping location.

Before I knew it, he was in a full tantrum. He started by throwing everything off his bed. He was lying on his back and kicking both feet on the mattress. He just kept screaming, "Leg hurts—somebody do something—leg hurts—somebody do something!" But when I would try to go near him, he would push me away. As his tantrum progressed, I realized there was no way I could reason with him, so I just let him have it out. This went on for an hour and a half. The more he kicked, the more he hurt himself, and as a result, the more he cried. All I could do was sit at the edge of his bed and keep reminding him that when he was ready I would comfort him. At one point, Sandy came and sat at the door, she too, fighting back the tears just trying to make sense of what was Jake was experiencing and how he was behaving. There was nothing either one of us could do, but her sisterhood helped me maintain the patience I needed.

Finally he said, "Mommy, if you want to make me feel better, you will take this fixator off my leg now." Of course, we both knew that was an impossible request. So the battle raged on!

I had such a range of emotions whenever he would throw these fits. Of course I was sad and often angry, too, but mostly I was concerned he was going to hurt himself. The fact that he had such trauma to his leg (both legs, for that matter) amplified the implications of his actions. In a normal situation, I would probably close the door and tell him to call me when he was done. But these were not normal circumstances. He had been poked and prodded for over 30 days straight with no end in sight. He had endured pain no child or adult should feel. He was lost, tired, confused, and angry. He was taking more medicine in a week than I had taken in my time on this earth, and it just wasn't fair.

I discussed the issue regarding Jacob's temper with Dr. Birnbaum at the next appointment. He said that this is very common for children and that Jacob is acting out quite normally. One time, Jake had gotten so angry he rolled off the bed onto the air mattress and crawled across the air mattress until he reached the floor. On the hardwood, he pulled himself to the door, then propped himself up to turn the door handle, all this because he wanted to go downstairs. I calmly watched the entire episode trying to settle him down.

He said, "I am going to walk downstairs." I just sat there allowing him to work this through. We both knew he could not walk or even put weight on his leg. He stared me down, wondering if I was going to stop him. I decided to give him his chance at independence and didn't say a word. The hair was standing up on the back of my neck the entire time; my heart was racing with anger and worry. But, I kept talking through in my head, stay peaceful, he is tired and frustrated. Just stay calm and steady.

He stood there propped up on one leg. His little body was shaking, his face red from crying, and his eyes begging me once again to "do something." Finally he sat down and dragged himself back to the air mattress. Once he was done and he had expended all his energy, I was waiting with open arms to run to his rescue. All I could think was bless your little heart.

This was so hard only because I knew he would not be better tomorrow or next week or even in a year. I knew he would probably have to learn to live with difficulty and often time pain. This would not be going away, and I knew that this would not be the last time his emotions would take over.

I just prayed God would continue to give me strength to stand beside him and say the right things and always provide the comfort he needs rather than let my frustration take over. I struggled hard with how to handle these fits and the roller coaster of emotions. I was trying to find the boundaries between compassion and discipline. I still had to be the filter of what was acceptable behavior.

In a short period of time, Brett and I had completely departed from our established parenting style. Under normal circumstances, we would not allow sippy cups to be thrown against walls, let alone condone hitting and biting.

We would not allow him to demand things. But in my heart, Jacob was intuitive and bright, and I knew he needed to somehow express his anger. I was torn between discipline and cheering him on when he would have an all-out fit; sometimes, everyone needs to just let it out. There was no guidebook for what we were facing. I know now that the medicine alone can wreak havoc on a child's little body and mind. On top of that, chronic pain, lack of movement, and immobility would be unbearable for an adult, let alone a child.

We didn't want to enable him; I only wanted to help walk him through this challenge. I knew he would need this courage, tenacity, and confidence going forward. I knew these were formative years and that our actions would have long-standing implications.

I knew Jake probably would not remember all the details of this experience, but I was aware it would certainly shape his character. And it was times like these that I prayed that we wouldn't make any mistakes and that we would guide him through this ordeal. He was counting on us. Even when he was throwing things at us!

At that point, I was a very tired mom.

CHAPTER 13

SNAP! Oh no!

Tuesday, May 18, 2004 10:15 PM (journal entry) Jodi
The beginning of the day was not as peaceful. When Jacob woke up he was already fretting about tomorrow. He was scheduled for his next surgery to remove the fixator and broviac. When he realized tomorrow would be another surgery tears welled in his eyes.

So on a whim; I suggested a visit to Gatorland. Well, the tears dried and the dimples appeared. So it was, Sandy, Katie, Jacob and I would go on a little outing. Although we were there for only a couple hours we had a great day at Gatorland.

When it was time to leave, I was loading Jacob into the car. As I slipped him across the seat trying to get him into the crazy position he needs to ride in—I heard SNAP! At that moment I realized we have just snapped his broviac!

It didn't get pulled out of his chest, but the tube tore right in half. As you can imagine, my heart dropped to my feet. Drips of blood began to spill out of the end of the tube. This tube runs directly into an artery and now that there was no clamp stopping the return blood so it could flow out freely.

So, as I started driving, I paged the pediatric surgeon on call at APH and Sandy jumped in the back seat to find a way to clamp off his tube. Within minutes a surgeon called me back. He knew who we were immediately and asked if we could come to Urgent Care. So, off we went.

When we arrived at Urgent Care Dr. Don Plumley was there in his shirt and tie (he was on his way to a meeting) waiting for us. We literally walked in and they took us to a room immediately, not because it was an emergency but because Dr. Plumley had to leave and if he didn't address it right away we would have to wait until the next surgeon was available. If this is the type of standards they hold at APH, they are a true testament of professionalism and human compassion. The way they handled our situation was not about a business or insurance companies or processes, it was about a little boy and how to make this experience as painless as possible. I was blown away.

So back to the story, Dr. Plumley quickly assessed the situation and told me we really had no choice but to remove the broviac. The general rule of thumb is to remove it while under anesthesia simply because it is so painful. In this situation, Dr. Plumley didn't want to leave it overnight and felt we just needed to go for it. It took him about 10 minutes; I waited in the hall this time. Once again, my heart was in my throat the entire time.

My poor little guy, we had one more day to live with that darn thing and look what happens. We have been flushing and changing and coddling that thing for weeks all for naught! When Dr. Plumley came out, it was all I could do to fight back my emotions; the tears were streaming down my face. He assured me it was going to be OK and commented how strong Jacob has been considering everything he has been through. I wasn't crying because of the broviac but really the entire experience. At that moment, the mysteries of life simply felt overwhelming. My heart was breaking!

All the way to the hospital Jacob was crying. Aunt Sandy was incredible, she kept his thoughts occupied and held his broviac to make sure it didn't continue to leak. She was a calming spirit for me simply because I feel like I am getting close to my tolerance level. She focused on Jacob when I couldn't, and I focused on driving and getting us there safely.

All the way, Jacob kept saying, "Mommy is it going to hurt? What are they going to do?" He is so sensitized to the situation that the anticipation alone for him must be overwhelming. I kept responding that I just didn't know and I avoided the question regarding pain. All and all the broviac removal was a success and Jacob once it was over, was fine. As for me, my nerves and emotional stability were once again tested to the extreme.

We decided to make it another party night in celebration of the removal of the broviac. So, we had a silly string fight in the backyard and did face painting. Jacob and Katie even decorated Jacob's ace bandages with paint and stickers. It was really fun.

My stories could go on and on but it is getting late. Tomorrow morning is going to come early. We are scheduled for surgery at 7:30 a.m. and we need to check-in no later than 6:00 a.m., Grammie and Pop are going to be here a little after 5:00 a.m. You see why I say it is going to come early! We are hoping to be home by noon. They have told me the surgery should not take longer than 30 minutes.

We will be in surgery when many of you are beginning your day, keep us in your prayers. Sweet Dreams to all. Love, Jodi

Wednesday, May 19, 2004 2:44 PM (journal entry) Jodi

The trip to the hospital was fine. We got checked-in and by then Jake had fallen back asleep. Around 7:00 a.m. the prep nurse asked me to wake Jacob. We gave him some medicine which made him pretty groggy and at 7:30 a.m. the Anesthesiologist carried him away. Bless his heart he just looked over her shoulder staring at me. So many things are just out of his control, he finally gave in.

Now he has a bright green cast on his right leg. They casted all the way down to his foot leaving the toes just peeking out. Dr. Birnbaum said they straightened his leg as far as they could, you can still see a small bend at the knee. That said, today was hard; the doctors were not enthusiastic and as usual they were definitely selective in their long term commitments. Really, the only definitive thing they told us is that they would see Jacob in two weeks. They plan to take the cast off then and hopefully put his leg in a brace. I asked Dr. Birnbaum if Jacob would begin walking immediately and he responded, eventually.

I know, they will do their best to give Jacob the quality of life we hope for him. But at the same time it hurts my heart to know what he may have to endure to get there. Bone lengthening, surgeries, physical therapy could be all options or none could be options.

It is clear the healing process will be long! We are lucky that with the blessing of parenthood God equips us

with patience, makes us durable and resilient and uncon-
ditionally committed to the welfare of our child. With these
coats of armor we will make it through the hard times!
Much Love, Jodi

Thursday, May 20, 2004 9:50 PM (journal entry) Jodi

Today was a relief after two days of emotional highs
and lows.

We started the day by attending Chapel with the students of PCCA (Jake's school). Today was the last day of
school and during Chapel Mr. Ritchhart presented Character awards to the students. Mr. Ritchhart presented the
"endurance" award to Jacob, through his tears he spoke of
Jacob's experience and how he admired his endurance.

When I wheeled Jake to the front of the church, the
entire congregation gave him a standing ovation. As you
can imagine, I was moved to tears. Following the presentation I had endless parents, students and teachers stop me
to tell me they prayed for us every day. The love and support we feel from that community is overwhelming.

When we got home we had another surprise. Jacob's
new wheelchair had arrived. This wheelchair has a seat that
is only 14 inches wide so his little body fits perfectly. He can
control the armrests, the wheels and the brakes. He was
amazing in this chair. It actually brought tears to my eyes
because as soon as I put him in he was wheeling around the
house. This wheelchair for however long he will need it will
be his key to independence. He was pleased as punch and
it was written all over his face. All good! Love, Jodi

Saturday, May 22, 2004 10:22 PM (journal entry) Jodi

Just when I am feeling like the toll of another day will
just be too much, I am blessed with a reprieve. I was so
tired from the week and when I woke today my spirits were
really down. Sandy left early around 8:00 a.m. and I
couldn't fight back the tears.

Incredibly a break came our way, just when we needed
it most. Jacob woke up in such a good mood; he was
smothering his Pop with affection all day. Pop hit the jackpot today!

Tonight I am so thankful for a day of peace we needed
to somehow invigorate our minds and bodies. I realize that

everyday cannot be this easy or this satisfying; there are many more challenges that lie ahead. But, don't be mistaken; I soaked up every moment. I am thankful and will use days like these as fuel to make us strong for the difficult days that lie ahead. Sleep well. Love, Jodi

CHAPTER 14

Under that cast miracles are happening

Monday, May 24, 2004 11:13 PM (journal entry) Jodi and Brett

Tonight I was reading the guest book entries, and there was a line that stuck with me. Tracy Caruso said, "Under that cast miracles are happening." How amazing is that? Under that cast miracles are happening. That is what I will go to sleep thinking tonight. Tracy, thank you for sprinkling me with hope.

As I have said before your words on our website have carried us through this crisis, you may never realize what an impact you have had on our lives, all of you. We would be in a very lonely place, perhaps a place we could never free ourselves from had we not had the arms of so many loving people to fall in to. Thank you for continuing to read, I will continue to write and hopefully together we can celebrate "the miracles that are happening underneath that cast." Love, Jodi

Friday, May 28, 2004 12:49 AM (journal entry) Jodi

Jacob is really adjusting to the cast. He is getting quite mobile; in fact this morning he and Pop were able to go for an outing to Bass Pro Shop. Tonight during our prayers, I asked him if he had any special prayers and he said to "keep his cast on forever and that his leg will not hurt anymore." Those are tall orders; I hope God can assist with the latter.

I spent much of the time while Jacob was away with Pop making phone calls and reading on the internet. Education is the next big step for us in this process. Brett and I have many decisions that lie ahead of us and we have a lot to learn. Now that Jacob is out of pain for the time being, we are going to use the time wisely. A week from this Friday, we will start over again. With the cast removal we will probably face a new set of challenges and decisions. We are going through the process of determining whether to obtain a second opinion and if so, how.

We would pursue this for no other reason than to leave no stone unturned. I am fully confident in the skills of the surgeons who have tended to Jacob however, this is our responsibility as parents to seek and provide the best care for his future. Shame on us, if we do not consider all options and avenues.

I hope and pray that "miracles are happening under his cast" but I also need to prepare if they are not. Brett and I have been discussing this at length and we are in agreement to research and educate ourselves. If nothing else, it will put our minds at ease that we have evaluated and considered all options.

Thank god for this reprieve, I think it will be a good weekend. I think the pain will be manageable for the next 7 days, so our primary focus will be to keep him entertained.

Tomorrow we will begin week seven. Tonight I go to sleep thinking about how far we have come. I look forward to bright days ahead.

As always—Much love, Jodi

Scooting was the next phase of mobility. Jacob had begun scooting all around the house on his rear. He would follow me from the living room to the kitchen. I would take him upstairs with me and he would follow me from room to room. Independence is a new gift Jake had not experienced in quite awhile.

He would sit on his bottom and use his hands to slide him across the floor. As he got more agile and daring, he would get on his knee, cast dragging behind and pull himself forward. The more mobile he got, the more he started to check out his leg and his toes. He couldn't see them, but he was starting to put his fingers in the end of his cast trying to feel them.

Brett and I continued to agonize over what would happen next in regard to Jacob's leg. I reached out to Dr. Birnbaum and he told me that he had just attended a conference for the American Orthopedic

Association and shared Jacob's case with colleagues and peers. He said after much discussion, he gained some ideas and perspective. While we discussed many issues including the growth plate, knee joint, and the trauma to the femur, there are still no concrete answers. In fact, Dr. Birnbaum indicated that many of the colleagues who reviewed Jacob's case agreed this was complicated with no easy solution.

With every call, every conversation, I was piecing together this puzzle. I was getting a crash course in the anatomy of a pediatric leg, and I had an insatiable appetite to understand the intricate details. I needed to know the magnitude of our circumstances and be a participant in the evaluation.

Dr. Birnbaum told me what to anticipate in the upcoming appointment. That Jacob would wear a brace 24 hours a day once the cast was off. We would take the brace off only for bathing, swimming, or any other water activity. Dr. Birnbaum was hopeful that Jacob would begin to apply pressure and eventually walk in the upcoming weeks. We knew he would have very limited movement in the knee joint for a long while. Probably the most important piece of information was that we knew the bone cement and brace were temporary solutions and that until the doctors understood how the growth plate was going to respond, we were at a standstill. We had so many unknowns to discover.

All in all, we were still unsettled. However, we were confident that our doctors were leaving no stone unturned.

Thursday, June 03, 2004 12:05 PM (journal entry) Jodi

For the most part yesterday was a normal day, we made creepy crawlers, baked a cake, painted pictures, went on a nature hunt—you know just the normal stuff!

We took a walk in the yard, Jacob was in his wheelchair. We were looking for creepy crawlers. Jacob would say "mom, flip that rock over" so, I would flip the rock and he would wheel in real close to see what we could find. I was game for the search until I flipped the rock and there was a giant earwig and I hear Jacob say "Grab it mom!!" "What?" I said—But Jake insisted—"Grab it mom!' Oh the fun just keeps coming!

Lots of love, Jodi

CHAPTER 15

Reveal and adapt

Friday, June 04, 2004 9:28 PM (journal entry) Brett and Jodi

Today was a big success, although difficult for the little man, there is no doubt today was a milestone. He was a little sad to see the protection of his cast go, but was a trooper nonetheless. When we arrived our first stop was the ortho technician. He sawed the cast off as quickly as possible. When Jake's leg was finally revealed it looked surprisingly good. From there we went and got x-rays. The x-rays were painful because we had to lay his leg straight, knee pointing up which was really difficult for him to do. He has limited control of his muscles and more importantly with that small bend it was really uncomfortable.

After the x-rays, the "brace man" prepared a special brace for Jacob. It goes from his ankle all the way to the top of his thigh. In Jacob's situation, this brace will allow him to eventually stand and walk. Without the support of the brace his leg would bow out and simply could not support the weight of his body alone.

Our next appointment is in 30 days. So the waiting game begins. Our job for now is to nurture Jake to begin to adjust to his "new" leg. Get him acclimated to his brace and the visual of his leg and toes. Tonight has felt much like the night after he had the fixator installed. He cannot move it around on his own, he is sort of helpless and it hurts an awful lot. We keep moving positions, hip to hip trying to find a spot that offers the most comfort.

For the first time his toes are exposed and there is no support around his ankle so this feels strange. We put a sock on his toes, which seems to provide him some peace. They still look like they hurt! Tonight and probably most of this week will simply be a transition.

As for his spirits, he seems to be in the "zone" again. Get through the pain and onto the next phase. He is truly a fighter. Even through the tears he is a tough little guy. Brave, tenacious and beautiful.

Brett tried to stay in the room for as much as possible. He was awesome; he never allowed Jacob to see his anxiety and cheered him on the entire way. Did I mention Pop? The amazing Pop was there with us the entire time. I was holding Jacob in my lap and Pop had his hand.

Anyway, the day is over. I think of where we have come in eight short weeks. I still find it amazing how instantly your life can change. Everything you thought was important is no longer. The many things you had planned get diverted but the love that anchors our family is stronger than ever. Life becomes a little clearer every day.

We have hard days ahead but nothing we can't handle. I cannot see your face, but as you read this I hope you are smiling because, I'm smiling too. Love, The Bainters

Monday, June 07, 2004 11:15 PM (journal entry) Jodi

The days continue to be long. It is sort of like having a toddler again, Jacob needs help with so many of the things we take for granted. The simplest things can bring him to tears for no other reason than complete frustration. I think under normal circumstances the patience of a four-year old is short fused, we have just compounded the situation. Each day the gap between the highs and lows is a little closer. Much love, Jodi

Thursday, June 10, 2004 8:59 AM (journal entry) Jodi

As soon as I got off the Lake Mary exit Jacob started to fuss. We never travel that far down I-4 so he knew we were only minutes away from Dr. Gupta's office.

Through his tears he agreed to allow Dr. Gupta to look at his toes first. He is so incredibly scared of the pain. All in all, Dr. Gupta said his foot looks great. As you can imagine after viewing the toes he was pretty upset by the time we got to his brace. So Dr. Gupta simply rolled his chair back and allowed Jacob to remove his brace at his own pace. The healing is coming along miraculously there are only several spots around Jacob's knee where the body has done what they call "over healing." It has actually created little skin tabs, three of them about the size of a dime each.

The way they are removed is to be burnt off. Dr. Gupta used a tool that looked like a skewer that had a type of dry acid on the end. He used the tool to "burn" the tabs. They don't immediately fall off but will over time.

He basically rubbed this skewer back and forth at the base of each tab (OUCH). Jake got pretty upset (justifiably so); one at the sight of all the blood and two because they were probably burning.

After Dr. Gupta was done we put gauze pads around his knee to stop the bleeding. He covered his whole leg with Vaseline (a real thick coat) and then wrapped one thin layer of gauze and lastly returned the "sock." By this time, Jacob's face was dry of tears and he was happy the whole thing was close to being over. We put his brace back on which is thankfully pretty painless.

I thought (or maybe hoped) we would be swimming by this weekend. While the weekend is not here yet, I know in my heart things like standing, walking, swimming are in the distant future. In fact today, our major accomplishment is touching the top of his foot with my fingertip. We haven't even made it to the bottom or heel and don't even mention the toes.

The saving grace is Jacob's positive attitude. He may not always do as he's told and often he gets frustrated but never is he discouraged. This fighting spirit will take him far in life considering the hurdles that lie ahead. Our sweet boy, my heart breaks as I watch the tears flow at the doctor's office and two hours later my heart soars as I watch him laugh with joy as Happy (his turtle) eats out of his hand. We are sending our love as we always do, thank you for the prayers today. I think they were answered. Love, Jodi

Saturday, June 12, 2004 12:09 AM (journal entry) Jodi

Today was our first bandage change with the newly burnt skin tabs so Jacob was very anxious. We took our time, unwrapping each bandage, slowly and carefully. After we had completed all the steps of treatment, before we put his brace back on, Jacob was holding his leg with one hand and gently rubbing up and down his leg with the other.

He looked up at me with big tears in his eyes, the kind so sincere and so childlike you don't even know where they come from he said "Mommy, look at me I am touching my leg." How awesome is that? "Mommy, look at me, I am touching my leg!" I am surprised you couldn't hear my cheers! We celebrated with a glass of Diet Coke! We both filled our glasses and sat on the kitchen floor like we had just climbed Mt Everest. We were laughing and gloating about what a great job we had just completed. We were both dreading today's bandage change and just like most things; it wasn't as bad as we expected. We are over the hump. Each day will get easier from here. One day at a time. Much love, Jodi

Monday, June 14, 2004 11:30 PM (journal entry) Jodi

I was talking to my mom on the phone last night and I made a comment like "When Jacob goes back to pre-school in August" and just then Jacob interrupted me. He said "Mom I can't go back to school like this, I can't go to school with my brace." I told him he would be walking by then (God willing) and he would go back to school just like all the other children.

He said, "I can't go to school until I can walk—how will I get to the lunch room?" Of course in my mind, I am thinking of all the much larger barriers of not walking. To Jacob, it is as simple as getting to the lunchroom. I think mentally he just cannot comprehend that he is going to walk again.

Today scooching is satisfactory as long as he can get to where he wants to be. Each accomplishment makes him seem to crave more so eventually, there will be no slowing him down.

Well, enough for today. Brett and I were able to spend some quality time together. We still have lots of emotions to work through and each dressing change is a constant reminder. We keep working to stay strong, optimistic and most importantly connected as a family. Goodnight and God Bless, Jodi

Wednesday, June 16, 2004 11:34 PM (journal entry) Jodi

Today I suggested we fill the pool and to my surprise with a little nudging he agreed to go out and sit in his lawn chair beside the pool and splash around in the water. The idea of water touching his leg really scares him for fear that it will hurt.

He made it very clear to me he was not getting in. I filled the pool, we positioned his lawn chair right at the side of the pool and he began filling his buckets, floating his boats just enjoying the thrill of being outside.

After about 15 minutes of splashing poolside, his swim trunks were getting wet along with the rest of his body. Soon, he said, "Mommy, if we take my brace off will you get in the pool and I will sit on your lap? Just don't let my leg touch the water." Of course, I was thrilled so I said "absolutely." He got a big smile and started unstrapping his brace. He was moving so quickly, I knew he was excited. I sat him on my lap and propped his leg on the side of the pool where it wouldn't get wet. He went on playing and the more he played the further he sunk down into the pool. The next thing I knew he was sitting on the bottom of the pool and I was holding his leg. While he was distracted I just slowly over time allowed his leg to ease into the water. When he realized what had happened he looked at me with shock and excitement. He said "Mommy, oh my gosh look!" He pointed to his leg with a big grin from ear to ear, and then he said, "Mom my leg is all the way in the water and it doesn't even hurt!"

While I know this probably doesn't sound exciting but if you could have seen Jacob's face. We called Daddy to tell him to hurry home from his lunch appointment and we called Pop to tell him this unbelievable news! Really, it was an amazing feeling. We were both so happy. He played in the pool today like he did when he was a toddler, as if he was doing everything for the first time. Today was just good ole' fun! We have not had some of that in a long while.

Before we got out of the pool, I was able to really "loofa" his skin and calf area on his right leg. It is covered in dry, dry, dry skin and the hair on his leg has been really growing so the combination makes his leg very itchy! When we came in the house after swimming, it was quite the production to get him re-wrapped, gauzed, Vaseline and everything in between! Those darn skin tabs are still pretty open and sore, but thankfully they didn't bother him in the pool. In fact the water was probably good for them.

So, as always we are so thankful for our gifts today—the good, the bad and the in between! Goodnight and God Bless. Much love, Jodi

Thursday, June 17, 2004 10:31 PM (journal entry) Jodi

This morning, when Jacob woke up I am sure you can guess what his first request was "Mom, can we fill my pool and go swimming?" When we went downstairs Pop's blue truck was already in the driveway, he couldn't wait to see the swimming extravaganza. Jacob was still extremely cautious getting in the pool; it took him a little while to get comfortable again. But, in the end I think he even enjoyed himself more today than yesterday. Maybe because today Pop was swimming with him.

I thank God for the small favors, and I look forward to what tomorrow holds. Love, Jodi

CHAPTER 16

Finding "Our People"

Probably one of my greatest lessons through this journey is that you can do nothing on your own. Over the years, I have begun to talk about "finding your people." It's a concept I sort of coined while trying to navigate my own heartache and emotional journey.

Once Jake started to heal, I found myself with small increments of time and I was obsessed with finding "my people." I just felt the need to meet other families who had experienced what we were going through. Fellowship is one of God's greatest gifts. Giving us the capacity to feel empathy and connect with others is so therapeutic. I started spending my evenings, often the middle of the night searching the Internet. The specific focus of my search was to find other families who had experienced an accident like ours, more specifically a lawn mower accident involving a child.

I soon learned through a Shriners Hospital report that statistically one child is injured in a lawn mower accident every day within the United States. So I knew we were not alone. Looking back, I think the obsession really stemmed from trying to find hope for Brett.

In the months following the accident, Brett was diagnosed with post-traumatic stress disorder. I struggled to understand what this meant. I desperately wanted to help him and throw him a lifeline. He was drowning, and I was just standing there watching.

He continued to struggle with what life had dealt us. And even though each day brought new smiles and healing, deep down in the core of Brett's being he was still fighting a demon and punishing himself, leaving him in a place that I knew would not be healthy for any of us long term. I guess my thinking was if I could find other fathers who were either living with the same guilt or had recently been through a similar situation maybe Brett could relate to them. Maybe, just maybe, he could find solace in a stranger who could identify with his pain. I knew talking openly and sharing the story with someone who could relate would be healing for both of us.

The first flicker of hope happened when I connected with the chief of police in a small town in Utah. I came upon a story dating back to June of 2003 about a little boy and his father who experienced a very similar situation to ours. Bless the Web, I was able to locate this police station online and send an e-mail to the Captain. I told him of our story and my purpose to try and connect with the family. I gave him the information regarding Jake's website to confirm the validity of our story.

Within 24 hours, the Captain responded. Not only did he respond but also he provided the information from the other family. In fact, he said, their son is doing great and they would love to talk to us.

I remember we coordinated a call. Brett and I were both on the phone. We spent over an hour on the phone, both couples sharing our stories. While their little boy did not sustain the injuries that Jacob did, he did experience major trauma to his foot. And he has faced a long and difficult road to recovery. They related the story to us about the day the accident happened and what the next six months to a year looked like for them—the sadness, guilt, anxiety, and hope for the future. They felt the same emotions that we were going through. I remember Brett was fairly quiet through the conversation. When I walked into the room to see if he was OK, he was just sitting there silently crying.

That phone call would be one of many that we would experience over the next five years. Through the years to come, this was a common theme: We would search and find families. I even sometimes found the tables turning as I started to be a comfort to other moms who were in the early stages of a traumatic situation. When we would get on the phone or communicate via e-mail, we would feel immediate connections. It's like when you meet someone who is from your hometown or went to the same college, you immediately have a compatibility based on experience.

I knew that none of these connections were going to solve our problems, but they did provide validation in our journey. Knowing we were talking to someone who had walked a mile in our shoes provided a sense of peace I couldn't find anywhere else.

Again, fellowship can be a life raft in a world that is completely unknown and unfamiliar. These acquaintances were our own GPS, they were lighting the way, having already traveled the road on which we were embarking. I am still somewhat crazed with the Internet searching when I am seeking support. What I have learned is that I never have to look far as there is always someone who has already walked a similar journey.

Knowing this gave us renewed hope, and finding "our people" gave us the boost we needed to push on.

CHAPTER 17

Milestones

Three months into our new life, we were starting to get a rhythm, moving from intense day-to-day survival mode to actually thinking beyond the moment. Our life had turned into a series of small milestones that marked progress, and this was our attempt to put our life back together.

In July we let the air out of the mattress on Jake's bed and moved his top mattress back. We did a "goodbye air mattress ceremony." There was a time when it was simply too painful to sleep on a standard mattress. I thought he would resist, thinking he still needed the air mattress. However, he welcomed the change. I could see Jake's bedroom floor again. For three months, we had turned his bedroom into a makeshift hospital room. The dressing change baskets still lined the walls, but the floor was clear. We talked about how far he had come and that this is a sign of healing.

One day Jake asked, "Mom, did God see my accident happen?" I told him I don't know, but probably. He thought about that a little and continued on with other questions. He said, "How did you know I was in an accident?" I said, "I was called at work." He said, "Who called you, God?" I told him, "No, Daddy called me." He looked at me and said, "Daddy was sad I got hurt." Jake was starting to process and talk about what had happened. These were all milestones in our walk back.

Friday, July 16th, was 100 days since the accident. I had promised not to count the days, weeks, and months forever, but at that time in my life it was a significant milestone. It was proof to me that we could do this. In 100 days we had been through the biggest whirlwind of our lives. I have this slideshow that plays over and over in my head. Of the nights at the hospital, walking in the courtyard of

APH, the endless visitors, sleeping in our living room on an air mattress night after night watching "Tarzan." Laughter, tears and victories they all still seem surreal. In 100 days, so much had happened.

For a period of time, Brett and I completely lost touch with what was happening in the world. At that 100-day mark I remember journaling that I knew through all the sadness, good would come. I had seen the goodness in people, family, and friends a million times over in those 100 days. We had watched our son celebrate small victories despite the trauma he had incurred. We had so much to be thankful for; I just couldn't wait for the day when Brett could enjoy them with me. I knew even then his day would come. So I kept counting days and milestones.

Another milestone was the start of physical therapy (PT). As I was sitting in the waiting room of the Arnold Palmer Children's Hospital Rehabilitation Center for my parent orientation, I knew this was another turning point. I was eager to visit prior to Jacob's first visit simply to have a picture of what to expect. I needed to understand for myself before I could prepare him.

The facility was designed for children. They had a big, open room filled with tumbling mats, big bouncy balls, small stairs for climbing, hula hoops, hopscotch, and so many other activities for children to experience. It sort of reminded me of an elementary school classroom or play area. As we walked through the facility looking at all of this miniature equipment, I could feel the emotions welling up. It occurred to me this would be where our son will learn to walk again or at least gain the confidence to try. We will probably see him take his first steps here, just like we watched him do in our living room three short years ago. Our next visit to physical therapy would include Jake and we were ready.

As Jake demanded less of my time, Brett and I were beginning to spend more time together. All of life's demands continued, despite this crisis we were in. Brett was still required to work; thankfully, I was still on leave. The bills were due, and life responsibilities still existed.

We made a point to make sure each week we found time to talk. We would sit down and just reconnect. For a period we ran our marriage kind of like a business. We would make lists so when we had our "marriage staff meetings" we could be sure not to miss anything. We would assign tasks and timelines, and brainstorm on the big topics. Literally, this is what went on!

Often we didn't agree on next steps, but we were aware how critical compromise was for our family to survive. So we would agree to disagree or go through a pro-and-con exercise until we could land on a feasible option.

There was so much happening in our lives at that moment, and communication was our only lifeline. If we had not kept the lines open, our marriage might have disappeared. I had slept in Jake's room for endless nights; often the days were too burdensome; and Brett and I were both irritable at night. Without this commitment to our "talks," I think we would have found ourselves at distant ends of the world by the time Jake finally recovered.

I continued to give Brett his space when we weren't having our "staff meetings." I let him know we loved him and would support him through this process. It broke my heart to know how bad he was hurting.

At times there would be the flicker of the old Brett, and occasionally we would sneak out for a date night. In fact, Jacob had his first sleepover at Grammie and Pop's in late July. Pop had pitched the tent (despite the 80 degree temperatures), blew up the air mattresses, filled the tent with supplies like flashlights, walkie-talkies, snacks, and more. It was a fun night of soul food for all.

Jacob's mobility was definitely a turning point. While he was not walking, he was scooching everywhere. He would spend the afternoon's scooching around the grass and sidewalk looking for and catching creatures. He had a pretty good system for getting from point A to point B. He would tell us where he was headed, then Brett or I would have to transport his necessary equipment, which consisted of nets, bug catchers, magnifying glass, pretend tweezers, and so on. His slow mobility could not hinder his quest to continue to discover all that lived in our backyard.

It was the end of July before I finally fully understood the impact of medication. As I looked back on the weeks following our stay at APH, it was clear to me that not only the pain but also the medication took a major toll on his body. When we were finally able to transition from pain medicine to Motrin, there was a dramatic change in Jacob's disposition. Quite literally, he went from miserable to happy! Even today it still breaks my heart to think of how he must have felt for all those weeks. He was in chronic pain and experiencing extreme side effects from the medication. After I pieced everything together, I learned that he experienced severe withdrawals from the morphine when we first came home from the hospital. That first week home was probably one of the hardest, almost unbearable. That memory is hard to shake. If I knew then what I know now, maybe I could have handled it better. I am a believer in medication; when your child is in the kind of pain Jake was in, you have to give him relief. However, with everything comes cause and effect, and with pain medicine in a child, the side effects are great. Over time, I think we have learned to better manage his medications, but there is no doubt that managing pain is one of the most challenging things I have ever done.

There were times in the journey when I felt like I didn't even know who Jacob was; he was so out of his mind. Knowledge was a powerful weapon as we traveled this road, and I knew I would be better prepared for medicine in the future.

We began physical therapy in late July. I chuckled because before we left, Jake came scooching down the stairs and told me he packed a box of raisins, Buzz Lightyear, and a flashlight. All things any child would need for his first day of physical therapy!

When we arrived, Miss Kelly Fagan took us to the big open room where all the "action" happens. Jacob did not hesitate for a minute. As soon as we entered the room, we sat down on a big tumbling mat. He was out of his wheelchair immediately and bouncing around on the mat. We spent the first 10-15 minutes just telling our story. Miss Kelly wanted as much detail as possible specific to the injury.

She asked many questions and to no surprise to anyone, Jacob had many of the answers! He really interacted, doing a complete show and tell. When he stood, he informed her he was not ready to stand on his right leg. He was willing to just lean on something.

As Miss Kelly watched him, she said, "Have you ever tried a walker?" I quickly said, "No." I didn't even think they made walkers that small. So as he played, she left the room for a few minutes. When she came back she had a little bitty walker. It looked exactly like an adult walker, just built for a four-year old. She set it down in front of him and said, "OK, step gently with your right leg, tilt your weight forward." Before she finished the words, he was halfway across the room! We couldn't believe our eyes. He could walk with the walker without putting any weight on his right leg. He used his upper body and would swing his leg through.

The thrill of seeing him upright and moving across the floor, the sheer liberation he must have felt was almost more than a mother's heart could bear. Brett and I were grinning from ear to ear, and so was Jacob. Such a little thing—a walker—left such a huge impact.

That appointment was the first time anyone had tried to measure the movement of his knee. Miss Kelly tried to bend, and then straighten, his leg. His leg hardly moved. They tried again, and he participated, but not much luck. That would be the first of hundreds of visits where they worked on straightening and bending Jacob's knee.

The first thing Jacob wanted to do with his new walker was show Grammie and Pop. So we headed to their house immediately. I called them on the way and told them they couldn't come outside, that we would meet them at the door because we had a surprise. When we pulled in the driveway, Pop was at the front door waiting.

He went to the front stoop but waited with his eyes covered. Brett and I got Jacob out and set up his walker and off he went, straight to Grammie and Pop. When they opened their eyes they couldn't believe the sight. The flood of emotions was simply beautiful. Pop could hardly get the words out he was so moved. They loved this little boy beyond words and to have lived alongside him every day, every minute watching his pain, his endurance, his determination, and then to see him with this simple gift of a walker was more than we could ask.

Pop immediately "souped up" the walker. He put tennis balls on the back legs so they slid a little easier. Also, Don and Sandy Neal made an adorable handmade bag to secure on the front of the walker! This was a very important addition because then when Jacob moved from one place to another he could take his supplies with him Mi Mi, bug net, pack of Juicy Fruit and sippy cup, you never know what he was going to need.

The next day Pop and Jake decided to go on a small adventure with the walker looking for bugs, geckos, and anything that flies. I suggested that Jake try putting tennis shoes on his feet, that he may actually feel more comfortable using his foot if his toes were protected. For the first time in months, Jake agreed to put on shoes, although he kept laughing, saying his right foot felt funny but thankfully no pain.

As the summer came to a close, it occurred to me that an entire summer had almost passed and we had been doing the same thing the entire time. Dressing changes every day, physical therapy three times a week, constant pain management, the days and nights blurred. It was strange to think that school had let out, families have enjoyed their summer, and that school would soon be back in session. I just kept thinking, I know that time will heal.

We were pretty isolated that summer. Bug and gecko catching, fishing, and swimming in the kiddie pool became our "signature" summer pastimes. All of which made Jake very happy during some long summer days!

Every night when I would go to bed, I would check on Jacob. His little walker sitting at the end of the bed would put a lump in my throat. At the same time, I would find myself smiling! They say God does not give us more than we can handle, and I knew Jacob was proof. He had taken everything life had thrown his way and made the best of it. Despite everything that had happened, Jake parked that walker at the end of his bed because he knew tomorrow would be another morning that he could walk downstairs by himself! I really knew there would be nothing that could hold him down.

Strength, strength, strength is what Miss Kelly focused on during Jake's physical therapy. We had lots of at-home exercises that I made part of our daily activity. His rehabilitation was constant, and the responsibility on us as parents was great.

Pop would frequently join us at PT, and he provided great moral support for Jacob. It was definitely a family affair. Brett, Pop, and I were all committed to helping him anyway we could. One of the hardest challenges for him was going up and down the staircase at physical therapy. He would go up willingly, but coming down, he wasn't so happy. With every step, he would cry, not a loud scream, but worse, the mouth wide open, no sound, can't-get-your-breath-but-tears-are-rolling-down-your-cheek cry! I knew this would not be pain-free, but at night I would plead with God to have mercy on the boy. How much pain could he endure?

We prepared for Jake's return to school by meeting with the principal of Jacob's lower school, the family counselor, and his new teachers. We brought Jacob along, so he could show off his walker and all his tricks. He was very excited to visit the school. As always, Pop came along so he could entertain Jacob while we had a brief parent/teacher conversation. In the end, the teachers and faculty were great. They told us they were "up for the challenge" and would welcome Jacob into their classroom. Brett and I couldn't hold back our emotions. This was all part of the healing for us. I knew that with faith, a little bit of luck, and a whole lot of hard work, Jacob would eventually be walking to the lunchroom, chapel, the playground, and anywhere he wanted to go. It just took a little longer than I expected.

Thursday, August 05, 2004 10:45 PM (journal entry) Jodi
Tonight we attended the Welcome Back to School Event. Jacob was thrilled to be on campus and seeing so many of his friends. He trekked across campus with his walker like the Mayor of PCCA. So many people were saying "hello" to him and waving. I was waiting for him to start

shaking hands and kissing babies or maybe even sign a few autographs!

I can feel the presence of something great on that campus and when Jake arrived I could see the lift in his spirit. Sending our love across the miles, especially to our families in Michigan. We love you all! Till tomorrow. Love, Jodi

August of 2004 was a month of many milestones. It was our first steps in Jake gaining his independence. He started physical therapy, using a walker, and preparing for preschool. We were beginning to see the healing for Jake, both physically and emotionally. It was a beautiful place to be.

CHAPTER 18

At last something normal

Monday, August 09, 2004 11:55 PM (journal entry) Jodi

When I woke up around 6:00 a.m., I wasn't alone; I heard a little voice upstairs calling me. When I went up he said, "Mom, is today my school day?" When I told him yes, he decided to get up; it was time to get this day started!

Fast-forward two hours Brett and I parked at PCCA we loaded him, his backpack, lunch box, walker and supplies in his new wagon and off we went across campus to his classroom. When we arrived at his classroom, he climbed out of his wagon and used his walker to enter the room. He navigated his way though everyone and found a spot in the front of the class on the big area rug. I briefly talked to Mrs. Shelly Durichek (his amazing k-4 teacher), we gave him a kiss and said goodbye.

Around 10:00 a.m., I couldn't stand it anymore so I popped by the school to check in, not for him to see me but to simply observe. When I arrived the children were out on the playground. For the record, I will probably not do this again. The reason is that it only made my anxiety greater! You see, the playground is covered in mulch. This can be really difficult for maneuvering a walker. As I watched him he stayed mostly near the fence while the other children were running around, swinging on the playground. He was looking for bugs and geckos but mostly just watching the other kids. He even lost his balance a couple times in the mulch and tipped over. Mrs. Durichek was there with a watchful eye; and she would help him up right away. Nonetheless, as a parent, the sight is heartbreaking.

My feet felt like cement as I walked away! The tears rolled down my cheeks, but today I knew I had to give him space.

When I picked him up this afternoon he could barely put one foot in front of the other yet he announced "I had a great time at school today!"

We know this is a huge step in the right direction. Who would have ever thought we would come so far in such a short time. We are certainly blessed.

I am sure there will be more excitement to come this week. Much Love from the Bainter house, Jodi

Wednesday, August 11, 2004 12:20 AM (journal entry) Jodi
The day has finally come. I will be returning to work this Monday! Thankfully, my leaders are allowing me to begin by working three days a week. Tentatively the plan is that I will work Monday, Tuesday and Thursday. On my off days I will take Jacob to PT and/or school. Brett will help on the days that I cannot do it. I definitely have mixed emotions. While my heart is not ready to leave Jacob for any amount of time, I know that he will be fine. I do not know what the future holds, but for now, returning to work is the best decision for our family.

Till Tomorrow—Love, Jodi

CHAPTER 19

Hurricanes ... really?

I n August, Hurricane Charley whipped across Central Florida and walloped our house on its way through. Along with 1.5 million other Central Floridians, we were without power. The *Orlando Sentinel* stated that it would take a week to regain power for all residents in Central Florida. Our neighborhood was a mess, trees down, roofs wrecked, cable and phones lines down. It was really unbelievable.

It was an interesting experience to watch the destruction of Hurricane Charley and all the inconveniences it created. However, having lived through the last five months, my perspective was simple. Is everyone safe? If the answer was yes, there were no worries! Life experiences like Charley are out of our control. I have learned that we simply have to take what comes and put things back together when it's over.

A week after Charley, we began chanting "Go away, EARL!" That's right; we still had no power at the Bainter house as the next hurricane was on its way to the Florida coastline. No power in Florida during the summer is a major bummer, especially for the little man with a big brace on his leg. We had spent the first week after Charley hit cleaning up the yard, and Jacob was an absolute trouper. He had trekked through the yard with his walker, tolerated the blazing heat and for the most part kept all complaining to a minimum.

PT was canceled for multiple weeks following Charley because of downed trees and power lines, although Jake was getting plenty of therapy in the cleanup operation. There was certainly some irony in the Charley experience. I had been planning for weeks how to return to work and coordinate schedules, and then the week of the "big event" when I was finally supposed to return to work, Hurricane Charley strikes. Every day, every life experience continued to shape me, I was reminded that I am not in charge of this show. There is a much greater power at work. How I respond is what really matters.

Our hearts went out to all whose houses were damaged in the storm. This was my first experience with a natural disaster, and it was heartbreaking for the families who had lost so much!

I finally made it to work on Friday, August 20. Our power had been restored, and our life was seemingly back to normal. I had so many emotions driving to work that morning, and thinking of returning to my office brought back memories of the day that I had received that awful phone call. I had some time on the drive to think about things, clear my head, and prepare for a new beginning. My team surprised me by rearranging my office, and I was welcomed with cookies, flowers, and other surprises! It felt really good to be welcomed back so warmly. I was surrounded by some very special individuals who cared so much about me and my family. Again, I was feeling so incredibly fortunate.

Changing my office was a brilliant idea. I don't think my team knew, but it made my first day so much easier. Facing my office as I left it that day would have been difficult. Instead they allowed me a fresh start. How great was that?

All in all, my first day back went well. By noon, it felt like I had never left. Funny, how you can simply pick up where you left off. It was a nice change to allow my mind to think about something different. Although I was completely exhausted at the end of the day, I found myself looking forward to the weeks to come. I just needed to build up my mental endurance. Thinking about work and still having the care of Jake weighing on my mind would be taxing, but I knew in my heart it would get easier as time passed.

Upon my return to the office I was disappointed to learn that Roger the plant man no longer serviced our building and that he had been transferred to a new location. Roger had heard about the accident and came to the hospital. There was so much happening, we only had a few minutes to talk, but it was incredibly nice of him to come. I asked the new horticulture team about him and they assured me he is doing well. I know he is still servicing plants in Orlando and probably having an impact on other people's lives the way he did on mine. I hope that someday our paths will cross again, maybe when he reads this book!

Shortly after school started, Jacob began actually lifting his foot and taking a step without the support of his walker. We visited Grammie and Pop's; he was walking about five or six paces from the table to Pop, who was sitting in a chair. He would go back and forth. He had the biggest grin I have ever seen; he was so proud, he was beaming! He continued to embrace life with zest and intrigue. Even though he had once walked with no effort, those steps for him were exciting and new.

CHAPTER 20

PT, PT, PT—oh my!

As we rolled into the fall, physical therapy was starting to become the bane of our existence. Everything else was in motion in this stage of our lives: I was back to work, Jake was back at school, but still we had this giant hurdle of rehabilitation to overcome.

Miss Kelly, our physical therapist, was making me increasingly aware of the importance of getting Jacob adjusted to his "new" toes and leg. There were still so many things he was doing to protect his foot and leg that it was preventing him from fully using the limbs.

We had made it every day practice to put cocoa butter in my hand and rub it over his toes. He absolutely hated it, and he cringed the entire time. His toes felt funny to touch; there was no soft tender tip to the second, third, or fourth toe, just bone and skin. There was not much left of those three toes, but it was enough to be bothersome. I know how strange his little foot felt in my hand, and I cannot even comprehend how it must felt for him.

Monday, September 13, 2004 10:11 PM (journal entry) Jodi
Today, I could feel the ache in my heart and found myself once again fight back tears as I watched Brett in the waiting room at Dr. Birnbaum's office. He sat quietly, playing with Jake; I think I know what was on his mind. I know as we sat there he was replaying it over in his head. Days like today are particularly hard because there is no hiding from what happened. I am so sad for him. I wish I could change the circumstances. I can only imagine the pain his heart must feel.

Dr. Birnbaum's major concern is that Jake's growth plate is closing. If that happens, it will add new complexities to the long term reconstruction on his knee. This was just another gentle dose of reality. When I asked Dr. Birnbaum what he thought the prognosis would be he said, "Mom, unfortunately, this will be a marathon for your family, this will take lots of time and the distance is long." He went on to say, this is a waiting game, waiting to see what his leg does. When it grows, how it grows, they will respond accordingly.

As a piece of good news, Dr. Birnbaum agreed to arrange a second opinion. We pressed the issue today and asked that he facilitate the process and collaborate with the other surgeons on Jake's care. He has recommended a pair of doctors who specialize in pediatric orthopedics, specifically leg deformities and lengthening. They are based in Baltimore and from my understanding are fairly renowned in their practice.

We left today with a script for three CT scans at APH, 12 more weeks of PT, two new types of PT (aqua therapy and biofeedback therapy), a script for a new brace (he has worn the gears out of this one!), two toys from the toy chest, hope for a second opinion and again a very heavy heart.

Brett and I walked quietly down the hall to leave; Jacob was already outside with Pop. We walked in silence, both of us trying to collect ourselves and digest everything. We walked through the doors outside only to be greeted by the biggest dimples ever!

Jake said, "Look mommy, look daddy" as he began walking down the stairs using the railing. All the way down he went and then at the bottom with the biggest grin turned around and walked back up holding the railing for strength and balance. Thank you God for reminding me, it doesn't matter what we throw his way, he is a fighter.

I needed that at that end of a long visit. He has definitely been equipped with special coping skills. Thank you for keeping us close in your prayers. Love, the Bainters

Saturday, September 25, 2004 9:58 PM (journal entry) Jodi
Well, things are getting a little more difficult at PT. I think the newness has worn off and Jacob has figured out

what this "gig" is all about and frankly he is not interested. Having said that he does cooperate but he is somewhat hesitant.

Today, Kelly bared his skinny little leg. It is so shaky and he is so protective. I couldn't help but have a lump in my throat as Kelly put her hands around his leg.

She gently started rubbing his shin and calf muscle. As Jacob was playing she would point things out to me. She commented on how much muscle mass he has lost and all the scar tissue she could feel under the skin. She took his knee into her hands and cupped it. She looked at me and said, "When he is not here this is what I want you to do." Allow the warmth of your hands bring his blood to the surface and penetrate his skin. She said to me, "If he will allow, close your eyes and focus on his leg—think positive thoughts—focus your energy, do whatever you feel comfortable with—Pray" she said. I was particularly moved by her compassion, her hope and her guidance. It was a really beautiful moment.

She told me while this is not a traditional method of PT it is comforting for Jake and so important for his leg. The more we can hold his leg in our hands, touch his muscles and skin the more confident he will feel, the less protective he will become. You see, what I am learning is this is not just a physical injury we are trying to overcome, mentally; Jacob will have many milestones to cross before he can freely expose his leg.

His poor skin is so pale and tender and as Kelly said, "the areas of the injury look lifeless." Her goal is to put life back into those remaining parts and make his leg function again. WOW, so much work to be done. The burden sometimes is more than I can comprehend. Love, Jodi

Biofeedback was another layer of therapy added that fall. It was an intimidating procedure for sure. Miss Trish Anderson (biofeedback therapist) was so gentle and kind as she would attach cords and stickies all over Jake's little leg to run the treatment. The hope was that the nerves and muscles could be reprogrammed over time to help Jake better operate his knee. It was pretty complicated stuff and yet Jake's little knee continued to remain unresponsive.

CT scans, x-rays, aqua therapy, biofeedback physical therapy— OH MY! There was a period of time that this became our lives. The schedule was hectic, the demands were great, but we knew rehabilitation was critical. The days were definitely blurry, and my worry was that poor Jake's childhood was being consumed with continuous doctor's appointments.

Thankfully, Jake's fascination with the outdoors continued to come to life and be some of our best methods of therapy. The rainy season had brought an abundance of tadpoles and baby frogs. Jake spent hours in the garage sorting and separating the tadpoles. Those with two front feet in one container, the tadpoles with tails in another, the tadpoles that were almost frogs would go in another. Each group had its own container and sorting order. He was meticulous in the process and observation. All the while, I would suggest doing therapy with his foot and leg! The distraction was terrific for my therapy strategies.

Each day brought new learning, and slowly I was trying to step outside of the day to day and try to vision the path for our future.

"With man this is impossible, but with God all things are possible."
— *Matthew 19:26 (New International Version)*

CHAPTER 21

83,600 and counting

Sunday, November 28, 2004 10:29 PM (journal entry) Jodi

83,600, that was the number of visits tonight when I logged onto Jake's blog, it is amazing to think that over the course of the last 7½ months over 83,000 times someone has stopped what they were doing and logged onto our site to check on Jake. All I can say is thank you for all the encouragement! This is a hard stage right now.

This is the stage where you are expected to return to the old routine however all of the players (Brett, Jodi and Jake) have changed. Life just requires extra steps. I am reminded of this so often it sometimes makes me mad. Like when it is time for Jake to get dressed and his shorts don't fit over his brace. When bath time is over and he is confined to the couch until I can help him put his brace back on. Sometimes it's just another day and I go through the motions without noticing, other times it is a struggle. We are caught somewhere between recovery and moving on, AND the dreaded self pity.

So, in this stage here is what we have decided, the trick (key to survival) is to set no expectations, be constantly adjustable, have the capacity to accommodate and stay positive. I don't need to explain how hard that can be! Each on their own can be forever challenging, but for Brett and I, that's the agreement. That is our goal each day, the last point being critical.

So, when the schedule changes on a daily basis or Jake's walker gets left at home by accident, Brett and I remind ourselves to be adjustable. When we visit PT for three months and the only progress we see is a little more wiggle from the big toe, Brett and I remind ourselves to set no expectations.

When bath is over and we are running late, rather than becoming flustered with the process, I remind myself how to accommodate.

And last but not least when I see Brett get up from the conversation about Jacob at Thanksgiving and go outside, I later remind him how critical it is for us to stay positive. We are lucky to have each other because none of these could we do alone. We trade back and forth; I fill in for him when he can do no more and vice versa. This is what keeps our head above water, being able to count on one another.

On a fun note, Jacob saw Santa on Saturday. He said, he is asking for a Bunny, a kitty, a hamster and a guinea pig! Of course Santa said he would do his best, this could be an interesting Christmas!

Let the Christmas countdown begin! Love you, Jodi

We had crossed into a period of our lives where the crisis was somewhat behind us and normal living was upon us, only now our lives were beginning to be defined as appointments and treatments. So when people would ask, how is Jake doing? The real answer was he is doing great. He felt none of the worry that Brett and I felt. He saw none of the agony over what his future will hold. He saw each day only as a new adventure, no matter the outcome of his leg.

He woke up happy every morning despite the sleepless nights. He came home from school happy despite struggling to cross the mulch with his walker. How can this be? I guess it is the gift of being a child. Sometimes I wondered if he just believed at age four, this is what every child experienced and he was no different.

As Brett was slowly emerging from his depression there were flickers of his old self, and although we still had a long way to go he was teaching me lessons along the way. If Brett hasn't proved to me "how to adapt when things don't go your way, and survive," I don't know who can. In fact, as we arrived at the eight-month mark, Brett continued to show me his ever-growing strength, his faith and how we will get through this as a family.

He had taken the lead on running around, taking Jake to therapy, picking up, dropping off, making dinner, cleaning house. You name it, he was doing it. He was helping to hold this family together, and I was grateful. Physically he was functioning, yet emotionally it was touch and go. On the surface, things probably looked pretty good. Underneath it all, we continued to muddle through. We were swimming as fast as we could. Because giving up on Jake, our marriage and each other was just not an option.

CHAPTER 22

Cookie power

In early October, I was getting really antsy for a second opinion. Dr. Birnbaum had sent a note of introduction to Dr. Herzenberg, a well-regarded pediatric orthopedic surgeon in Baltimore, who is highly accredited in bone lengthening and deformities. I was waiting patiently. A couple weeks had passed and we had not yet heard anything, so I decided to reach out to him again. I spoke to his head nurse and she told me he had received the information from Dr. Birnbaum and was reviewing Jake's case. I was so hopeful that he would grant us the opportunity to bring Jacob to his clinic for a consult and further evaluation.

After a couple of additional weeks passed, I could not wait anymore. I called Dr. Herzenberg's head nurse again and she told me that he was going to review Jake's file soon. I was disappointed but I knew he was a busy man.

Sometime in early December, I could not wait anymore. I decided I needed to shift to more extreme measures to get his attention. So, Brett and I sent Dr. Herzenberg a photo cookie bouquet. This was not just any bouquet; each cookie had a picture of Jacob standing in the backyard with his walker! 12 Big Sugar Cookies with the little man looking right at you! And we attached the following note:

Dear Dr. Herzenberg,
Our four year old son was severely injured in a lawnmower accident on April 9th of this year. Jacob's orthopedic surgeon, Dr. Birnbaum from Nemours Children's Clinic in Orlando has referred us to your clinic. We are seeking the

best possible options for our son and your reputation is unprecedented.

Like many parents, we are hopeful you will take the time to review Jacob's file soon. We are ready and waiting to book our flights to Baltimore!

Please feel free to contact Brett or me at the phone numbers included, or Dr. Birnbaum at his office.

We realize you are a busy man, so thank you in advance for your time.

Warm Regards, Brett and Jodi Bainter

Thursday, December 16, 2004 10:20 PM (journal entry) Jodi

Today, I received a voicemail from Dr. Herzenberg's (our Baltimore doctor) assistant. She left me a message asking me to call her at my earliest convenience. Of course, once again my heart was racing and my mind was spinning. For months I have been trying to make contact with these doctors and now it actually happened!

So, I called back immediately. When she answered, I told her who I was and that I was returning her call. I could hear the excitement in her voice. She said, "Mrs. Bainter, we received your cookies yesterday. Not only were we floored by the creativity, but more importantly, we were moved by the photos and your story."

She went on to say that even Dr. Herzenberg was moved and felt bad that it took such drastic measures to catch his attention! Nonetheless, she said, "I am reading the notes that Dr. Herzenberg wrote on your letter. He has asked me to contact you and let you know that he will be in Boca Raton over the holidays. He would like to know if you could bring Jacob to Boca Raton on Sunday, December 26th at his parents' house and he will see Jacob there!" Can you believe this? Not only have we made contact but now he is willing to see Jake and within the next 10 days.

I couldn't stop crying, not because I was sad, but because I was so overwhelmed. She went on to tell me that Dr. Herzenberg likes to make a point to see the children if he is traveling in the state in which they live to save the family the cost of coming to Baltimore. Can you believe it? I like him already.

So, I gathered all the details, confirmed the date and time and then began the phone calls to Medical Records to obtain all Jake's information by Thursday of next week. Between photos, charts and x-rays, it took a while to make sure his file would be inclusive.

As you can imagine, Christmas came early for Brett and I this year. And even though we have not yet met Dr. Herzenberg, I really feel peace knowing we are doing the right thing for our son. And, the fact that Dr. Herzenberg is going to see us while on his holiday vacation is truly remarkable. I am sure this is common practice for him since he has committed his life to helping children. But, that day will be monumental in our lives, and never forgotten.

Thank you for your prayers, I am confident they continue to be answered. I realize that there are no easy answers or maybe no answers at all, but I have to know we tried. We will continue to be persistent until we have exhausted all options. And at that point, I bet we meet success!

In the end, the cookies were a success. Brett said that is the best $50 he has ever spent! I hope you are smiling as you finish reading this entry. I can't get that feeling out of my heart, of anxiety, excitement and gratitude. And I am relishing in the idea of hope.

For now, sending all our love, The Bainters

We had a wonderful Christmas that year. We were blessed to be surrounded by our family and friends on Christmas Eve and Christmas Day. On Saturday afternoon (Christmas Day), we went caroling at Arnold Palmer Hospital for Children. Nathaniel's Hope, a local nonprofit, coordinates Caroling for Kids every year, and we thought it would be something special to do on Christmas day. I was feeling incredibly compelled to find a way to pay it forward and this seemed a perfect way to encourage other families. Jacob chose not to go; he was still apprehensive about returning to the hospital, no matter the reason for the visit, so he and Pop stayed home. From the moment we arrived, we were very emotional. Just standing there in the lobby of the hospital singing "Silent Night," I closed my eyes, and was overwhelmed with emotion. Sadness for all of the families who would celebrate such a special holiday in the hospital, and gratitude for the blessings we received over the last nine months.

On the seventh floor, we were singing "O Holy Night," and straight ahead of us was Jake's old room. The door was open, another child lay in the bed where Jake spent 17 days, and the parents were standing in the doorway. It was really more than we could bear. I wanted to run down and give the family a hug, reassure them that they, too, will get through this, but instead, I allowed them to enjoy the carols and the gift of hope that all these people were offering to them on Christmas Day.

We drove home in silence that evening, too much on our minds, with incredibly heavy hearts. The first year of Caroling for Kids was hard, but we have since made it a family tradition, with Jake joining in. We understand that desperate feeling when your child is in the hospital but we want those families to know that better days come. That they are not alone and that God will provide.

Sunday, December 26, 2004 11:42 PM (journal entry) Jodi
Well, we started the day around 5:30am. We (Brett, Jacob, Grammie and Pop) were on the road by 7:00am, headed to Boca Raton. The trip was no problem. When we arrived, my cell phone rang. To our surprise, it was Dr. Herzenberg's mom. She was calling to make sure we weren't having trouble finding the house. Brett said, well I think we are parked out front. She walked outside and greeted us in the driveway. She was extremely warm and welcoming. She invited us all inside. When we walked through the front door, we were greeted by Dr. Herzenberg's wife and two of his daughters. They made us feel welcome straight away. We small-talked for a few minutes, and then Dr. Herzenberg's wife, daughters and mom left, so we could visit in private. Grammie, Pop, Brett, Jacob and I found a place on the sofas, and Dr. Herzenberg pulled up a chair.

We immediately got down to business. He asked a lot of questions, watched Jacob "get around" by walking and scooting and how he was using his leg. He reviewed all the files we had brought which took about 15-20 minutes then he viewed Jake's leg. We took off his brace and sock; Dr. Herzenberg had a great bedside manner. He talked to Jacob, asking him about his Christmas, while he was inspecting his leg. He had him do a few small exercises, like try to straighten his leg and bend or move toes and ankle. All of which Jacob willingly participated in. He, by the way, was a great patient. He cooperated and followed direction with no problem.

I had told him during the week that we were going to see a very special doctor on Sunday, and his cooperation was so important. I told him that this doctor might be able to help him use his leg more. As always, Jacob soaked up my words and responded as I had hoped. He is a smart little guy and extremely aware of the situation.

After Dr. Herzenberg checked out his leg, Jacob was free to goof around with Pop while we chatted. Rather than regurgitate the exact words of Dr. Herzenberg, I will give you the quick "Jodi" summary.

The situation is this. Jacob currently has little or no movement in his leg. It is essentially frozen in the position it is in today. Because of the trauma and scar tissue, it is optimistic to think he will regain any considerable amount of motion. Not impossible, but unlikely. The position it is "stuck" in currently is not the best position. It is sort of awkward, and not necessarily good for walking.

So, option 1 would be to fuse his leg in an almost straight position. Dr. Herzenberg presented this first, because it is the easiest and the end result is pretty guaranteed. This would mean they would remove the damaged knee joint and put a steel bar or pin where the knee was. His leg would be in a permanent slightly bent position. This option would accomplish a couple things. It would give him the stability he needs long term to walk without assistance or a brace, and it would free him of future surgeries, etc. This solution would be a somewhat final remedy.

If we put the fusion option aside, our other options are pretty limited because there are no easy ways to fix the femur and knee joint on a child so small. There was some discussion on a procedure where they actually fill the gap with a cadaver bone. He did not offer many options, simply because there are not many ways to mend the bone. We even discussed amputation, however, he feels that Jake has such a strong healthy ankle; a fused leg would be more functional and easier than becoming an amputee.

One of the big overriding challenges is the lack of movement. Because, the theory is, why do all the surgery to fix the femur and mend the knee joint, when because of the trauma, he can never regain motion anyway? You put him through all the surgeries to end up with a leg that still doesn't move.

On the other side of the coin, if we could regain motion, then it makes all the sense in the world to try and treat the injuries. Put him through the surgeries if we knew that there was potential to have a somewhat healthy leg long-term. Who knows these answers? We will only learn more and be able to make a more educated decision over time.

After spending about 40 minutes in discussion with him, we closed with this. He is taking Jake's slides back to his office. He is going to discuss Jake's case with some of his colleagues and Dr. Birnbaum. He committed to follow up with us sometime around the second week of January. Then he suggested we make a trip to his facility in Baltimore. He would like Jake to see his physical therapist team, to see their recommended course of action for more movement.

Since Brett and I are not yet sold on the idea of fusion, we are eager to visit the clinic in Baltimore. We are committed to continue to try and help Jake gain some movement. If he can move his knee, then Dr. Herzenberg is more likely to consider other options, like the cadaver bone to rebuild his femur.

The bone cement Jake currently has at the base of his femur is only temporary, and it will wear over time. There is not a real sense of urgency, but this does remain in the back of our minds. Dr. Herzenberg said he would prefer Jake to use his walker as it provides less stress on his leg. Help the bone cement last longer.

Yesterday was really difficult. The long-term implications of this accident were reiterated and the decision you never want to make as parents is unavoidable. I grieve with Brett because we both go back to that day and how everything can change so instantly.

We left feeling sad yet satisfied. I have no doubt in Dr. Herzenberg's abilities. He was extremely compassionate, articulate, and I trusted his opinions. We have some big decisions to make over the next 6 to 12 months. I pray that when we go to Baltimore that there will be more options. That Jacob through his therapy will regain motion in his leg.

Brett and Jake are already asleep in our bed tonight, I think I am just going to join them, something we normally never do but it just feels right tonight.

I think having them both close will provide a peaceful sleep. I love them both so much. I just want the pain go away. Free Brett's heart and heal Jake's leg. I know as we enter into 2005 this will be another difficult year. We have the good fortune of unconditional love from our parents, brothers and sisters, extended families and friends. My peace comes from knowing how blessed we really are. So, while this weekend was difficult I know this too shall pass.

Dr. Herzenberg is truly a God- send. He provided a quick reality check, options and hope. He is in the business of mending children, and I know whatever the decision, he and Dr. Birnbaum will guide us to make the best choice for our son and our family. That is really all we can ask for. Someday, when Jacob reads my writings, I hope he will know that we agonized, we loved him, and we tried to make the best choices possible for his future.

Well, as we all know, in life there are lots of things we don't deserve, and many situations alter our lives like divorce and death, but the true test is what you do with the outcome. Hopefully, even though Jake or Brett "Didn't deserve this" and "it has changed their lives," they will prevail despite of the adversity.

Thank you for listening. I feel like I just conducted my own personal therapy session. We are praying for good things to happen. Sending our love, The Bainters

CHAPTER 23

Baltimore

WOW is what kept running through my mind as we sat in the waiting room of the Rubin Institute for Advanced Orthopedics at Sinai Hospital. Wow, how life can change in a year. It was the first time since the accident where we blended in with the crowd. Practically every child there used a walker or some sort of walking device. There were children in casts, external fixators on their arms and legs, all types of contraptions much more complicated than Jake's. In some strange way, it was very therapeutic for all of us.

We spent a couple days in Baltimore meeting with Dr. Herzenberg and his colleagues. Together, they were able to provide us a really detailed overview of Jacob's injury, and some recommendations for next steps.

Dr. Herzenberg knew that we were not 100% convinced on fusing Jake's leg. Therefore, after much discussion, we all agreed we would continue to work hard at gaining function in his knee. The plan was to try a special orthopedic brace and see if it would be possible to achieve a greater bend over the next 6-8 weeks. Before we left Baltimore, they actually casted Jake's leg, then cut the cast off as part of the process for creating the brace. When the brace was complete, an orthopedic technician put the brace on Jake's leg and tightened the restraints. Well, that about shot Jake right through the roof! It was extremely painful for him, and he was screaming to take it off, literally screaming.

I remember that Brett disappeared; it once again broke his heart. I tried to comfort Jake; we quickly relieved some of the tension, and removed the brace. Jake looked me straight in the eye and said, "Mom, that brace is stupid! In fact, I am never wearing it again!" I have never heard him say "stupid," so I knew he was trying to come up with a word that would catch some attention. And that he did!

We returned home with a plan to wear the brace a couple hours a day and work into wearing it through the night. The goal was to achieve a straight extension of the leg in 6-8 weeks.

During the trip we gained a great insight. We learned that there were two key considerations in our decision; form and function. Meaning, just because the leg may not be in the form you are looking for, if it has the function, you can find satisfaction. I found that advice to be profound, and I would reference it later in our journey.

Many tears fell following those days in Baltimore. My emotions were sadness, anxiety, worry, and probably just sheer exhaustion. I kept thinking that we can send people to the moon, but we cannot fix a little boy's leg.

A few days after pining over the options, I decided to write to Dr. Herzenberg a note. The one option that had not been discussed was amputation. There were doctor visits during the past nine months in which it had been brought up, but only for a fleeting moment and then everyone agreed to table it as a last resort.

But, after much thought, knowing the available options, amputation in my mind began to become a viable solution. So I decided to ask Dr. Herzenberg three questions. The first was, is it our right as parents to make the choice of an elective amputation? Second, what does this surgery entail? And finally, what are the risks and recovery?

Now, certainly we could never make a decision based on this information alone, but it was a starting point to see if Jake was even a candidate. I explained in the e-mail that as gruesome as this choice may sound, in some ways it seemed the best of the worst options we had be given.

You see, in many ways I felt amputation could have the potential to offer Jacob the lifestyle we so craved for him. It would give him the form and function that we had discussed. It would not inhibit him like fusion, and it would possibly free him from endless surgeries, therapy, and the other obstacles that could lie ahead with a bone graft operation.

I told Dr. Herzenberg that I was not asking him to make our decision, but to simply educate us, and let us know if this could be a viable option. I had thought about this option all day. The more I thought, the more convinced I was that we needed to explore it further. Certainly there are all kinds of mental and physical challenges that come with amputation, all of which I took incredibly seriously.

But, in my mind, I was thinking if we could find the strength to get through the process, we may be doing Jake a service in the long run.

Dr. Herzenberg provided a quick response. He did not recommend amputation at that point. He recommended first to continue the plan to get Jake's leg straight and moving by using the special brace we received in Baltimore. Then, IF Jake gained the flexion, he suggested moving forward with allograft (donor bone graft).

If this procedure was not effective, the next choice he recommended would be fusion. And should Jake not be satisfied with fusion later in life, amputation could always be a worst-case scenario. Writing this now, I find it funny that amputation was characterized as the "worst-case" option.

After much discussion with Brett, we agreed with Dr. Herzenberg. It was important that we stay the course. It seemed that it was too soon to consider amputation. It was one of those moments where I think I was in a sprint, yet the marathon had just begun. Making that kind of decision before we had turned all stones seemed premature. I had to slow down, and we would walk as a family, slow and steady, and see what the future would hold. I knew the topic of amputation was not over, but the truth was that, at that point, we just didn't have enough information.

So we forged forward. We committed to working hard on gaining an extension over the next six to eight weeks. At the time, I had no idea where this would lead us; I just knew we could sleep at night knowing we tried everything. I knew our job as parents would be determining when to draw the line. What are we willing to put Jake through? The answer would come in time.

CHAPTER 24

Jake and the dreaded brace

Monday, January 24, 2005 11:55 PM (journal entry) Jodi
Today was the day to start the daily brace routine. Since it is a plaster cast you need to pull it apart and slip his leg in so it is a two man job! Brett was a great help even though he dreaded being a part of it.

Once the brace was on I pulled the bands to tighten the tension, which was immediately painful. Jake would look at me with tears and say, "Mommy, that is hurting real bad," I would say OK look at the clock we only have 10 more minutes. I was reading a book to keep him distracted. This went back and forth until we had completed 20 minutes. I told him when the big hand was on the 12 we were done, and sure enough at one minute till he watched intently until the clock struck 12.

We set up a chart where we measure his leg. We committed to e-mail photos to the team in Baltimore every 12-14 days. We took some pictures tonight to send as a starting point. So, keep your fingers crossed. I am not sure exactly where extension will take us but I have faith in Dr. Herzenberg and for today that is our assignment. Since all three of us are pretty competitive this should be interesting!

So every day we will use his new brace. We started with 20 minutes and this week we will work to 45 minutes and the long-term goal is 3-4 hours a day. Whew, I am tired thinking about it. The thing about this brace is I have the feeling he is going to need our undivided attention. It will be like PT and he needs the support of both Brett and I to cheer him on! So, we will have to carve out time daily to dedicate to the task. I am thinking Brett and I will alternate to give him time with both of us.

So, this is where we are today. Although I desperately want to look six months ahead and picture our lives back to normal, I just have no idea what this year will hold. Without a doubt, it will hold more hospital time, more tears and painful decisions. But more importantly, it will hold lots of smiles, time with family and friends and hopefully a few special miracles! Much love, Jodi

Tuesday, February 08, 2005 11:58 PM (journal entry) Jodi

Today was day 18 of using our new brace and we continue to work hard on our new assignment. We put it on everyday for a minimum of 3-4 hours and we were even able to get Jake to wear it through the night a couple nights this past week. All this being said, the truth is he really hates it (and so do Brett and I!). Every day when it is "brace time" he comes up with 50 excuses why he cannot or does not want to wear it. Of course, Brett and I insist, he doesn't cry too much and generally cooperates after some persuasion. Although, when we pull the tension on the orthopedic bands he does cry and beg us to loosen the straps. It is a tough one because you don't want it to be completely uncomfortable but it needs to be tight enough to be productive.

The brace is really uncomfortable to sleep in. It is sort of big and bulky and gets tangled in the sheets and blankets. Nothing he can't handle but it is just sort of annoying which causes him a restless sleep.

Last night we measured his leg, we have a simple process for measuring which includes charting his progress on a wall chart. He sits on the floor against the wall, stretches his leg as far as it will go and then we mark where it falls on the chart. So, drum roll please, according to my chart, his leg has not moved at all!

Not a millimeter! I thought this can't be true but I think it is. I can definitely feel his tendons and muscles loosening and his leg seems to be bending more but it has not moved any further into an extension. It seems to be in a "hard lock" position and movement to a straight position is just not yet happening.

Well, enough of that. Tomorrow is Pancake and Pajama Day at Jake's school and he is really excited. He plans to wear his power ranger PJ's to class! I moved PT and bio around this week so he could go! I am excited for him because all work and no play is a big drag! So no more therapy till Friday, but it will be a double header and we will still have to "do" the brace!!!

I am going to end here, it's late and I am tired. Love, Jodi

Exploring and researching, that was my life in early 2005. We thought we were making great progress after our trip to Baltimore but started to get discouraged when the brace was not providing any improvements. We began to wonder, what the point of the brace was if we are not seeing any improvement; only pain and angst for Jake.

I decided to make another call to Dr. Birnbaum, and in that conversation we toppled upon another idea. We talked about the ideas that the Baltimore team had offered, and when we got on the topic of bone graft, he mentioned that maybe we should consider talking to Dr. Douglas Letson. He was a surgeon based out of Tampa and well known for his care of pediatric cancer patients and his work with bone allograft. Dr. Birnbaum told me that Dr. Letson visited Nemours Children's Clinic in Orlando once a month and that he would get us an appointment to see him.

I knew this was another turning point, and we were ready. At the same time we were casting a wide net, I sent our application to Shriners knowing they treat many lawn mower cases each year. I had talked to one of the social workers from Shriners in Tampa, and she was very helpful. I knew if nothing else, they had an unbelievable network of families and resources that we could potentially tap into. Tampa was so close, and at that point I was just seeking options.

It was sometime in February of 2005, that I finally made the decision to step down from my leadership role at Disney. It was a difficult choice because I really loved my job and my team, but Brett and I decided it would be best if I could move into a part-time role at Disney and reduce some of my professional responsibilities. It was an absolute blessing to learn I would be able to stay in my division and begin working part time. I was so grateful for the mentorship of Ed Fouche' and Trisha Warne; they exemplified what we all hope for from a leader, looking out for me as a professional and as an individual. My heart was conflicted about the change, but I knew I just didn't have the capacity to be an expert at both work and home during that time in my life. Taking a reduction in pay was certainly worrisome, but we made the decision thoughtfully and were prepared for the sacrifices that would come. The good news is that I found peace in my decision. I knew how much Brett and Jacob needed me, and this allowed me to make them my priority.

My commitment to my professional role remained the same. On the days I worked, I knew that was my priority. I would work hard to clear my thoughts on the drive into work and focus on the task at hand. Some days I would drive in silence just processing my thoughts. Many days I would play my beloved Wynonna Judd soundtrack; *Her Story: Scenes from a Lifetime.* So many songs from that soundtrack spoke straight to my soul. Silly as it may seem, it was my therapy!

At that stage, life was literally one day at a time, but work took a little more planning. I was quickly learning that organization was critical to my success. I would look five days out knowing what was expected for that week. That way, if something went sideways at home, I still knew the work expectations/deadlines. Even though I was lucky enough to begin working part time, it continued to be a constant juggling act to find balance, and I worked hard to find my rhythm. I wanted to maintain my role at work; for one, we needed the paycheck, but more importantly, I loved my job, the company, and the people I worked alongside. I knew that someday, when the dust settled, Jake would be healed. I did not want to lose myself along the way. I was fearful that I would become "Jodi, the mom of the boy with the injured leg," then when Jake was healed or gone, who would I be? This kept me motivated to maintain perspective on my professional life while working to solve the dilemmas at home. It wasn't easy, and certainly there were days that the whole house of cards could and did come tumbling down. But it was not for my lack of effort. I worked hard to keep all elements in motion for me, for Jake, for Brett, and for my employer.

Organization and planning became key elements of my survival. On Sunday night, I would review my calendar and the expectations for the week ahead. This literally coupled with the conversation I had in my head everyday as I drove into work, helped keep me calm. It was a constant and deliberate mental game. I worked hard to leave my burdens at home and not cloud my attitude for the day. This was a never ending balancing act yet served a valuable purpose, allowing me to keep my career and family afloat.

CHAPTER 25

Renewed hope

Sunday, February 20, 10:55 PM (journal entry) Jodi
Friday morning we met with Dr. Letson, the oncologist who specializes in orthopedic cancer patients. He is well known for his limb salvage techniques and Dr. Birnbaum had arranged for us to meet him on Friday during his rounds at Nemours.

When we arrived at Nemours around 9:00 a.m., Dr. Birnbaum was there waiting for us (on his day off I might add!). Instead of the normal orthopedic waiting area we met Dr. Letson in oncology, he was great and from the moment we met him we felt really comfortable with his words. He was extremely articulate and made us feel at ease.

For Jacob the base of the femur is where he received most of the trauma. The bulb on the right side of the femur is called the lateral condoyle and in the accident Jacob lost almost the entire right lateral condoyle. In addition, he lost the tissue and mass to the right of this bone that supports the lateral side of his knee. So he basically had a big hole, everything that was supposed to be there was gone.

The blade also cut through the growth plate at the bottom on his femur. Any trauma to the growth plate can trigger what the doctors call growth arrest, causing that portion of the bone to stop growing. Long term this would result in a limb-length discrepancy.

When the accident occurred Dr. Birnbaum used a temporary solution called bone cement and secured it at the base of Jake's femur. Without a substance to fill in that gap, Jake couldn't stand complete weight bearing. One challenge is that the body does not like a foreign substance rubbing against a natural substance. Meaning the material of the bone cement does not wear well in Jake's knee joint so long term this material must be removed.

Dr. Letson said that Jake has lots of good healthy leg left so let's try and preserve that. His recommendation would be to try and mend the lateral condole with a piece of human bone from a cadaver. The theory would be that they locate a bone and basically carve it to fit his knee.

So, at this stage in the game, a bone graft seems to be the top recommendation.

The optimal outcome would be that the bone takes as planned. In 12-18 months Jake begins using his leg out of a brace and/or cast a he regains function at a "normal and acceptable" level—meaning; bending, walking and maybe running. He may not be interested in high impact sports but without basic functionality we will not consider this a complete success, per Dr. Letson!

I am cautiously optimistic. I hope and pray that the miracle of modern medicine can allow Jake to use a bone from another's body to give him back the use of his right leg. There is always the chance that we begin this process and one surgery leads into another and so on, it can be a slippery slope. But, we cannot NOT try! It will be our job as parents to monitor how much is too much. Only time will tell.

I am already beginning the mental preparation. We may face another summer in Florida in a CAST. We will have to pull out some of last year's tricks for entertainment. A trip to Michigan is always good for a little distraction and cool weather!

In the meantime, we keep using the orthopedic brace. On Friday, they took new x-rays of Jake's leg so they could measure the space and begin the search at a bone donor bank. We will wait to hear from Dr. Birnbaum to determine next steps! Sending our love, Jodi

Wednesday, March 09, 2005 5:12 PM (journal entry) Jodi
Today I learned that Dr. Letson has sent Jake's x-ray file to the doctor at the University of Miami to find a proper match. Dr. Letson's assistant said they are locating a

donor bone and then Dr. Letson will Michelangelo the bone to fit Jake's tiny femur.

I was telling my mom that at no point did Dr. Letson even call to say "now, can I gather your insurance information because I am sending Jake's files to Miami" Instead, he just kept pushing on after our gratis visit at Nemours. I know we will work out all those details in due time but it is just another example of the type of surgeon he is, he is doing exactly as he committed to do, find a bone and have it sculpted (or Michelangelo'd) to fit Jake's small knee! Talk about passion for your work! I like him already. For today, Jodi

CHAPTER 26

Egg hunt and Easter reflections

Sunday, March 20, 2005 9:07 PM (journal entry) Jodi

Friday was Jake's Easter Celebration at school. Pop and I were able to go and participate in the festivities. At the end of the party they had an Easter egg hunt. Pop and I helped some of the other moms hide the eggs while the children waited in the classroom.

The entire time we were hiding the eggs I kept thinking to myself, this is going to be interesting. How is Jake going to "run" around and gather eggs? I was mostly thinking the children will all be able to maneuver so much better than him that he may not be able to gather any and get discouraged. And how was he going to use his walker, carry his Easter basket and move quickly across the mulch.

Well, let's just say, that's why I am the MOM, I do all the worrying and he makes it happen!

When the classroom door opened, he was leading the group with his walker. He was grinning ear to ear as he headed to the gates to the playground where Pop and I and some other mom's were standing. When they reached the gate, all the children stopped behind Jake and Mrs. Durichek. I hadn't said a word or shared a single thought about how this was going to unfold.

As if she could read my mind, Mrs. Durichek said, "OK children, I am going to open the gate and allow Jake to get inside and get started and then everyone can follow." As simple as that the children all said, "OK, GO JAKE"! Off he went, giggling out loud and instantly he was filling his basket with eggs and the other children came running in behind him. Mrs. Durichek and I caught eyes; she gave me a wink and continued on!

The children were all gathering eggs and shouting to each other. Some would even say, "Hey Jake, over here." Well, needless to say, Jacob managed his walker through the grass and mulch, he had Pop carrying his basket and all in all he nabbed 21 eggs! And I think they had a 20-egg limit! Now, if the truth were known I think Pop may have hidden a couple special eggs in close proximity for Jake to find but we'll keep that as our little secret.

All in all, he didn't miss a beat and the Easter Egg Hunt was a complete success. I think the lesson for the day was, never underestimate the will of a child, especially when there is candy involved. My nerves were tapped but Jake had fun!

This will be an interesting week and weekend for us. Although Easter happens to fall in March this year, last year it fell on April 11, just two days after the accident. Good Friday of 2004 is the actual day the accident happened.

Today, Jake and I pulled out our Easter decorations and I have to say, it brought back some memories. I remember coming home Friday night (April 9th, Good Friday 2004) while Jake was in his first surgery. After they wheeled him into the surgery, Crystal drove Brett and I home. We ran to the front door and I remember the Easter Bunny hanging on the door and the house being filled with Easter decorations. We were only home for 15 or 20 minutes but strangely I remember it well. Seeing the decoration again was eerie, I could almost feel the ache of those initial hours.

After some reflection I watched Jake place the Easter decorations around the house and that Bunny is even back on the front door AND I am excited. We have so many gifts to celebrate this Easter it truly is a time of renewal. We are home and 12 months stronger!

We have been invited by Bert Lace to attend the Easter Sunday service at Orangewood Presbyterian Church. Ironically, we met Bert and Pastor Jeff Jakes last year on the Monday, following Easter Sunday. I remember the visit well, Jake was still in ICU, Bert and Jeff had heard about our accident from a mutual friend. They showed up at the hospital filled with compassion and the hope for healing. They took Brett and I to a private room and we sat hand in hand—all four of us. We cried, prayed and shared a moment of such sadness and despair. From that day on, Bert continued to visit the hospital what felt like every day and continued to come to our house long our days at APH. Also, the members of Orangewood Church brought us meals and gifts for many weeks following our return home from APH.

Anyway, it seemed to us like the perfect place to spend this Easter Sunday. I will be proud to share with the families of Orangewood how far we have come and how fortunate we were to have been loved by so many from their church during such a difficult time!

I guess I am getting a bit sappy but to have been at our lowest of lows on Easter of last year—to today—is really something to talk about. Our worship this Easter Sunday will undoubtedly be one of renewal and thanks. Thank you for all of God's blessing over the last 12 months, for no infection, all the people who have crossed our paths leading and guiding our choices and our faith, Jacob's strength and tenacity and Brett's courage to pull it together. The list could go on and on.

Well, on that note I will end here. Tonight I am thankful for:

The Easter bunny on the door

The 60 second lead at the Easter Egg Hunt

And Bert for extending such a special invitation to our family.

It is interesting how this week in particular is different for Brett and me. This year has brought so many things but our spiritual journey has been most important. We will go into this weekend with such a different perspective and appreciation from years past. We will spend this weekend with our eyes raised toward heaven knowing this journey would not be possible on our own.

Much love, Jodi

Our lives had become such a roller coaster, I wrote the next journal entry just two weeks after spending a prayerful and reflective Easter weekend. You see it wasn't uncommon to find us rejoicing one week and in anguish the next. The uncertainty of what the future would hold never left our minds. God was teaching us a powerful lesson in patience, and I must admit I didn't like it at all!

Sunday, April 03, 2005 11:35 PM – Jodi

Tonight I have mixed emotions, primarily I am feeling frustration.

My frustration resonates from the fact that a whole year has passed and while Jacob has made amazing progress in so many regard, in the end his initial injury is still as stifling today as it was in June of last year. I was watching him out the window this afternoon the front yard. Each step he requires such energy and effort of his little body.

Brett and I feel the same way about this. We know we have no choice but to accept watching him struggle as he tries to keep up with his friends in the yard or his worry over keeping up with the kids at the Easter Egg hunt. I think even after 12 months it's just too soon to put all those "hopes" aside. And if it is hard for me, you can only imagine Brett's struggle. Learning to raise Jake with this disability is a job onto itself. Sometimes we don't even know what to do. Do you rescue him? Do you let him flounder? Do you talk to him about it? Do you act like it's not happening?

He generally does not get mad or frustrated over "trying to keep up", at least that is not the emotion we have seen display. He generally gets quiet and watchful. As parents, we will always struggle with when to reach out and when to let him find his way. We don't want to enable him yet we want him to feel our compassion and support. In the end, we follow his lead; I guess he will be our best guide.

Today is harder in some ways than those initial days. The days in the hospital were physically exhausting, today is a complete mental game. Brett and I are working hard to hold it together. We are always learning, unbelievably willing and forever faithful.

I am passionate about the next steps for Jake. If we can try this bone graft, if nothing else when the cast is removed his leg will be in a better position for walking. Today it is too bent to have a normal stride, which makes his walk so awkward. Well, enough for tonight! Love, Jodi

CHAPTER 27

We have a match

Tuesday, April 19, 2005 11:44 PM (journal entry) Jodi

Around 3:00pm the phone rang today. At the time we were getting ready to walk out the door to go to Brett's parents house for dinner. My mom answered and the person on the other line asked for me. Mom, trying to expedite our departure, said, "I'm sorry, Jodi is not here right now, this is her mother can I take a message?" The lady responded by saying, "Do you know when she will be home, this is Chris from the bone and tissue center in Miami and I need to speak with her, it's very important." Of course mom immediately handed me the phone.

The rest of the conversation went something like this, "Mrs. Bainter I am calling to notify you that we think we have located a bone match for your son." WHAT, I couldn't believe my ears. My heart was racing. She went on to tell me that they are pretty confident they have found "a bone match" and that I needed to notify Dr. Letson to initiate the necessary paperwork to obtain the bone.

My mind was reeling, you wait and wait for this call … and when the phone finally rings and you hear the words through the receiver your mind goes blank.

I was speechless.

Chris was all business, short and to the point. She said, the next step is to notify Dr. Letson and he knows what to do from there. I prodded her a little to try and extract more information. I said, did you have the bone at your bank or did you obtain it from another bank? She said, "We obtained it from another bank." My heart sank to my feet. The emotions I was feeling at that moment were incredible. Joy was pumping through my veins, this is what we have been waiting for but, I could not help but think that as I celebrate another family was grieving. That ache was indescribable.

The words that still hang with me are, "We are pretty sure we have found a match." This means they are not 100% about the match so I am trying to contain my expectations. I am hoping to know more tomorrow or by the week's end.

I still cannot believe today we got the call. Mom and I of course dissected the call analyzing every word as only a mother and daughter can do like, when will the bone be ready? How quickly will this all come together? Will my insurance cover the transplant or slow this process down? Then, after we had said our peace, we put it to rest.

I couldn't help but look back at what we were doing on April 19 last year. I pulled this from my entry on April 19, 2004.

> *I must admit, I was feeling discouraged earlier today. It often feels like we take 2 steps forward and 3 steps back. But, then after a difficult decision like using the feeding tube, I am reminded of our purpose. Jacob needs Brett and I to make tough decisions, to hold his hand through the ouches, to smile even when we want to cry. He needs us to push him forward even when he wants to stop. I am hopeful that someday in the not too distant future, he will be pushing us and we will have no choice but to follow his lead! I know in my head how critical these small painful steps are to his recovery; it is my heart that I keep trying to convince.*

After reading that entry I found it ironic that those words I wrote would be so applicable on the same day one year later. "Jacob needs Brett and I to make tough decisions, to hold his hand through the ouches, to smile even when we want to cry." This will be one of those decisions. We have a long road ahead and I pray that we will make the right choices. We will need the rally when this special little bone finally makes its journey into Jake's leg becoming part of his body. WOW! Much Love, Jodi

From that first phone call, things started to move quickly and it was decided that Jake's bone allograft surgery would be scheduled for early July. Dr. Letson requested we do the surgery at All Children's Hospital (ACH) of St. Petersburg, Florida, because he felt most comfortable surrounded by the staff who supports him in this type of surgery.

He told us we should anticipate that Jake would spend three to five days in recovery. He would then spend a couple months in a full leg cast, in a straight extension.

Dr. Letson let me know that he would like another surgeon to help out with surgery. This doctor was also located in Tampa, and he specializes in pediatric orthopedics. They had worked together many times on cases that involved growth plate injuries such as Jake's, and this surgeon was skilled in the details associated with a growth plate injury. Little did I know that Dr. Scott Beck would become a very important part of our journey. He became a beacon of light guiding us through the surgeries and decisions to come. He became a friend and a trusted confidant. We will always be grateful for the care he provided our whole family, not just physical, but many days emotional. He is a special man.

There was a point in one of my conversations with Dr. Letson, when I asked if this bone allograft was going to work. His response went something like this: "All the other options are bad, so we can only hope this will work but there are no guarantees." He went on to say that there would be many variables that will determine the success: how Jake's body accepts the bone, for instance, and then how he grows and how the donor bone supports him as he grows. He said it would be 12 months for sure before we can determine success, then another 12 months to see how it holds up. So I began to process what two more years of working and waiting would look like.

The major variable was whether he could regain movement. There was so much scar tissue that when it heals the risk was it could freeze even worse than it was. A big unknown! Once again, we found ourselves in a wait-and-see situation. We knew the timing for the June procedure was good because that piece of bone cement was beginning to wear away from the bone. And with each day, Jake seemed to be losing more mobility and gaining more pain.

It was definitely time for the next step. More and more, we could see Jake's physical limitations, but thankfully there was no break in his spirit. I couldn't help but feel like the other kids his age were growing strong and learning to ride bikes without their training wheels, or swim in the deep end, or play baseball, while we were back to floating with swimmies and riding a tricycle. Jake was maturing, and his awareness was growing. He was asking me things like, "Will my toes grow back?" Finding the words to explain that they would not be growing back was sometimes hard to do.

He knew another surgery was coming and that he would wear a cast for a while. He also knew they were planning to use a donor bone, in fact he told his classmates that news. I often wondered what his comprehension was for these major events, but like most things, somehow I think he understood.

The next step was to meet Dr. Beck. The good news is that everything went seamlessly. Dr. Beck was already waiting when we arrived; he had reviewed Jake's x-rays and records, so he was prepared to chat. I liked him immediately. In summary, here is what I know: Dr. Beck, like all the other surgeons, was optimistic yet realistic. Meaning, they all agreed this was our best option but there were no guarantees. That being said, we remained cautiously optimistic and ready to proceed.

CHAPTER 28

When you can't walk - be carried

Sunday, April 24, 2005 10:04 PM (journal entry) Jodi

On Wednesday of this week, Jake's school hosted a walk-a-thon for as a student fundraiser. Well, when I first received the flyer I thought, "This is going to be interesting!"

I had talked to Jake's teacher ahead of time and she told me she would find Jake a good spot to sit and watch the walk-a-thon. She reassured me he would be fine. Tuesday night I just couldn't get it out of my head. I thought I hate it when he can't participate. Since they were walking in a field neither the wheelchair nor walker would work. Plus, they had thirty minutes to do as many laps as possible so there would probably be a lot of running; I mean they are four-year olds!

So, I dropped him off on Wednesday morning and Mrs. Durichek once again re-assured me she had everything under control. When I got home from dropping him off, I said to Brett what do you think about going over there and just checking out what's going on?

Brett and Grandpa Mike (my stepfather) headed over to the school. When they arrived Jake was sitting on the bench and the children were lining up getting ready to begin. Brett sat down beside him and said, "Hey, what are you doing," Well, Jake shouted "DADDY!' Brett said "You ready to walk?" and Jake said "Yes!" and gave him a big "thumbs up!'

Brett proceeded to put him on his back "piggyback style" and the two of them walked/ran 10 laps. When Brett was sweating and his arms tired, Grandpa stepped in and walked the final four laps with Jake in tote. All in all, Jake completed 2½ miles in the walk-a-thon. Every time they came around the course, they would get their lap card notated and Jake was smiling ear to ear! He even took two water breaks!

I share this because it really touched my heart and I know it will touch yours, too. You see, regardless of your circumstances, anything is possible—sometimes you just need a little extra help!

Now, I don't think Brett will be signing up for any "major" walk-a-thons but he certainly made one little boy really, really happy on Wednesday of this week.

As always Love, Jodi

Thursday, May 12, 2005 11:14 PM (journal entry) Jodi – Fractured Femur!

"What?" That was my response today when Brett called me from Nemours! Jake had slipped in the bathroom the night before and since I was working, Brett picked Jake up from school and they headed for Nemours for an x-ray.

When Dr. Birnbaum walked into the patient room the nurse had already put the x-ray films on the light on the wall. He took one look and said, "Well, he broke his leg." Brett about fell over, he said, "What how can this be?" With closer inspection it appeared that indeed Jake has fractured his tibia on the right leg. He has a small crack right where the pin was inserted last summer with his external fixator. It was plain as day on the x-ray!

I asked him what happened next and he said not much other than a clear directive from Dr. Birnbaum to TAKE IT EASY! Meaning, keep Jake off his leg as much as possible between now and the next surgery.

I called to check on Jake on my way home from work, he said, "Mom, guess what, I broke my leg and next time you shouldn't let me run around without my brace on!" Thanks Jake, good thing I have him around to keep me in check.

Keep your fingers crossed that we have no more "accidents." We are in extra safety mode at this house! Love, Jodi

Tuesday, May 31, 2005 11:03 PM (journal entry) Jodi

Last Thursday was Jake's last day of school for this year and the pre-k students put on a show for the parents and grandparents.

When the music began it was a western theme and one by one the children began skipping down the center aisle riding play horses dressed like cowboys! To our surprise, in came Jacob, he was riding in a "covered wagon" being pulled by Mrs. Durichek. They had creatively transformed the class wagon into a covered wagon for the sole purpose of allowing Jake to participate in the entry and ride around the sanctuary just as the other children did on their pretend horses! As Mrs. Durichek pulled him around I could hear parents commenting, "Oh look there's Jake." He was sitting in the wagon grinning from ear to ear.

We could hardly see through our tears. It is this strange feeling of pride, happiness and a tinge of sadness all at the same time, almost impossible to put into words. I cried openly as I watched. I was so proud of him and how far we have come. The other piece of me cried as I watched the tears roll down Brett's cheeks, knowing how hard this tugs on his heart!

When they finished circling the pews, they found their places up on stage. Mrs. Durichek lifted Jake out of the wagon and took him to his spot. She had not overlooked a detail. Not only did she find a way for Jake to join the children in the fabulous entry, on stage she arranged for a special spot on stage. He was sitting on a rocking horse positioned next to the risers where the class stood. Since there was a long period of standing, singing and dancing around and he was able to participate from his rocking horse! It was perfection.

Much love, Jodi

Jake's last day of school was the end of May. July 1st was just around the corner and he would be once again undergoing another surgery, this time to receive the much anticipated, donated bone. I felt the need to hunker down, yet Jake was feeling free. I knew what the weeks ahead would bring, but I didn't have the heart to smother his enthusiasm. That would all happen soon enough.

In collaboration with our closest friends, the Worden and the Davis families, we officially designated June 2005 as 30 days of fun!

And that is exactly what we had. We kicked off the first weekend with an airboat ride on the St. Johns River, then a weekend at Cocoa Beach to include a fishing tournament for the boys, followed by a weekend of playing on the lake at the Bainters' house. The kids would say, "See you next weekend," but that even ended when we began to meet for dinners, cookouts, swimming dates, just hanging out on the days in between. It was a very special time. We enjoyed lots of laughter and really some of the first carefree days in a long time. As the month came to an end, July 1st was on the horizon. We were tanned, relaxed, and loved.

Those 30 days were a life raft in so many ways. It allowed us to free our minds and just enjoy the friendships we had missed so much. It was a really beautiful time, and we have often said we should initiate another 30 days of fun, although there was something so priceless about those weeks, I am not sure they could ever be replicated. We will treasure them in our hearts always.

CHAPTER 29

The great bone transplant

Thursday, June 30, 2005 9:57 PM (journal entry) Jodi - writing from St. Pete

So we made it! We arrived in St. Pete today around 4:00 p.m. Brett and I were able to check into the Ronald McDonald House, St. Petersburg while Jake, Grammie and Pop went to their hotel to swim. The house volunteer gave us the "lay of the land," we also met some other families. It is always heartbreaking to hear other stories and see other families suffering. I have only been here for six hours and I have already counted my blessings on several occasions. Tonight when we returned to the room after dinner I had a chance to talk to Jake about tomorrow. We have been talking about the idea of surgery and cast for months but I wanted to fill him in on some other details. I mostly just wanted to prepare him, no surprises. And for a little boy who is going in for major surgery tomorrow I think he is doing pretty darn good. Not a sour word today. No grumbling or sadness—nothing. He never ceases to amaze me.

So with our strong little man leading the way we are all ready for tomorrow. Brett and I have said our prayers, we have cried our tears and we have found peace in our decision to move forward with this surgery. We are optimistic that tomorrow will open another door for Jake, giving him all the opportunities he deserves.

Well, I probably will not get much sleep tonight, but neither will Pop, or Grammie or my mom, or my dad, or our siblings and so on. We are loved by so many I know that tomorrow at 10:30 a.m. the prayers will be abundant. And have no doubt the little man will be strong!

Jake is sleeping without his brace tonight, I thought I better let that little leg enjoy one more night of freedom before that yucky cast! I was looking at his leg wondering what it will look like six months from now. Hmmm, I can't imagine—straight and bending—strong and sturdy—tan and healthy—no more pain, I can only pray.

Thanks for all the messages today; it is good to be loved! Goodnight and Blessings. Love, Jodi

Friday, July 01, 2005 10:34 PM (journal entry) Brett & Jodi
Right now I am sitting in Jake's room, he is sleeping pretty soundly. First let me report that today was a success. We are thrilled with the initial report from the surgeons.

We had an opportunity to talk to Dr. Letson and Dr. Beck prior to the surgery and get some of our questions answered. In fact, after our battery of questions, Brett asked Dr. Letson if he slept well last night and he said, "I always do," He went on to say, "I work hard and sleep good." He put his hand on my arm and said, "We will take good care of him mom." I knew Jake was in good hands; call it mother's intuition.

When they rolled him down the hall at about 12:10 p.m. Brett and I stood there holding hands waving good-bye, giving the little man the thumbs up sign. OOOOHHHH those moments are so hard. The love for your child is indescribable. Deep breaths help.

Sometime between 3:00 p.m. and 5:00 p.m. the surgeons came to the waiting area. They had big smiles on their faces and were full of optimism. They accomplished our first goal, which was to implant the cadaver bone at the base of the femur.

What's next? Well, he will certainly be in pain so this weekend will consist of pain management. He is currently taking antibiotics and Dilantin (another form of morphine) administered through an IV drip.

So, needless to say today he is full of medicine and not feeling too good. He has been mostly sleeping and will probably be groggy through the night. I have made our bed alongside Jake. Brett and I will be close by if he decides to wake up. Grammie and Pop will stay at the Ronald

McDonald House tonight. Brett and I are lucky to have them with us, they are such a God sent.

He is in a splint wrapped with ace bandages and he will be in this for the next 10 days then a cast. Tonight we pray for no infection. I also pray to give him some relief, he is pretty miserable, so medicated; in fact he has already vomited once. If only we could trade places, I hate to just stand by and watch. The narcotics are so hard on his little body. Well, this is the hard part. Tomorrow will be better. For now, Love, Jodi

Saturday, July 02, 2005 9:45 AM (journal entry) Jodi

All in all Jake is pretty miserable! Brett slept with us last night so we alternated between the roll away bed and the chair! It was nice to have him by our side, we have come a long way since APH. I forgot how cold and "unfun" hospitals can be. So we are going to get this little man well quick so we can bust out of here! Love, Jodi

Sunday, July 03, 2005 11:04 AM (journal entry) Jodi - morning update from St Pete

Today Dr. Beck came by to see us during rounds. He said, "Let's just give his body time to recover." He went on to tell us that the surgery was major reconstruction of bone, tendons, muscles, nerves etc. and unfortunately bone pain is extremely difficult to manage. Therefore all the pain and misery he has been experiencing is normal and to be expected.

Despite the pain, I will say Jake is getting his wits about him. When Dr. Beck left, the muscle spasms continued and we were waiting for a new medication. Jake looked at me and said in his "assertive five-year old grumpy voice," "Mom, where's that doctor, I want him in here now!" He went on to say, "I want to know what he is going to do about this." I said, "Honey, we are waiting for the pharmacy to get the new medicine" and he said, "Then get the nurse; I want to talk to her!" The good news is within 20 minutes they were able to obtain the new Valium prescription and within the hour it began to work.

Whew, thankful for the medicine today. All of our love, Jodi

Monday, July 04, 2005 8:58 PM (journal entry) Jodi - Happy 4th of July

Each day we make some progress. We are moving at a slow pace but making progress nonetheless. We do have a little cabin fever after completing day four in the hospital. The days are long and quiet. Jake is in and out of sleep and we are mostly spending our time managing pain. Stressful when he is awake, trying to rest when he rests! A little bit of déjà vu.

We did get him out of bed twice today. Since they don't have a reclining wheelchair we were able to "rig" up a wagon for transport. We took him one time around the hospital and the only time he perked up during the outing was when he was looking at the snails in the aquarium and the grasshoppers' outdoors!

Our release date is still unknown. Lots of stuff needs to happen between now and then.

I keep telling myself that miracles are happening under that splint. May you each enjoy many Blessings, Sparklers and Fireworks today!

Love, Jodi and Brett

Tuesday, July 05, 2005 12:15 PM (journal entry) Jodi - Medicine, medicine, medicine

Recovery is hard. It is like chasing your tail, "this medicine" stops the pain but makes you lose your appetite, the fluid IV helps to feed and hydrate him but until he can get off the IV he cannot leave. The Benadryl they give him for the itching (side effect of Morphine) makes him sleepy; when he's sleepy he doesn't want to get out of bed for PT and on and on and on! Until he participates in PT he can't leave. And lastly all the medicine and not eating made him throw up this morning so they gave him another medicine to settle his stomach!

I do think we are gaining on him feeling better, but it is a never ending juggling act. Last night he only bottomed out once with pain and he needed morphine again. His heart rate jumped up to 170 (80-100 is normal for a child) and his temperature was climbing due to the pain. After about 45 minutes Jake's sweet night nurse and I were able to calm him down and get him back to sleep. Then the rest of the night was great. He did wake up at 3:00 a.m. to watch a little TV and have a bag of chips! I was happy because food is good. Even though it was 3:00 a.m.! I am hoping soon we will be resting comfortably, eating, drinking and playing with Cozy (his beloved Guinea Pig) at home! We are tired for sure, and anxious to get back to Orlando. Hopefully tomorrow, keep your fingers crossed. Keep the messages coming—they bring a smile to a long day. WE LOVE YOU! Jodi

CHAPTER 30

Home sweet home (or something like that)

Wednesday, July 06, 2005 10:54 PM (journal entry) Jodi

We started out a little tired today but were pleased when the "on call" doctor came by and announced we were ready to go home! When they released us from the hospital we walked across the street to Dr. Beck's office, which is attached to ACH by an overhead walkway. Jake kept asking me what his leg was going to look like under the splint. I reassured him it looked the same as before the surgery with the exception of an incision. He was pretty nervous. It was hard for him to understand that it would look nothing like his original injury. When we arrived Dr. Beck's team took us directly back to their "casting" room. We put Jake on the table and he was extremely pensive. We had given him a dose of his pain medicine about 30 minutes prior to make sure the change was as painless as possible.

Dr. Beck began unwrapping the splint that had many layers of gauze and ace bandage wrap. Jacob was fretting the entire time. I was holding him trying to ease his anxiety but he did not take his eyes off Dr. Beck's hands. When they reached his leg and they were cutting the final bandages away, he was now crying with fear. When his leg was exposed and he realized there was one long incision and not more cuts he was absolutely relieved. He literally exhaled and said, "Whew, I was so worried"! It was really sweet.

It took them about 10 minutes to cast his leg and another 10 to dry and we were almost done. Dr. Beck is really remarkable and so kind. He took his time with Jake when removing the splint and recasting and handled his little leg with such care. Then he spent an equal amount of time answering questions and just having a conversation about what lies ahead.

The final story on our "journey to All Children's" was when we left. By this time it was 12:00 p.m., Jacob was exhausted and we were ready to load up and go home. Well, Brett had gone home on Tuesday night and returned this morning but what we didn't know was when he returned he brought COZY! So, when we opened the door for Jake to climb into the truck there she was in a travel case. He actually squealed with delight! It was so exciting for him it brought tears to our eyes. What a great reward for such a brave little man. He held her all the way home. When we got home he and Cozy got comfortable on the air mattress on the living room floor (Déjà Vu) again! And he has been there ever since. We fought over medicine and he moved around a lot trying to get comfortable but in the end he fell asleep and is now resting quietly.

We are thrilled to be home. All three of us are worn out. Tomorrow will be a day of recovery, just getting acclimated to being home and establishing our schedule. I am hopeful by the weekend we can wean him from the meds and resume some normalcy.

Thanks Grammie and Pop, I am not sure how I got so lucky but when I gained you as my "in-laws" there is no doubt I hit the jackpot! We could not have gotten through this weekend without you. We love you!!!! Great days ahead. Love, Jodi

Friday, July 08, 2005 3:34 PM (journal entry) Jodi - Hanging in!

Well, we have survived two nights at home. YAHOO!

The nights seem to be harder than the days at this point. All considered Jake is doing awesome. He is adjusting to once again dragging around the big cast. And as much as he hates it he eventually gets the medicine down and cooperates as best he can!

Wednesday night was tough; we didn't actually get to sleep until 4:00 a.m.! He had all kinds of problems, a tummy ache, and achy leg, uncomfortable and itchy. You name it, he had it! Once we were able to work through all the issues he was able to fall asleep! The nights were so incredibly difficult.

Thanks Uncle Todd for looking up courage, according to Webster's *COURAGE is defined as*: mental or moral strength to venture, persevere, and withstand danger, fear, or difficulty. You brought tears to my eyes, the affirmation fills my heart. I am so proud of Jacob.

We are seriously thinking about a trip to Grandma's in Michigan. Escape from the heat and hurricanes. Brett and I continue to pull each other close, knowing our stability and love will be Jake's foundation for healing! Much Love, Jodi

CHAPTER 31

Together we go

The aftermath of a tragedy is a really complicated place to be. The challenges we faced as a family were in some ways no different than anyone else. As Jake was healing, all the other life challenges—like finances, emotions, work—still existed. Brett and I found ourselves battling over things like "who was more tired or how could we pay our bills?" even "who was going to do the dishes". We were feeling angst at every end of the spectrum from the big stuff to the small.

There were a few things I learned, and I have stood behind them every step of the way. First, none of us is to blame. We are all tired, and there are no slackers in the family. The days when Brett could not find his footing are the days I needed to step up. Often times it had nothing to do with the accident; it was just the normal pressures of life, work deadlines or bills to pay. However, when you lay those challenges on top of an already tumultuous day, week, month, year, the situation becomes a pressure cooker.

There were moments like the middle of the night when I thought I could not go on—could not face one more screaming fit—meet one more looming deadline at the office—face one more medical bill—when we turned to each other. On the days I could not go on, Brett was waiting in the wings to help and me the same for him. Now it didn't always work seamlessly because there were days we when both felt we didn't have the energy to carry the burden, but a conscious awareness that one of us needed to step up was key. It was work, it required both of us to not lose compassion for one another and more importantly maintain respect for our individual journeys.

We tried not to point fingers at who had been through more, or keep a score card of who had more burden, we just committed to be there for each other no matter the angst. This is easier said than done, and trust me we were not always perfect. Often on the days when we were both exhausted, whoever got tasked with the "extra work" was bitter for sure. But we always worked through it.

Another valuable lesson we learned was to think before we spoke. How important it was to take a moment to evaluate the outcome of the conversation. This was an exercise of continual consideration—it was not about me, or about Brett; it was about us. There were two people in the relationship, and we each deserved full consideration, respect, and grace. We practiced this constantly through our journey, we tried to give each other space when needed, and we ultimately made a choice to work at our marriage. To be honest, many times this simply required both of us to stop talking, walk away, and let things cool down.

I would say our lifeline was a constant understanding of sacrifice and empathy toward one another. Empathy to your partner is such a gift. We could never lose sight of the other's trials, and whether they were greater or less than our own it didn't matter. They just were. This is such a valuable lesson, because now years later when the dust has settled we still have each other to lean on. We do our best to continue to practice those valuable lessons we learned. We are not perfect but we are perfectly capable!

I remember sitting in church (Discovery Church, Orlando) where I often found great moments of solace and encouragement. This particular morning (the amazing) Pastor David Loveless was teaching us a passage from Ephesians.

> *[10]Finally, be strong in the Lord and in his mighty power. [11]Put on the full armor of God, so that you can take your stand against the devil's schemes.*
> — *Ephesians 6:10-11 (New International Version)*

He asked the congregation, "What is the armor in your marriage?" This really made me stop and think. In this tutorial on marriage, I was learning that compassion and empathy were the armor that was allowing Brett and me to survive. It was becoming clear, that with those, the devil could not work his way into our marriage. For us, that just wasn't an option—so with our armor we stood strong.

Early into the summer and subsequent to a variety of conversations with Jake's pre-K teacher Mrs. Durichek, we made the decision for Jake to not start kindergarten until the fall of 2006. The list of reasons was long. However, the most important reason was to give Jake a fighting chance. His little body had just been through so much, and we wanted him to start kindergarten strong and ready.

So, with that plan, we prepared him to return to preschool in early August. We agreed we would continue a three-day school week schedule until he was comfortable and able to attend more. We knew he would return to school in a cast and using a wheelchair because his cast was not weight-bearing. All of this was a continued distraction for Jake. Mobility is an incredible gift, and without proper mobility all things in life quickly become more complicated.

Our whole goal for the 2005-06 school years was mostly socialization and just integrating Jake into normalcy. Knowing he would spend another year in the safe environment of K-4 with a teacher he knew and loved him was the only option. In the years that have passed, Jake has said many times "my mom and dad held me back" and he is a little annoyed that he won't be graduating high school with his friends who were born the same year. But someday when he is an adult, I think he will finally understand the mountain he faced. As parents our only intent was to make the climb easier. And during that time, in that summer, K-4 again was an easy decision for us.

I love this photo.
Jake's first day of Pre-K3,
August 2003

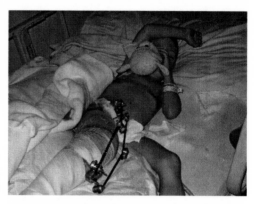

Jake in ICU at Arnold Palmer
Hospital for Children,
April 10, 2004

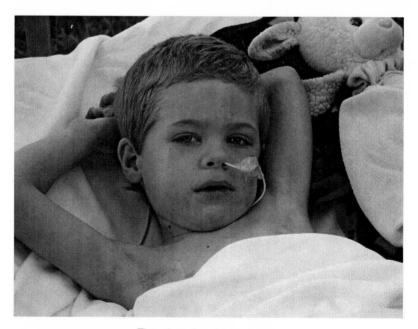

This photo breaks my heart.
We were approximately 10 days into our hospital stay.

A moment of pure bliss, sitting by the lake enjoying the sunshine.
May 2004

We took this family photo for our thank-you cards in August of 2004;
we were trying to put the pieces back together.

Jake and his new walker. That was such a liberating moment after being off his feet for five months!

Jake's first day of Pre-K4, August 2004

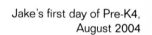

Jake posed for this photo during one of our many visits to Physical Therapy.

Jake and Pop in a terrific water fight! Summer 2004

A little relaxation after a big day in the kiddie-pool.

Many hours were spent navigating the yard with his walker, catching bugs and geckos.

141

Jake and Pop find a moment of quiet before the bone allograft surgery in July 2005, at All Children's Hospital in St. Petersburg Florida.

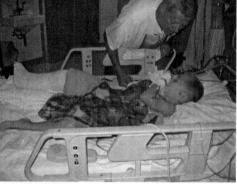

Pop was by his side after the surgery, July 2005.

When asked to pose for a picture, this was Jake's response! We were happy for the neon green cast, and ready to go home from St. Petersburg.

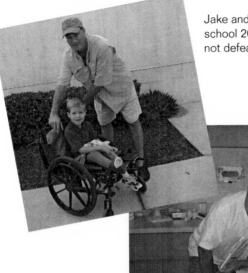

Jake and Brett, on Jake's first day of school 2005. A wheelchair and cast but not defeated!

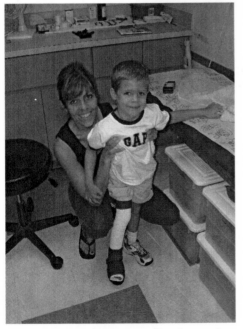

Jake and Pop in between cast change in Tampa, Florida.

Jake and I, another new cast!

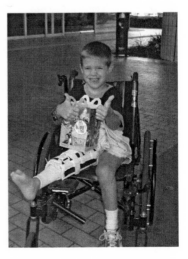

September 2005, cast off and a new brace. This was a new phase in healing and Jake was ready to go!

An afternoon doing what Jake loves the most… fishing!

Jake at Shriners of Tampa for gait analysis testing in the Spring 2007

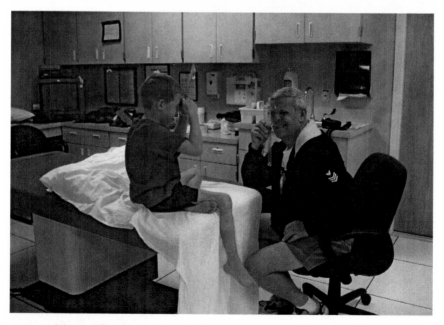

Jake and Pop passing time in the patient room at Shriners of Tampa

Jake and the amazing Scout during our meeting in Michigan, August 2007

A rare photo of Jake swimming without his brace, August 2007

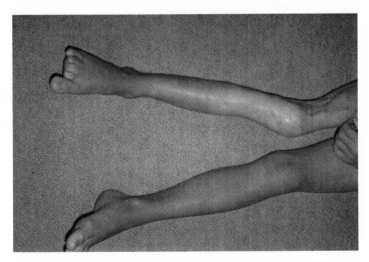

I kept a photo journal over the years to track the progression of Jake's leg. This photo was taken seven months prior to the amputation.

I snapped this photo the morning of Jake's amputation, when we met Boston Bill on the roadside. I had no idea how special Bill and this photo would become.

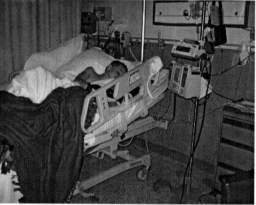

Our brave boy sleeping, following his amputation surgery. A new beginning was unfolding. February 20, 2008

Just 5 days following Jake's amputation surgery, a smile on his face and ready to go home!

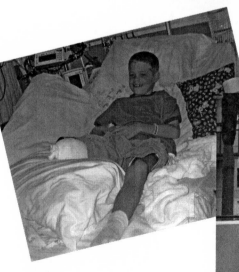

This was a giant milestone. The amputation was complete and we were ready to go home. Jake and Pop posed one last time in front of the hospital, ready to close that chapter of our lives.

Jake meets his idol, Kevin VanDam.

Jake and I during the awful
dressing change and the first
time reveal of his new leg.

31. Jake and Pop doing sand-art to pass the days

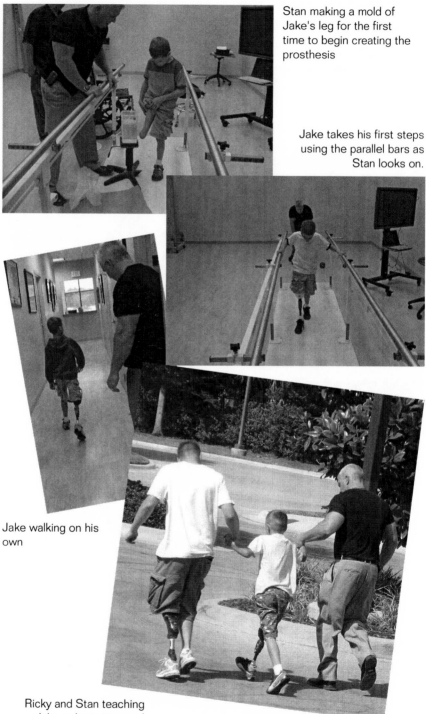

Stan making a mold of Jake's leg for the first time to begin creating the prosthesis

Jake takes his first steps using the parallel bars as Stan looks on.

Jake walking on his own

Ricky and Stan teaching Jake to learn to run. I loved this moment!

May 2008, life is good

At last, a summer without
surgeries!

Jake knee-boarding, Summer 2008

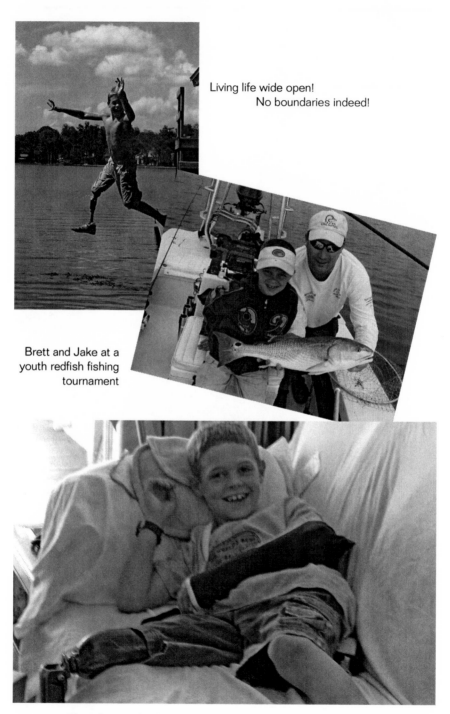

Living life wide open!
No boundaries indeed!

Brett and Jake at a
youth redfish fishing
tournament

The infamous broken arm, a minor setback in December 2008

Boston Bill presenting Jake with his first run-leg on behalf of the Challenged Athletes Foundation, Prosthetic and Orthotic Associates and Ossur, at the Challenged Athletes event in San Diego, California. October 2009

A new run-leg ... Jake was feeling strong!

The three of us just enjoying the moment. Healing had begun!

"Got one!" Jake; Summer 2010

Jake and the INCREDIBLE Dr. Novick in December of 2010. How far we had come!

Boston Bill completed his ride across the United States in July 2011. Jake was lucky enough to join him on his hand cycle for the last mile of the ride.

Jake and his best friend, Cooper Davis, had the unique opportunity to meet Winter the Dolphin in July 2011.

Jake and I, my sweet boy's fifth grade graduation.

Jake fishing in Key West, Florida Summer 2012

Peace at last.

CHAPTER 32

Cast on, cast off

All summer long, we traveled back and forth to Tampa. Dr. Beck established an orthopedic plan for Jake that required a "cast change" every three to four weeks. With each cast change he would attempt to stretch Jake's leg to gain a better extension.

Each visit, Billy Maxwell (the orthopedic tech) would saw off the old cast and replace it with a new one. Jake was always nervous because his leg had become increasing stiff, tender and weak. In fact it was so sensitive; just being exposed to the air caused him pain. Billy always worked quickly and did a great job of keeping Jake's mind on other things. He was absolutely awesome and Jake grew to trust him completely. Thankfully, Pop made every trip and was right there in the thick of things trying his best to comfort Jake.

I will say that one of the highlights of the frequent cast changes was Billy's cast artistry. He did a great job of entertaining Jake by creating designer casts to match the Power Ranger colors. He started with a bright green cast. Then he began to explore his creativity with a solid red cast and black stripes. His finale was my favorite, solid yellow with bright blue stripes.

The trips back and forth to Tampa made for a long summer, but I have to say, the timeframe when Jake's leg was in a cast was probably some of the best days for him. The cast kept his leg completely protected, fairly straight and pain free. It was actually a pretty liberating couple of months.

We had gotten a little spoiled with the protection of the cast and once again I found myself wondering what would happen when the cast was removed. Brett and I prayed until our hearts ached that God would grant Jake the gift of allowing the bone graft to work, to save him from more surgeries and to let him heal. That, too, was always the goal of Dr. Beck and his phenomenal staff and we will always be grateful for their tender care during the summer of cast changes!

Monday, August 15, 2005 10:03 PM (journal entry) Jodi: MUST HAVE ICE CREAM!

Today the ice cream truck came through our neighborhood. I was upstairs and I heard Jake yelling for me, I heard the front door fly open and by the time I made it downstairs with $1 and he was already half way down the driveway—ON HIS BUTT! He was scooching at top speed across the concrete, then stop to wave his arms and then keep going. Here comes the clincher; the ice cream man didn't see him sitting at the end of the driveway, arms in the air waving like crazy while he tried to catch his breath. And he drove right by!

We could hear the music fading away and he drove down the street. He turned and looked at me, his lip curled and eyes welling up with tears. Well, that was it, I scooped him up and off we went first on foot. But he was too far down the road. So, I said, "OK Jake we are going by car." I tossed him in the back seat we both buckled up and off we went on an "ice cream man mission"! He seemed a little surprised when I came wheeling up behind his truck, three blocks over but was happy to accommodate Jake's ice cream desires! When Jake finally had his ice cream he was smiles from ear to ear.

All I can say is that he is strong and healthy right now. He has made the best out of the situation and a cast does not stand between him and ice cream. He is eating well, sleeping well and playing full throttle! We are for the moment in a good place. There is no doubt that we have been cradled by God's grace. We are catching our breath and ready for what happens next. Blessings, Jodi

Wednesday, September 14, 2005 11:34 AM (journal entry) Jodi

The cast is off! I am so happy to report that yesterday was another successful visit. In fact, Dr. Beck said in terms of where Jake should be at this point and how the x-ray's looked we probably scored a 95%! We headed out yesterday morning, Brett, Jake, Grammie, Pop and me, a family affair. These Tampa visits are an all day event.

After the cast was off we moved onto x-ray time. Jacob is wearing a leg immobilizer which looks similar to his last brace although it keeps his leg in an extended position. Keeping his leg straight is critical.

We see Dr. Beck again in four weeks. Jake is free to walk on his leg with the brace. However, it will take a couple days to a week before the stiffness resides and it doesn't hurt to bear weight. Everything on his leg is stiff and sore all the way down to his foot. So, we will have to ease into walking over the next couple weeks so, back to scooching and wheelchair for now.

When we got home he went upstairs on his bottom and straight to his bedroom. He called me and when I walked in he was sitting on the floor, he said, "Mom, I knew this was going to be a problem, how am I going to carry Cozy downstairs if I have to use my hands to scooch?" It was his first moment of disappointment; you could hear it in the tone of his voice. Although, in true Jake form, it was short lived. By the end of the night he had figured out a plan. Cozy goes in his backpack, his backpack goes on his lap and off he goes on his bottom!

There is no easy fix in this situation so again the little milestones are all we can ask for. His leg looks great. It is straighter than we have seen it in 16 months. And, the shape is better; to me it looks more like a normal leg. I would go as far to say, I think it is even getting a little meatier! Not the same, skinny, scrawny leg it was before the surgery. We will continue to wait and see. Love, Jodi

CHAPTER 33

Choose joy

Thursday, September 15, 2005 10:11 PM (journal entry)
Jodi

Today wasn't one of Jake's better days. It started out a little rocky. He really didn't want to go to school. He said his leg was really bothering him and school would only make it worse! Amazing how quickly they learn these tricks. After some tears and negotiating we finally made it to school.

When we arrived at his classroom he was not interested in joining the class. He sat in his wheelchair very somber. I told him to have a good day; He said "OK Mommy."

As always, Mrs. Durichek came to the rescue. She said he was slow to come around, but eventually he joined in with the other children. In fact, she said he took his brace off to show the kids his leg. She said the children were very curious and Jake was happy to show them. I am not sure what that means, maybe nothing, but I am happy he felt safe enough to share that with the other kids.

Playground time was a bit of a bummer since once again he could only sit. He made do by looking for frogs and Mrs. Durichek said he seemed to enjoy himself. Whenever he is "land locked" the kids seem to move on without him, which is natural. They want to run and play and unfortunately they don't wait around for Jacob. In fact, after school tonight he told me that nobody played with him at playground time so he looked for frogs. He says it very matter of fact. I don't pry, I just say it sounds like you had a good day, looking for frogs is the best!

I was thinking this morning driving into work how deflated Brett and I were feeling this week. On one hand we are over the moon about how Jake's leg is healing on the other we are weary because the light at the end of the tunnel is dim sometimes even hard to see. Working toward an unknown goal certainly harbors frustration. All of this brought me to a quick reality check. As deflated as I was feeling this morning after the "morning battle", I was driving to work thinking it through in my head. What can we do different, how can we better prepare him or make it easier and so on. Then it occurred to me, if this is how Brett and I feel this week imagine how Jake must feel. Removing the cast and starting over again probably knocked the wind out of his sails.

I mean really, I get the luxury of taking a break. Today instead of carrying Jake to the kitchen table for lunch, I got to just take care of myself since I was at work. As for Jake, he carries it around with him all day. Literally all day he is faced with his leg. I get moments of freedom, he has none, and it's with him every day.

So I asked myself, what's my pity party all about? I have two healthy legs and the freedom to move as I please. My pity party was short lived.

I guess it all comes back to choosing your attitude. There is no doubt that must be hard to do when you are 5. Ironically Mrs. Durichek told me she had a talk with Jake today about making the choice of how you want your day to be. You can choose to be sad or you can choose joy. In the end he chose to make his day good, even though it took him a while he realized it is more fun to be happy. So after lunch he participated in the class activities for the rest of the day.

Let me just say, Jake by no means is any different than another child. He has the fits and talks back and everything in between. But he is a fighter and through that, he teaches me every day.

Tonight at bedtime after we took his brace off, I told him, "Wow Jake, look how strong your leg looks!" I went on to say, "I think we are getting closer to a leg that bends and works the way you want it to," he just grinned. He was thinking and then he leaned over and hugged me. He squeezed me tight. The HOPE for healing, it was so strong in his hug I could feel it. My faith is strong; I know that this will all be worth the wait, when the healing is finally complete. No sooner, no later—just when its time.

My dad has been telling me all my life that I choose my attitude, each day it is my choice to make my day what I want it to be. So today, just as Mrs. Durichek suggested to Jake, I choose Joy. I hope you do the same.

Love, Jodi

Sunday, October 02, 2005 9:04 PM (journal entry) Jodi

Jacob finally started walking again this week. He was taking gentle baby steps on Sunday evening and by Friday had a full stride. Since his knee is locked in an almost straight position and his leg is not completely weight bearing he does a "hop step." While it doesn't look like a normal walk it serves the purpose of getting him from one place to another. It is great to see him walking around the house again.

On Tuesday we saw Dr. Beck. It appears that the bone is continuing to form in the necessary places and the growth plate still looks clear. Dr. Beck has recommended a "high tech" x-ray and evaluation of his knee. So on November 10th we will travel to Brandon, Florida for the test. Unfortunately the procedure will require anesthesia and be done as outpatient surgery.

One of the things I really admire about Dr. Beck is he never overwhelms us by trying to forecast too far into the future, he just takes us in small manageable steps. Most importantly, he never leaves us standing still. And although Jacob's case is unique to anything he has done before, his knowledge and intuition seem to guide him and we are faithful to follow. As always, thanks for the never-ending prayers. We are grateful for every single one. Our love, Jodi

Wednesday, October 26, 2005 8:23 PM (journal entry) Jodi – FUN IN MICHIGAN

Today we arrived in Michigan for our annual Halloween "getaway." The whole family is going so it should be a great time. We are spending a couple days at my mom's house in Bay City and a couple days in Grand Rapids with my brothers and then a visit to Kalamazoo to see Aunt

Tammy, Uncle Corey, and cousins Luke and Gage. We have been counting the days and very looking forward to the cooler weather and time with family.

This past week leading up to our trip, Jake has been up in the night screaming in pain and begging us to do something, sadly Brett spirals right back to the beginning. So, for him the highs are high and the lows are low. And they leave him on an emotional roller coaster. Hoping for a restful and peaceful week in Michigan. I will write again this week, all I can say is brrrr ... Love, Jodi

Thursday, October 27, 2005 10:03 AM (journal entry) Jodi

This morning when Jake woke, his leg was bent in its usual position. That is what happens when he sleeps without his brace. It generally takes us 15-20 minutes to get it back in an extension and into his brace. He woke me up by tapping me on the shoulder whispering, "Mommy, can you wake up and start stretching my leg so I can get my brace on?" Basically he wanted to get up and run around but he knew he couldn't until his brace was on. I told him to get comfortable because it could take a few minutes, he said, "OK mommy."

His urgency was because he likes to crawl in bed with Grandma (Grandpa had already left for work) and wake her up. This is kind of tradition when we come to visit. I am pretty confident she is already awake but just plays along with the game. So, he was in a big hurry to get his brace on. In fact, I was laughing to myself because I had my hand on his knee applying pressure and he would sit up and press down as hard as he could, then he would say, "is it straight yet" I would say, it's getting closer, so he would try it again.

Funny, how he can help when he is trying to climb in bed and wake up grandma, but when I am trying to get his leg straight for his brace before school in Florida, he can hardly move!!!! So, things I am thankful for today:

Dr. Beck and his plan

Being pampered in Michigan by Grandma and Grandpa Bergen

Pop for taking care of all the pets while we are away!

My brother Todd, for entertaining Brett, and helping him have a great getaway

Tomorrow is the pumpkin patch, apple orchard, hay ride and all things of fun Michigan. Saturday is carving pumpkins and making caramel apples and the rest of the weekend will be filled with fun Fall activities! More to come. Love, Jodi

Sunday, November 06, 2005 7:14 PM (journal entry) Jodi

Trick or Treating was a blast. The only hiccup was that Jacob started on foot trying to keep up with the other kids and by house number five he was exhausted. He sat down in the grass and said he wanted to go home. At that time Uncle Matt shifted into action. He carried Jake to the next 10 houses while I ran home and got the wheelchair. Side note, Uncle Todd and Brett were already back at the house, inflating the tires on the wagon.

Together we returned with the wagon, Uncle Matt handed Jake back and off we went. Without skipping a beat, Jacob was then able to keep up with the kids and continued to trick or treat through the entire neighborhood.

All is well and Jake is doing great. We are now preparing for his next surgery this Thursday. For now, Love, Jodi

Friday, November 11, 2005 10:14 AM (journal entry) Jodi

Yesterday, the high tech x-ray procedure went seamlessly. Jake was really unbelievable. Brave and strong and when it was time to go with Dr. Beck not a cry or a whine just a wave goodbye. The results from the procedure were as expected, no startling news. Still lots of things that need to get "fixed" but there is nothing to indicate the healing is not happening as planned. As described by Dr. Beck, scar tissue is like concrete, very difficult to bend and stretch. So despite the news we push on. Much love, Jodi

CHAPTER 34

Finding our rhythm

In the end of May 2006, Dr. Beck gave us the summer off from appointments, surgeries and therapy. To quote him, he said "Let's allow Jake be a kid and enjoy his summer." For the last two years his summers had been a struggle, so as you can imagine we were making up for lost time.

We kicked off the summer with a trip to Michigan for a family visit. Then, we were lucky enough to take a trip to Arkansas to visit my dad where Jake spent six days fishing for trout on the White River. I must admit, it was complete bliss! In between trips, Jake had one thing on his mind, fishing, fishing and more fishing. He is officially a fishing fanatic.

The break from the regime of medical treatments was nice. Jake had been through so much and the struggle to resume a normal routine was ongoing. There was no handbook on what to do when your son is run over with a riding lawn mower. There was no Internet site, checklist, self-help, cliff notes or picture book—nothing. None of those resources were available. So we took it one step at a time. We learned every day. We learned Jake's boundaries, his abilities and we probably pushed him when we shouldn't have or just the opposite coddled him when we should have pushed. But, each day, just like every other parent we woke up and did our best.

At some point over those first two years we had shifted into "solve-the-problem mode": remedy Jake's injury and put Band-Aids on the broken hearts, tired souls, empty bank accounts and shattered dreams. Somehow dust ourselves off and move on. But I have to say, in our moving on, the pain and disappointment doesn't immediately subside. At one point, Dr. Nancy Cruce, our family counselor (Brett and I started seeing her following the accident) asked Brett what eats at his core, his biggest source of guilt. Brett responded with a long answer about how much it eats away at him that opportunities may have been taken away from Jake. Brett said it keeps him up at night thinking of Jake's disappointment.

After Brett finished, Dr. Cruce simply said, "You feel the guilt of making life more difficult for Jake." She followed that with God knows that life is difficult in general, let alone adding a disability to the mix. Especially in a society that glorifies athletic abilities and diversity. But God has a plan, and for Jake it will be great. We must be patient and not sad over what could have been. For what is yet to come may be better than anything you ever expected.

Our lives will continue to be that incredible balance of learning to live with both the celebrations and the sadness. The journey was long, and I knew our walk was not over. But when we began to embrace the unexpected turns our lives have encountered we found ourselves in places more beautiful than we ever dreamed.

We continued to grow closer as a family and draw strength from one another.

CHAPTER 35

Tissue donation – returning the gift

Monday, November 20, 2006 8:39 PM (journal entry) Jodi - TransLife Speech

Sunday, November 12th, Brett, Jake and I shared probably one of the most powerful days we have shared since Jake's accident. The reason it was so moving is after all the heartache we have shared we were finally able to give something back.

Last summer I was contacted by another mom (Dee Woolford) whose children attend Jake's school. She had heard me speak two years ago at the PCCA annual fundraiser and was aware of Jake's story. She worked for Translife (Central Florida's Organ and Tissue Donation Service) and contacted me to see if I would be interested in allowing Translife to use Jake's story to spread the good word about the importance of organ and tissue donation.

Shortly thereafter, I was invited by Dee to speak at Translife's Annual Remembrance Day Event. This is an event attended by 250–300 families who have lost loved ones and in their passing offered their organs and/or tissue to help another. The day is a time to remember their loved ones, celebrate their life and how they saved or changed other lives in their gift.

From the moment we stepped through the door of the Winter Park Civic Center (the location of the event) emotions were high. Brett, Jake, Grammie, Pop and I attended. We found our seats, which happened to be reserved in the very front. Jake sat right in the middle and waited patiently for the event to begin.

The emotion in the room was powerful and I was so nervous to stand before this audience and share my story. I prayed it would touch their hearts and somehow in all their grief and sadness, I could give them something to take home, maybe a little peace or a smile to know the impact their donation has had on people all over the country.

Jake's story would represent all the recipients, and even though they may never meet the recipient of their family member, he was a symbol of hope for them all. Whew, it humbles me just writing this and reflecting back.

After the speech I showed a short video of Jake and his journey. At the end, Jake joined me on stage. The audience cheered. I don't think there was a dry eye in the house. In fact, even the choir was crying!

Here is the beauty of this day.

Following my presentation people began to come to us. Each family shared their stories of the loved one they had lost. It was so meaningful to both of us, connecting the past with the future. At the day's end we were all exhausted. Our tears were dry and our emotions completely wiped out. But, our hearts were full. I think I actually caught myself smiling in bed that night.

I will always grieve deep in my heart for the things my husband and son have lost. But, I am open and ready for the ways this accident will continue to touch and change our lives and impact others. Much love, Jodi.

CHAPTER 36

A turning point

November of 2006 was poignant. I had a feeling in my heart that had been nudging me quietly ever since we met Dr. Herzenberg in Baltimore in January of 2005. There are moments in your life when something becomes so clear that everything else in your life falls aside. I had tunnel vision. In my heart, deep in my soul, I knew that if I could just get the courage to say it out loud, that maybe Jake would be better off without his leg.

I would lie in bed at night and think, how will Jake function with his leg like this. On the surface, our life had resumed some normalcy. But I found myself more unsettled than ever.

I felt Jake was caught between two worlds. He was not part of the able-bodied world, yet not part of the disabled world either. He was caught right in the middle.

I just could not stop asking myself, Is this the best we can do? I knew our son, and I knew this leg was holding him back.

In the fall of 2006, Jake had a series of incidents that pushed me further to question what we were doing. I felt that he started to take some steps backward. While he was craving to be more independent than he had been; his leg was not cooperating and ultimately holding him back.

Slowly, Jake began to not eat as well. His appetite at times was nonexistent. I spent hours planning meals and finding ways to elevate his energy. The nights were relentless. He would wrestle with pain until wee hours of the morning. It was common practice for me to still be in his bedroom at 3 a.m. This had become more normal than not in the recent months. The lack of sleep and food resulted in having a hard time focusing at school and just getting through the day. The pain often carried over into the day, and he had started taking

Tylenol at school. I would cringe every time Miss Sandy Larsen would call from the elementary office to let me know we were out of children's Tylenol, but I was running out of choices.

As a result of the trauma, Jake had several new problems progressively making everything more complicated. His injured leg was not growing at the same pace as his sound leg, and his knee had atrophied at a slight bend. Therefore, he was no longer able to stand flatfooted; instead, he was always propped on the ball of his foot. Further, as a result of the trauma and the amputation of his toes, his growth plate was affected in his foot so over time he had acquired a size discrepancy between his two feet. In the beginning it was not dramatic, but by that fall, there was a 2½ size difference between the right and left foot.

The combination of a small foot, frozen knee and limb length discrepancy began to affect his balance. As a result he was frequently falling, tripping, and losing his balance.

In September and October of 2006, we made three trips to the ER for falls. Well, actually we went to his pediatrician, and all three falls were so bad he decided to send us for x-rays. On the last trip to our pediatrician for a fall in which Jake hit his head, I was definitely at the end of my rope. Dr. Gregory Coffman could sense my frustration. I held back the tears as we talked through Jake's well-being.

While Jake went to find a treat at the nurses' station, I shared my thoughts with Dr. Coffman. I told him I felt like we had focused so much on saving the leg that we had lost sight of the "total" child. I told him I felt like the leg he was carrying around was so damaged it was dragging him down. I told him there were times when I thought amputation would be a better option. He offered me the gift of a listening ear and validation and I felt he understood my point of view.

About a week later, I was sitting at my desk at work. The phone rang, and it was Dr. Coffman. He said, this is probably not protocol and maybe I am out of line, but I have been thinking about Jake and I want you to know I endorse and support your idea. He went on to say, I think that with the advancements in technology and all the soldiers returning from Iraq, Jake may have a chance to have a more normal gait as an amputee. He said he thought Jake was not well, that this journey was beginning to take a toll on his little body. He commended us for exploring these difficult options and told me whatever we decide would be OK, but if we chose amputation, we would have his support.

I hung up the phone. My heart was racing. I closed my door, I put my head on my desk and I prayed. God knew exactly what I needed. I needed the courage to go forward. I was floundering and second-guessing myself, and that phone call from Dr. Coffman was just the motivation I needed to get going. It was time.

I began to craft a comprehensive plan. Sounds crazy, I know, but I knew this would be my greatest opportunity to improve Jake's quality of life once and for all. I would need to convince Brett and Jake's doctors that amputation may be an option to pursue. This was not a sales plan. I did not want to sell them on my idea. I wanted to educate them, to show them what I knew, show them the pros and cons and see if we landed in the same place. To be honest, I was running on a mother's intuition, it was time to get still and listen, and allow the Holy Spirit to be my guide.

There were so many variables to consider and so many moving parts. I had to do my homework, because the choice would be irreversible and the patient was the most important and precious gift in my life.

This journey, this decision, would turn out to be my greatest contribution to the never-ending search for what's best for Jake. I was on my way. I knew there would be no turning back. My first conversation was with Brett. He was not in agreement with amputation but he was in agreement that it was time to have a heart to heart with Dr. Beck to find out where we were going and what was next. I agreed and that was my cue to put things in motion. We would start with Dr. Beck. I knew this would not happen quickly, we would go through all the motions until our family could make a decision.

In my mind, amputation was not if but when. We said nothing to Jake … all in due time, he was too little and already carried a great enough burden. The time would come eventually when we had all the information we needed and we were convinced, and then we would present Jake with the option. At that point, it would be in God's hands to lead us and somehow make Jake whole again.

It was then that my quest began. I wanted someone to tell me: Why not? Why not amputate? I needed to know.

In December of 2006, I called Dr. Beck and asked if he would meet with us without Jake. I remember driving once again to Tampa, the trip we had made so many times over the last 12 months yet this time it was different.

We met with Dr. Beck in his office. We felt so close to him, I actually liked the intimacy of meeting in his office, surrounded by photos of his own children. This reminded me that whatever he recommended certainly came from his doctor vantage point, but more importantly he understood this decision as a father himself.

I was nervous. I had no fancy presentation for my case like I would do at work. This was all heart and mother intuition speaking. The words rolled off my lips as if I had scripted the whole conversation. I explained what Jake had been facing over the past four to six months and how we felt life for him was becoming increasingly difficult rather than somehow easier.

The cornerstone of my case was to no longer think about Jake's leg but think of Jake as a whole being. Stop thinking of growth plates and extension. Let's start thinking about what life would be like with a leg that is straight and never bends. What happens mentally, when every year you start your school year knowing you had another surgery on the horizon. What about all the missed field trips and afterschool activities for physical therapy and doctor appointments.

Although, despite all of those points, my greatest angst was the constant pain he endured. On days when I have a headache or I slept wrong and have a kink in my neck, I am completely unproductive. My focus becomes finding comfort and relief from the pain. This was how Jake had spent the last two years, distracted and preoccupied. The situation was always holding him back from fully engaging. I explained to Dr. Beck that he was falling behind in school and other activities. I felt like he was watching life pass him by.

As I talked, Dr. Beck listened. He was so gracious, and I think for a moment that he removed his doctor hat and was a friend, parent, and thought partner. He understood everything I was saying but with the grace I admired so much, he suggested we go through another step just to absolutely confirm we were headed in the right direction.

He suggested we go to Shriners in Tampa. Shriners could conduct a sophisticated set of tests and analysis to really understand Jake's gait and potential for improvement. This was part of our "leave no stone unturned" process, part of my "case for change." I needed facts and validation to support what my heart already knew. We hugged Dr. Beck goodbye. He looked me in the eye and said, "You will find the answers you are seeking." We felt so connected, and we trusted his advice. On the way home, we received a phone call from the assistant to the head of surgery at Shriners. Dr. Beck had already called them. By the time we arrived back in Orlando, our appointment was scheduled.

**Monday, March 12, 2007 2:10 AM (Journal Entry) Jodi -
Unraveling (only for a moment)**

In my personal journal I made this entry. You can see by my words that time and ambiguity were beginning to take a toll.

What is on my mind?

I am beginning to unravel. I started saying this in December, but I continued to repeat it since sometimes the words are coming out but maybe no one can hear me.

I am failing.

I feel like I am failing Brett, and I am failing Jake, I am failing myself.

Jake is struggling on so many levels, sometimes I wonder if it is real or my imagination.

He limps, he hurts, but he doesn't vocalize it. I have vocalized it for him to the doctors and teachers because I feel like he is too small to know it could be better, and it pains me that he has to just live with it. So I keep speaking out on his behalf.

All the things that concern me about Jake:

Becoming needy "sick" child – if you're sick for too long it becomes all you know

Becoming distracted by doctors, pain, disappointment, and not learning... I see that he is checked out at school; the teachers are teaching but he just cannot focus

He suffers daily from headaches, backaches, knee pain, extreme loss of energy and the endless peaks and valleys

What am I afraid of? I just don't want him to suffer anymore. Maybe I don't want Brett and I to have to watch it anymore. I know Jake can have a better quality of life. It is just so big; I am paralyzed with fear to take the dramatic steps to fix it.

What is going to become of his leg? The waiting and uncertainty is breaking me down. I cannot "wait" forever; I am not good at "getting by." It is so daunting—how can I manage this?

I am so desperate that I feel like I might be smothering him. I just can't stand it anymore.

Lord, please guide my way. I am unraveling.

How do I fix Brett? I kept thinking he would evolve, he would heal, he would be free of his guilt. Yet it still carries on. I feel very disconnected from him.

The tears are pouring down my face. How did we get here? I miss Brett, I miss my old life. I ache for the intimacy and friendship Brett and I shared. He is now so burdened with grief; he doesn't have room for me.

I am tired. I am losing myself in the process. I have never felt so alone, out of control, or insecure. I don't know what to do next. I feel restrained.

I feel like Brett is closing the door on me, he wants to just stay in this place, live in the darkness. He doesn't know how to get us out of here.

How can we teach Jake something we cannot do ourselves? I pray we do not fail him.

Every day I sift through the bills and wonder how we are going to do this. We are all making sacrifices and I feel anger welling up in me. I have hit a wall; I am not sure what direction to go.

I want the old Brett back. I want the strong leader of our family.

Sometimes I want to hide, not see Jake every day. Just avoid the problem, and maybe it will go away. I am unraveling—unlike anything I have ever experienced before.

Immediately following the accident I started running, running fast, never stopping, saving everyone, when will it end?

Here we are, Brett still buried in guilt. Jake has had a lot of surgeries but no better function, no big improvements and a leg that doesn't work.

And me, my body is tired, my mind is tired, my heart is numb, my dreams are hazy with unfamiliar images, my heartbeat is anxious, my focus unguided, my intuition unfamiliar, my judgment skewed, my intentions questionable.

Our finances are drained, my marriage distant, my life numb. Where are we now?

I have never been in a place where I am simply at a loss. What do I do?

I pray. On my knees I go, for I am learning when there is nowhere else to go, I am so grateful I have my God to lean on, "if I did not have you lord, what would I have?"

Tonight I will pray for guidance, I am ready, lord, I am ready. I surrender. This is yours, please show me the way.

Wednesday, April 11, 2007 2:17 PM (journal entry) Jodi

We started our visits to Shriner's in March, which was actually good therapy for me! One of the really amazing elements of Shriners is they have blended all the essential orthopedic services into one facility. Our first visit we met Dr. Cara Novick, she got right down to business. She came in and said to make this the most beneficial to all of us; I have pulled together a team so we can have this conversation with a perspective from all disciplines. Basically, I don't want to waste my time or yours.

Within a few minutes we were in a room with 6-10 people, representing many different orthopedic disciplines, everyone from pediatric orthopedic surgeons to the C.P.O's (Certified Prosthetist-Orthotist) and Physical Therapist.

She turned to me and said, "Well, tell us why you are here." I was completely flustered. I have said this so many times but in that moment, nothing came to mind. I said we just want to know if there is more—better—for our son.

Well, Dr. Novick not only answered that question but filled my heart with hope and validation. By the time we left that first day, she gave us hope that all the things we wanted for Jake were not out of reach. We just needed to find how to get him there. She went on to say, whatever the outcome of this exploration, we won't stop until you can find peace with his abilities.

On the first visit, they asked Jake questions to find out where he was emotionally and they asked him to perform tasks to figure out where he was physically. Brett and I just stood by and held back the tears.

He was totally unaware but this would be another milestone, a turning point in his life.

In fact, when we left that day, I had to walk around the corner and just cry. Brett was confused, he was happy and couldn't understand why the tears. But, what I felt was relief. They saw the things I could see. They endorsed my hope that we can do better. That he could have more, a new flicker of hope. The brilliant Dr. Novick was on the scene.

The first round of gait analysis was an all-day affair. That day we showed up at the hospital (mom, dad, Grammie, Pop, iPod and UNO cards in tote) and spent the day in the motion analysis center. Jake walked back and forth across the room about 100 times that day! They did everything from a full physical exam to have him walk across a sensor that tracked the pressure points of his foot and hooked him up to sensors all over his body to record the motion of his stride, really amazing stuff. Exhausting for a little person, but thankfully he went with the program.

Before the day was over they took another mold of his leg to design some customized braces. From the mold two different styles of orthotic braces were created. The goal of each brace would be to support Jake's knee and modify his walk to minimize pain and damage to other joints. At the last appointment, they fitted Jake for his new braces and conducted another round of gait analysis with and without the new braces.

On Monday, he will begin wearing the first of the two braces. He will wear it for four weeks; we will keep a very detailed log of pain, stamina and function. The second four weeks he will wear the second brace, same thing, we will keep a detailed log. The plan? Well, I keep asking that question myself. It is as simple as this.

So, can Jake's challenges today and in the future be managed with a specialized orthotic device? And, if so, is the device an acceptable solution for long term? Or are there surgical solutions that have not yet been presented or explored?

The answers to these questions will be weighed out against the data gathered through the gait analysis, all the input from the entire Shriner's team and Dr. Beck. Then we will be faced with choosing the best option for our son.

In the meantime, the next step is for Jake to try out this new brace. We ordered special shoes required to fit over the brace which arrived on Monday. My plan is to get him used to it over the weekend, and then we really begin on Monday.

It is a little cumbersome so I want to make sure he has mapped out his balance and ability before charging off to school. In late June or July we will return to Shriners and begin to put the pieces together.

In the meantime even though I have periodic melt-downs, I have finally surrendered to the idea that I cannot fix Jake. I cannot fix Brett. I can comfort them through this crazy journey, I can encourage them, and I can love them. Whatever the plans, wherever we land—we will be OK.

The difficult question that remains, is there an opportunity for a better quality of life? We hope those answers are on the horizon. Come on Dr. Novick!

Many Blessings, Jodi

Monday June 25, 2007 10:30 PM (journal entry) Jodi

In the beginning of June we received some surprising news, Dr. Novick decided to leave Shriners Hospital in Tampa and join Dr. Beck's practice. That was a little twist as we have done all of the testing and analysis under the direction of Dr. Novick. She has been incredibly professional in the transition. She suggested we follow up with the head of surgery for Shriners and he could follow the file and analysis to date.

Further, we still have the opportunity to take our learning's back to Drs. Beck and Novick for future conversations.

So this month we circled back with another surgeon at Shriners. He confirmed what Dr. Novick had already told us, that the test results from the gait analysis validated that Jake's gait had minimal opportunity for increased mobility and that orthotic treatments would deliver limited results. Meaning those dumb orthotic braces Jake tried were not the answer!

During our visit, he conducted a series of x-rays with a special system that he could manipulate Jake's knee during the x-ray which gave him a good view of the growth plate. Through this he confirmed Jake's growth plate was closing. Even with this knowledge he was still not a supporter of amputation. I was beginning to feel there was this professional struggle that maybe amputation would be considered failure in the surgical world.

That being said, he asked that we follow up with Dr. Letson (the surgeon who conducted the original bone allograft in July '05). I was definitely disappointed but respected his opinion so once again, we were faced with arranging another Dr. appointment. Unfortunately as often the medical process works, it took them all summer to arrange the follow up appointment with Dr. Letson.

Please keep us in your prayers, for today my hope is great. Love, Jodi

At that time, I was full speed ahead. Knowing that Dr. Beck and Dr. Novick were loosely open to the idea of considering amputation and learning the news of the closing growth plate, I was more encouraged than ever.

My mom instinct told me we were headed down the right path. I could see a flicker of light and I knew we needed to press on. Slowly, as we learned the facts, they were confirming the medical challenges with leaving Jake's leg as is. We are moving in the right direction.

CHAPTER 37

See it, feel it, touch it

June 2007 was really a turning point for us. Our efforts through Dr. Beck, Shriners, Dr. Novick, and Dr. Letson were beginning to validate the consideration for amputation. We started to shift into high gear to understand what amputation would mean. I knew that to get everyone over the hurdle, we would need to immerse ourselves into the world of disabilities and fully understand what life as an amputee would be like for Jake. And so, a journey of discovery began.

Extremity Games

I was spending hours on the Internet. When everyone would go to bed at night, I would stay up searching amputee blogs and web-sites. To be honest, sometimes I didn't even know what I was search-ing for, maybe community, encouragement, and facts for validation. There could be no regrets. One night as I was surfing the Net, I top-pled upon the extremity games website and learned that the 2007 extremity games were going to be held in Orlando, just minutes from our house. This had to be a sign!

I decided that would be my first opportunity to expose us all to the amputee community. I mentioned to Jake first, I told him the event was happening and suggested we drop in. I told him it was a sporting event of extreme sports like wakeboarding, skateboarding, dirt biking, and it was for athletes with limb differences. Step one, complete, he was interested. Brett was completely supportive, but as luck would have it, he was out of town the weekend of the event. So he encouraged Jake and me to go without him.

It ended up being a very informative and really great afternoon. When we got there Jake found a seat by the skateboarding ramp and was pretty quiet. I had a chance to sneak away and begin to talk to some amputees and families. I told them our story and our dilemma, and they told me about life as an amputee. Every time we began to talk to someone and I explained our choice, they would get very emotional. I felt so connected to these individuals. They were a lifeline to what I wanted for Jake. As each shared stories about how their lives are fully functional, I just ached. I wanted that so much for Jake.

This was the first time Jake saw an amputee in person. He watched what they could do and how they used their prosthesis. He didn't ask any questions or even talk too much. He was just processing. That visit to the extremity games opened the door to begin the dialogue. I didn't want to scare him or pressure him, I just wanted him to see and learn at his own pace.

Local Prosthetics Pursuit

The next phase of the amputee conversation didn't include Jake. It was for Brett and me. In order for Brett to even begin to consider the option, we needed to get educated about the mechanics of a prosthesis. We needed to see it, touch it, and understand how it works. The best way to begin the conversation was to meet some local prosthetists. Through friends and the Internet I was able to narrow down to five prosthetists in Orlando. I started calling and setting up appointments.

I took photographs of Jake's leg, and his most recent Shriners x-ray. I wanted the prosthetist to understand what we were up against and why we were considering such an extreme choice. Also, I wanted them to see the awkwardness of his leg and understand if there would be a challenge to fit him for a prosthesis. We started our meetings sometime in July. After each one, we would get back in the car and once again drive home mostly in silence. Slowly, through the interviews/meetings we were beginning to learn more and more, and with each visit I was more convinced this was the right choice for Jake.

Brett was incredibly inquisitive during each meeting. He was opening up and asking all the right questions and really trying to understand the mechanics of the artificial limb. How could this functionally make life better for Jake? We continued to ask ourselves that question over and over. It was sort of an out of body experience sitting there holding a leg and learning how the foot and knee work. I still couldn't wrap my mind around this leg in our house, fitting our Jake. Again the idea was just too big, but I was hopeful. The more Brett learned, the more I could see a flicker in his eye. He was conflicted with putting Jake through more pain but learning how functional a prosthesis could be.

Our last appointment was with Stan Patterson, Prosthetic and Orthotic Associates (POA). Ironically, when Jake was originally admitted to the APH at the time of his accident, a friend had given me Stan's business card. She thought should we ever need a prosthesis or advice, he may be a good resource. I was told about Stan again at the Extremity Games. We met a guy who had lost his leg to cancer. He was also a patient of Dr. Letson and had heard about Jake's situation. So, when I was surfing the Internet and POA popped up, I looked at the owner, Stan Patterson and thought that name sounds familiar. I went to the book of business cards I had been collecting over the last four years and wasn't surprised to realize I already had two of Stan's cards on file. I knew we must be destined to meet.

When I called Stan's office, a young man named Ricky Shultz answered the phone. I started to tell him my story and at the end he said, I was hit by a lawn mower, too, when I was Jake's age. I'm now a 21-year-old amputee (below the knee). My heart was beating out of my chest. There is something so therapeutic about talking to someone who intimately understands your crisis! I couldn't believe it. Even further affirmation that we were destined to meet.

Our appointment with Stan was in late July. Brett and I walked through the front door of POA and were greeted straightaway by Ricky. He was warm and inviting and made us feel at ease. The entire lobby of Stan's waiting room was filled with framed photos of amputees. They were engaging in all kinds of sports from bowling to skydiving. It was liberating, I had a big smile on my face. I knew we were onto something.

Stan took us to his common area with Stephanie Kingston, his office manager. We all sat down and we started to tell Stan about our situation. We had his undivided attention. We showed him photos and x-rays. We could not hold back the tears as we explained how conflicted we were. Brett was a wreck, his eyes were bloodshot and the tears just rolled down his cheeks.

Brett said, "Stan can you help our boy?" Stan told Brett he would never encourage amputation that it's not easy and it is a lifetime of commitment. But based on what we had told him and showed him, he thought Jake would have a better, more functional gait as an amputee. Stan explained the benefits and challenges. He spoke to us honestly about risks we could face like infection and phantom pain, but in the end he also told us the mechanics of prosthesis would give Jake the ability to run, walk without such a pronounced limp, and free him to do whatever he wants without worry of injury.

We told Stan we were really hoping to find a young amputee for Jake to meet, someone closer to his age and size to really see up close what this whole amputee thing is all about. We hoped for someone high functioning to show him what could be possible. That was how we met Scout Bassett. Stan told us about a patient of his, a young girl (18 at the time). She was adopted from China when she was six years old and had already lost her limb in a traumatic event. When she was 15 she began to travel from Michigan to Orlando to see Stan for prosthetic care. They had since developed a close friendship. Scout was an accomplished runner and cyclist, and soon we would be sitting in front of her to learn of her accomplishments firsthand.

By the time we left POA that day, we knew two things, should we choose the route of elective amputation; Stan would be the person to provide the prosthetic care, and second, I would need to track down Scout Bassett.

Hi, Scout, can we come visit?

By Wednesday of the following week we were on a flight to Michigan. I had called Scout over the weekend and after explaining the whole story to her, I simply said, "How would you feel about us flying up to meet you?" She was taken back, I think, because the next question was "When?" I said, "This week?" She said she would need to talk to her parents and call me back. Before the evening was over, we had talked again and I was booking flights. It was a long way to go, but because amputation was irreversible, there was no distance too far to explore before deciding. Michigan was an ideal location as my mom and brothers also live there, so we had the opportunity to add some fun for Jake.

I showed him a photo of Scout. I told him she is a young girl who is an amputee, I told him about some of the things she could do and how I thought it would be cool if we could meet her. He was completely open to the idea. I explained to him that this was about learning. Every person is unique. Scout happens to have only one leg, let's see how she lives and what life is like with one leg. That doesn't mean it would be the right thing for you or anyone else, this is about learning. He said, "OK, Mom," and that was it, zipped off to his room to begin packing.

I lay awake that night staring at the ceiling. Is this a complete boondoggle? Am I dragging my family across the country for nothing? Would it be realistic that we would ever send Jake in for an elective amputation? Brett was dipping back into his depression. The worry and angst over this decision was becoming a burden. I could feel his tension and uncertainty. I didn't want to overwhelm him or Jake, but we needed to keep moving. Time was of the essence, we were knee-deep into the idea of amputation, and there was no turning back in my mind until we made a decision on the option either way.

Thankfully, school didn't start for another week so we squeezed in this trip to Michigan. On Wednesday, we flew into Michigan, rented a car, and headed north to Scout's family's summer home. It was about a four-hour drive. I felt sick, I just kept thinking, I pray this works. I had no idea what to expect; I was running on intuition and Diet Coke. Thankfully, everyone was cooperating. I was watching the fields of Michigan farm country fly by, and I was dreaming of the day when all of this would be behind us. I wasn't sure how much more I could take. The roller coaster was incredibly tiring, and I was the only fuel for the family. If I stopped, we would all stop.

We pulled in front of Scout's house. I was so nervous inside but jumped out of the car with confidence knowing that Brett and Jake would follow my lead. We knocked on the door, hearts thumping out of our chests. I have never been so relieved to see a smile. The beautiful Scout Bassett answered the door with a grand smile and perfect grace. The rest of the day was no doubt another piece of the puzzle. We visited with Scout and her mom all afternoon. Scout showed us all her legs; she and Jake even had a little footrace. She showed Jake how she put her legs on and off and how they worked. He didn't ask a lot of questions and acted as if he was more interested in the nearby frogs he found, but I noticed he had his eye on Scout at all times.

We left at sunset, followed by hugs and tears. There was an immediate connection and forever friendship built in one afternoon and grounded in common circumstances.

As we were leaving, Jake had already gotten in the car, and Scout was standing there with Brett and me and her mom Susi, Bassett. She said I have been an amputee all my life so I know nothing else. She told us there have been things that are difficult and certainly obstacles she has had to overcome. But living as an amputee, she wanted us to know that if she had the choice she would choose not having a leg than having the leg Jake had. She said, it just seems too damaged and he could do so much more. It was such a powerful testimony, it made the hair stand straight up on my arms. I thanked her over and over, on the drive to my mom's house, we rolled down the windows, told funny stories, let the wind blow through the car and we all just settled into what we had learned.

We were back in Orlando by Sunday. Brett and I were exhausted, but there was no time for rest. We had an appointment with Dr. Letson that week. I was feeling so accomplished. Scout and Stan were key pillars to our quest, particularly for Brett, and I was feeling the momentum. We were checking the boxes of "would Jake be functional as an amputee," and it was a big giant checkmark.

Back to Dr. Letson

Next was, what does this surgery mean? Who would do it? What would the recovery be like? What are the risks? Most importantly, what would the impact be for Jake emotionally? How do you prepare, recover, and live?

We reconnected with Dr. Letson at the Shriners in Tampa on his clinic day. He was great as always and pleased to see us and Jake. He reviewed the x-rays and concurred that the closed growth plate posed a big problem. He outlined the options he felt were the most viable for Jake. They were: amputation AK (above the knee); the "Van Ness" procedure, a treatment in which they would take Jake's foot, remove the shin and make his foot the new knee (we were not keen about this idea); and lastly a prosthetic knee joint that would be implanted into his existing leg and would expand as he grows.

To be honest, I did not expect Dr. Letson to suggest an artificial knee. Doing so sort of threw us for a loop. I left the appointment feeling completely deflated. When we walked out of the building, Brett and Grammie were sort of jubilant. Dr. Letson had offered some kind of hope to avoid amputation. I was completely frustrated and, to be honest, angry. We had come so far, how could he throw out another option at this juncture? This was a giant barrier, and I wasn't sure I had the energy to bring Brett back.

While Dr. Letson was talking I could feel myself holding back the tears. Pop had taken Jake for a walk so it was just Grammie, Brett, and me. Looking back, I understand their excitement; they were not as far along as me in the idea of amputation. Plus, I felt so close to the pain with Jake that at this point I just wouldn't accept any other solution. I was the only one who had been there every minute of every day living his pain with him. Brett was there, but the trauma for him was too deep, so I think he separated himself, and his guilt was holding him back from thinking clearly.

When we walked out, I wanted to scream. I could feel the anger just bouncing around inside me. I wanted to scream, What? Now? Really, you are going to suggest this now? I have dragged my family around the country, we have traveled to endless appointments, and I have spent every day of the last three months researching amputation. Now you want to suggest something that we had not even considered I hoped I had the energy to do this.

As we drove home from Tampa once again, Pop and Jake were giggling in the backseat, oblivious to what was happening. I was fuming. I was feeling upset with Brett for even going there and getting excited about this option. I was fighting this fight for us—for our family—and here he was stepping off the train midway.

When I finally was able to get myself together, Pop and Jake had their headphones on, so I asked Brett and his mom to explain why they thought an artificial knee was a good option. Of course, their response was that we can save his leg! But I just couldn't shake it. Save what? Save a foot that is not growing at a proper pace, a calf that has already lost half of the muscle and a thigh that only has 30 percent muscle function? How will he even operate the prosthetic knee? I just felt that even to consider this option was so naïve. I listened to what they had to say, as the tears of frustration poured down my face.

I knew I needed to pull it together. I couldn't let this unravel me. It was OK that Dr. Letson posed another option, what if we would have proceeded with an amputation, and then learned of this prosthetic knee? That would leave us with "what-ifs," and possibly regret. He was actually being a great surgeon and advisor; I just couldn't see it in that car ride home from Tampa.

I found myself once again on our bedside on my knees. Praying that God would direct, how could we come so far and then learn about this option? Maybe it was the solution, but I didn't think so. I was so confused and tired. I asked the lord to make my shoulders strong and help me continue to be a clear thinker leading our decisions based on facts and not on emotions. This was a lot to ask considering the decision, but I needed clarity and I needed continued compassion for everyone involved. If I began to lose the ability to see what was important to Brett, we would become idle and too paralyzed to make a decision. I begged God to scoop me up and help me find where to go next. I crawled in bed with Brett, I curled up next to him, and he pulled me close. We had to do this together; there was no other way, a united front. I knew we had to explore this option from

Dr. Letson. I laid there looking at the ceiling; I wondered how a leg could cause such angst. My answer was simple, because it was attached to this incredible little boy.

That week, I was able to collect my thoughts and prepare what we would need to do next. I knew we needed to investigate both options (the knee prosthesis and the Van Ness procedure) in addition to amputation. The truth was, we didn't know much about either of the alternatives and again we could not make a decision until we had exhausted every option. I called Dr. Letson's office on Monday and asked if we could follow up and meet the girl in Orlando who had the prosthetic knee.

It took about a week or two, but eventually I was able to connect with the family in Orlando. When we told Jake about the procedure I am not sure he could fully understand, but we explained that some kids have a man-made knee in place of their own. Just like every other family we have met in this journey, their response was warm and of course empathetic and completely open to arranging a visit.

It was almost impossible to tell the difference from artificial knee and the normal knee. There was a very small incision that ran along the side the knee but other than that, you would have never known. The parents told us that it didn't cause pain and probably the only drawback was that their daughter was limited to a more sedentary lifestyle, no high-impact sports or things like that. We had a great visit and learned a lot about the procedure. After we left, we talked to Jake on the way home, sort of asking him what he thought. His answer was classic, "Nope, that's not for me." What? How could he know so quickly? Well, what really deterred him was the cautionary note about high-impact activities. He said, what would happen if I fall and break the knee? Well, we would fix it. His reply, nope, it's not for me. And that was sort of that.

Brett and I sifted through the pros and cons; probably the biggest difference for Jake is there was nothing pristine about Jake's knee. The damage was already so great that it was hard to imagine inserting a new man-made knee and getting solid results.

In short, we were able to quickly eliminate that option. Even Brett was not convinced it was a good alternative. Then Jake's response pretty much solidified the choice. While we hadn't yet chosen amputation, we had at least eliminated the prosthetic knee. For the same reason as the prosthetic knee, we also eliminated the Van Ness procedure; through research and consultation we agreed that the existing trauma to Jake's knee was just too great to assume he would regain adequate function through this procedure.

Time to reconvene

It was early August, and we had already accomplished so much. We had not held ourselves to a timeline, but we had come a long way since our initial conversations about amputation in January. The only sense of urgency was the fact that Jake seemed to be limping more, hopping on one foot more, and, most importantly, he continued to have increased pain.

During my research, I continued to read more about a specific procedure called the Ertl procedure. It was a highly regarded procedure for the actual amputation that created a durable and functional residual limb. The procedure included steps of how to tuck the nerves away and close the end of the stump. Without consultation with Dr. Beck, Dr. Novick, and Dr. Letson, I reached out to the Ertl group. There was no question that Dr. Novick or Dr. Letson could perform the surgery should we decide to do it. But there was so much pressure in this decision, I just could leave no stone unturned.

Our friends and family continued to ask what they could do, but the only thing that mattered were answers. I was living day to day with a smile on my face. Jake had just started first grade and I was still working part time and juggling all the normal daily life commitments. It was the researching and evaluating and then committing that was gnawing at our hearts. Putting a stake in the ground and setting the date was daunting. It was not like we could return our purchase if we were not happy. Jake would have to live with this decision for the rest of his life, and so would we.

When surgeons like Dr. Letson threw "hope" into the equation, I could not just ignore it and press on with amputation. We had to slow down and explore all options because, someday, I wanted to be able to look Jake in the eye and promise him we tried everything. No regrets.

August 22, my 39th birthday – I wrote this note to my girl-friends

Do you really want to be bummed out on a Thursday? I could say yes it was fantastic, but since you are all my true friends I think you will appreciate this. Oh by the way, don't be too depressed, the story gets better at the bottom :)

I woke up late in a frenzy to get Jake out the door for school. Brett slept in because he was "tired." By the time he got up I had already argued with Jake to get up for school, brush his teeth, wear his belt and that he was having eggs and sausage for breakfast not brownies. Brett strolled down to make his coffee and walked us to the door.

I dropped Jake off, turned around to pick Brett up to go to our 10 a.m. appointment with our therapist. We drove in silence because I was extremely irritable. We spent an hour with Dr. Cruce talking about things that make me physically sick to my stomach. Jumped back in the car only for Brett to tell me he needed me to follow him to the mechanics to drop his car off. Between it all I was back and forth on the phone with a surgeon / nurse etc. in Oklahoma trying to figure out how I can get on their schedule so they can see Jake.

Then I took a glance in my checking account because I thought I could slip in a little shopping—Oops sorry—Banks dry!

So, I swiped my finger across all the dust that has collected on my dresser, stepped over the laundry stacked in the hallway, took the dirty glass from the bathroom downstairs to sift through the pet hair in the entryway and set the glass in the pile of dishes already stacked in the sink. Sigh—then I lay down to take a nap. As I fell asleep I thought about how I can get myself through the next 6 months. My heart is breaking over what our son has to go through and I just can't control the anxious feeling that swells in my heart every day. Money? Well, it would be nice but better days will come. My dirty house? Well it would be nice if it was clean but who really cares. But my son, my husband and my family, the heartbreak we have experienced only time can heal.

Everything thing else doesn't really matter. I just want Brett and Jake to be happy and worry free. I know, for today, this is the place we are in as I have said many times, we are back at the bottom of the mountain but I know it will pass.

Needless to say, I didn't feel much like celebrating today. And Brett is so low himself he couldn't possibly lift me up.

However, here is the silver lining. Around 4:30 p.m. I woke up to a little hand on my face and a whisper in my ear. "mommy, are you awake?" It was my sweet Jacob. I opened my eyes to those big dimples and missing front tooth and my heart melted. He crawled in bed with me and we snuggled and talked about his day. Then he said, "Are you hungry?" I told him yes. So off he went about 10 minutes later he returned with a tray/ On it, Baked Lays potato chips and dip, a bag of Oreos, a tall glass of ice and a can of diet coke. He was grinning ear to ear. He suggested we have a little snack party. And from behind his back he pulled out a bag of marshmallows! And he said "these are just in case, it is your birthday"!

So, we sat there at 5 p.m. eating chips, dip, Oreo's and marshmallows. Now, honestly, can there be a better way to celebrate a birthday?

Around 6 p.m. Brett and Jake ran an errand, I called my mom and had a good cry. The beautiful thing about life is, I feel better. Let's really celebrate next year. For now, I am not in the mood to be too much fun. But I know that we will have fun celebrations in years to come.

We are slated for dinner tomorrow night with friends. I am going to try and put on my best Jodi face. But I would be lying to say that I am not dying inside. Oh by the way, don't be afraid to talk to me, I promise I won't cry. I am better today. I don't want to scare you off with my message. Sometimes you just have to say what's on your mind and I don't want to waste valuable lunch time to say all this.

Thanks for loving me. Your friend the 39 year old basket case!

CHAPTER 38

No stone unturned

Oklahoma City (September 4-6, 2007)

So enters Dr. William Ertl, a young guy, maybe early forties (at the most), quiet, well-spoken, friendly face, respectful approach, and a website and résumé complete with testimonials for his work in the amputee community.

Our appointment was Wednesday, September 5th, in Oklahoma City. Yes, I once again dragged the boys across the country! There we were once again sitting nervously in a waiting room, me tapping my foot, pretending to read magazines, while running through my questions and thoughts in my head. All the while Brett and Jake played UNO. I remember we were the only ones in the waiting room. It was super cold and quiet, the perfect environment to sit and get nervous.

When we met Dr. Ertl, we did some quick introductions, and then he climbed up on the examination table next to Jake and leaned back against the wall. He folded his hands in his lap and said, "So, Jake what do you like to do?" Jake thought for a minute and said, "I like to fish." This opened up a whole dialogue on fishing. He would ask Jake questions, Jake would answer and Dr. Ertl listened intently, laughing and responding in all the right spots. After about 15 minutes, when Jake was feeling comfortable and warmed up, Dr. Ertl said, "How about letting me take a look at this leg?" Dr. Ertl did a simple exam, and we went through the usual drill: Does it hurt? Does it ever hurt? Where? How often? Can you bend? Can you straighten? Etc.

After the quick exam, he sat down in a chair and started asking questions. At this point, Jake was excused from participation. This is when he lies down on the examination table, puts on his headphones, his sweatshirt over his head, and completely tuned us out!

Dr. Ertl was a champ, he asked all the right questions, used the right disposition, humble, yet confident, to gain our trust. And the most beautiful piece of the equation is that he understood the details of Jake's injury.

I explained to him, the big dilemma now seems to be whether to amputate through or above the knee. We have gotten conflicting opinions from prosthetists and wanted to make sure we had all the information. Dr. Ertl immediately understood the dilemma and the reason for the conflicting recommendations. He agreed that amputating through the knee would serve Jake better to avoid cutting bone. However, he also agreed that there may be too much damage around the knee joint to leave the base of the femur.

This is a man who specializes in musculoskeletal traumatology, amputation revision, and reconstruction. He immediately zeroed in on the complexities of Jake's injury, and endorsed the idea of amputation. He consulted us on our options and really helped to articulate the pros and cons of both amputation approaches. He set forth some follow up work, including an updated CT scan, to allow him to get a better view of the knee joint. We left feeling satisfied, and he was completely open to continue further with Jake's care should that be our choice.

That evening before dinner, when I was taking my shower, I finally had a moment to take it all in. Strangely, I felt this wave of relief, something I had not felt in quite some time. No racing heart, no tears –just a little bit of relief.

You are probably asking yourself "Relief? How could she feel relief?" Who in her right mind would feel relief after a 2½-hour meeting in a 4-by-4 examination room with five strangers, Brett, Jake, a crazy x-ray of Jake's knee that is already showing signs of arthritis, bone deficiencies, muscle loss, a closed growth plate, rotated tibia (strange phenomenon), 2,000 miles from the comfort and safety of their home and loved ones, talking about a topic that has changed our lives, drained our bank account, and would ultimately change Jake's life forever? How could I feel relief?

Well, with every meeting, I knew we were getting closer to a plan. It was as simple as that. We were doing the work of "to amputate or not to amputate," and while we had not yet put a stake in the ground, I think Brett and I both knew that amputation may be the inevitable outcome.

In that case, determining the best type of amputation for Jake was a critical step. All these surgeons were thinking of how to get an optimal prosthetic fit, a functional and comfortable residual limb with the highest functionality, and most importantly offering Jake best quality of life, which for me was RELIEF!

We seemed to be getting closer to a plan, and for that moment—I could breathe.

CHAPTER 39

Jake's decision

September 2007

September was a month of much reflection. We had spent the summer traveling and seeking answers. So we decided in the fall we would just be still, stop talking about options, stop searching the Internet, stop, stop—stop. Just be still. And that is exactly what we did.

We resumed life, Jake was in school, I was working, and Brett was busy as ever. Sometime in early October, I received a phone call from Mrs. Melanie Baucom, Jake's first-grade teacher. It was then I learned Jake had made his decision. During prayer time that day, when it was Jake's turn, he told his class that he would soon have a prosthetic leg. In his 7-year-old maturity, he told them that while his legs would be different, he would be the same old Jake. I had been praying for God to send me a sign, little did I know it would come through Jake!

So that was the turning point. We talked to Jake and told him about our conversation with Mrs. Baucom. He was very matter of fact and told us that he thought his life would be better. He wasn't interested in a lot of deep discussion, his decision was made.

CHAPTER 40

December 2007

W e were once again sitting in the sterile patient room at Children's Orthopedic and Scoliosis Surgery Associates in Tampa. We had made the trip at least a hundred times over the last four years, but this visit was different: We had reached a turning point, and the next time we would visit this office, Jake would no longer have his leg from the knee down.

We had reached a crossroad like nothing we had ever known. Quite honestly, everything in my world seemed like background noise. All I could think about was how are we going to get through this? Our sweet, sweet, precious Jake, just seven years old but the bravest of us all, was sitting on the patient table, once again suited up in his armor of courage and waiting to see Dr. Novick. To him, the decision was already made.

Prior to this visit, we had spent October and November exchanging e-mails with Dr. Novick, sifting through questions and concerns. Jake knew the purpose was to ask our final questions and schedule a surgery date, and his position was unwavering. The only remaining piece of the puzzle was Brett. I had spent so many nights trying to put myself in his shoes. I knew that as Jake's father he wanted every possibility in life for Jake, but to choose an elective amputation seemed like further destruction of a small body that had already been so compromised.

Finally, after about a 10-minute wait, Dr. Novick knocked on our door. "Hey Jake! How's my favorite kid?" He was all smiles and equally happy to see her. Dr. Novick is a petite woman with very short, black, wispy hair. Although her frame is small, her presence is commanding. When she begins to talk about the intricacies of a child's body, you can tell this is her God-given talent. From the moment we met, she was concise and to the point. I loved this about her.

I knew she thought this appointment wasn't necessary, since we had seen her just a few months back. No physical checkup was required. She already understood Jake's leg intimately and had given us a clear overview of how the surgery would unfold.

In the end, that wasn't enough; we needed to see her one more time and hear her say the words. If nothing else, Brett needed to hear her say the words. Really, all that was left was to put this surgery on the calendar. Dr. Novick's nurse had brought the surgery scheduling book to the room, and after some discussions about Dr. Novick's availability, they suggested February 19, 2008. Of course, Brett said, "so soon? No need to rush." I said, "I was thinking maybe sooner." It was clear we were still in such different places.

Finally Dr. Novick said this is a big decision. Rather than debate, go home and let it settle in; we can always move the date. She looked at the nurse and asked her to make a note in the file: waiting for mom to confirm. I will never forget that, waiting for mom to confirm.

Dr. Novick asked Jake if he had any questions. My heart was sinking for him. But he was very mature and he simply asked where she was going to cut. He was sitting on the patient table with his leg stretched in front of him. He took off his orthopedic brace, and Dr. Novick used her hand to show him where the amputation would be. She took her finger and drew an invisible line across the middle of his knee. She told him that his kneecap was already gone and that they would basically dissect his leg between the two major bones. She told him she would be cutting only tissue, no bone. Then he asked about how she would close the incision. When she began to tell him about the stitches, he was already putting his brace back on. He seemed to be tuning her out. Dr. Novick paused. It was clear that Jake had heard enough, and Dr. Novick understood.

Out the door Jake went, and the room fell silent. We all looked at each other. We were finally out of questions. We knew how the anesthesia would work, how she would manage the existing skin grafts, how rehab would be handled. We had done so much homework; there was nothing left to ask.

Dr. Novick looked me in the eyes and said, "You know how to reach me if you need anything." She gave me a hug. "You have everything you need. I will wait to hear from you."

We said our goodbyes. As we walked down the hall to leave and pay our bill, I couldn't help but notice the festive office mood. Everyone was finishing up the day so they could head to the holiday party.

I felt so sad and distant. I knew in my heart we were making the right choice for Jake, but I was scared. I felt as if we were back at the bottom of the mountain. A mountain I was sure we had already climbed in April of 2004.

Following the appointment our family fell silent. Brett set the tone, and it was clear he didn't want to talk about it. And, quite frankly, Jake didn't want to talk about it either. So I just gave them their space. I sort of thought we would get through the holidays and then reconvene. But the more the days passed, the more anxious I began to feel. As a family we needed to finalize this decision and begin planning. We needed to stop living in ambiguity; it was time to move forward.

One night after Jake went to bed, I walked downstairs. Brett was in the kitchen. I slid onto the countertop and watched him washing dishes and getting coffee ready for the next day. I finally said, Brett can we talk about this? "I can't," he said. "You can't talk about the surgery, or you can't go through with the surgery?" "I just can't do this," he replied. He turned to face me, tears rolling down his cheeks. He said, "I can't make this decision. I already hurt him so badly, how can I choose to put him through this?" I had always felt that this decision had to be made as a couple, as parents—two people agreeing on a common goal and supporting each other, no matter the outcome. But with Brett's resistance, I was feeling unable to proceed. I knew if somehow this was the wrong decision, Brett would never forgive me. It was hard to breathe.

I knew Brett wanted whatever was best for Jake, but to put him through another surgery of this magnitude was risky. We had already been through so much. What if Jake had regrets? What about infections? From the beginning, Brett could not see beyond the actual surgery, the physical pain Jake would endure and the emotional pain we would face when he was returned to us without a leg. I, on the other hand, could see only the future. I could see five years down the road and nothing but freedom for Jake.

Somehow we had to find a middle ground. I decided to let it go for the night. I hopped off the countertop, gave Brett a kiss, and went upstairs.

The rest of the week was quiet. We were going through the motions, but the indecision was killing me. At night, Brett and I slept with our backs turned to one another, not in anger but in complete despair. I finally reached a point where I knew that to wait any longer would only cause further complications for Jake. Each day was taking us closer to February 19, the date we had identified for the surgery and we would need to prepare. I needed to get Brett to agree and call Dr. Novick's nurse to confirm.

The weekend came. I knew if I continued to give Brett his space, we would never move, he would never come to me, he would just hope it would go away. I asked him if we could talk. Once again, we were in the kitchen. I was sitting on the countertop, and he was standing across from me, leaning against the counters.

I took a deep breath and tried to lay out my thoughts in a clear yet not overbearing way. I went through all the reasons we had to go forward with the surgery. I reminded him of all the people we had met and how I knew in my heart that if we could do this for Jake and get through the next six months, we may just set him free.

Brett just stood there sobbing. He asked me all the questions that scared us both: What if there are complications? Infection? How will he live his adult life as an amputee? What if he changes his mind and resents us for this decision?

There was no perfect response other than if we left his leg the way it is, he could have all those challenges as well. I knew this was in God's hands and that as parents the time had come for us to hand Jake over.

I finally said all I need is for you to say yes. I will do everything from there. I just need to know you said yes. We sat there crying, just staring at each other. I wondered how either of us even had any tears left. Finally, he looked me in the eyes and said, "OK." And that was it. I called Dr. Novick's office and confirmed the 19th.

Having received Brett's nod, the next thing I wanted to do was tell our friends and family. We had been agonizing privately for weeks, and I was ready to open our world and welcome their love and encouragement. I had actually written a letter a few weeks earlier trying to figure out how we were going to share the information. Up until this point, the decision was a note in Dr. Novick's scheduling calendar, but sharing this decision would make it real. It would be the first time we would finally say it out loud, and now we would need to begin the walk that we had prayed would go away.

It was hard to even read the words I had put to paper. When I handed it to Brett to read, I just sat on the couch and watched his face. This man I had loved for the past 18 years was so tired and vulnerable, his heartbreak so visible. He finished reading, and looked up at me, the tears rolling down his cheeks. OK, he said. It was so important to us to share our decision with the important people in our lives. They had followed us through every step of this journey, and we knew the next stage of the journey would be impossible without their love and support. Phone calls seemed too much for us to bear. We will write it once and send to all, and then wait. I knew that some would be surprised by the decision and that others would wonder what took us so long. The reasons on both sides were complex, and we had been living with those burdens for four years. I knew it was time to set this family free.

I was sitting in Brett's home office sometime in early December 2007. The air in the room felt too thick to breathe. Everything was silent, yet I could hear the humming of the refrigerator downstairs, a rhythm that matched my racing heart. I just couldn't believe we had finally reached this place. The four years prior were flying through my head—a slideshow from the first call to 911, the nights of tears and pain, the never-ending doctor appointments and physical therapy, the distance between myself and Brett, all leading to this decision.

When I finally pushed "send" on the first round of letters, I knew that our closest friends, Jake's teachers, and our family would soon all know our decision. I knew they would sit at their computers and cry. Maybe they would tell a friend or someone close to them. I knew they would go home and hug their own loved ones. I knew they would ache for us and be grateful for their own blessings. I knew that after hitting "send," we would be one step closer to going through with the surgery.

I am not sure I have ever felt so vulnerable, finally saying out loud that we were proceeding with the amputation, made everything feel so final. I crawled into bed with Jake that night. He was sound asleep. I laid there and cried. I cried for everything he had been through, I cried for all the pain my family had felt. I cried for what lies ahead. I knew I could not get him to his final destination without giant sacrifices and suffering on his part. In my entire lifetime, I had never faced such a challenge as this small person. If I could, I would have given him both my legs. But I could not do that for him. I cried for my little boy. I was not mourning a death, but I am not sure my heart has ever ached so hard. He had already given up so much; he missed summers, school days, vacations, and just the treasure of having a carefree childhood. I was most saddened knowing he would miss much more before he could finally be free.

I just wanted to protect him, but that was beyond my motherly arms. I could only surrender and turn him over and know that our Heavenly Father would cradle him in the times when my arms could no longer provide.

I was scared, I was excited, and I was eager. We were finally ready for the possibilities of, what if? So, I hit "send."

December 12, 2007
Dear Friends and Family,
I have contemplated over the past few weeks about what this letter would say. Every person we are sending this to has been there since Jake's accident. You have prayed for us, cried with us and celebrated our turning points. There is certainly no handbook about how to handle life circumstances and while we have tried to handle this gracefully I would be lying to say it has not been rocky and at times more than I thought we could handle. But, today, is another turning point.

After a long year of learning and researching we have finally made the decision to proceed with an above the knee amputation for Jake. This is a decision we have not taken lightly and as parents a responsibility that has consumed our lives. Every day of the last 3½ years has been focused on how we allow Jake to gain the most functional lifestyle. Unfortunately the complexities of his injury were just too great for modern medicine to solve. So, we were faced with this. Jake could receive a lifetime of surgeries, try experimental procedures and work hard at rehabilitation. This was an option but there was no guarantee, in fact it would be highly questionable as to whether he would ever gain more function than he has today. He would face challenges such as stiffening knee joint, severe arthritis, limb length discrepancy, atrophied muscles. All of these challenges on their own are difficult but combined almost impossible to overcome. Together they would continue to restrict his ability to use his leg like other children resulting in physical limitations. No matter how hard he worked or sought solutions, these challenges are real, they cause pain and simply cannot be overcome.

In the end we had very few options. In September we made our final travel to Oklahoma to visit another renowned surgeon. When we returned home we finally had all the information we needed to make an educated decision. We knew all the options, the pros, cons and more importantly the risks and rewards.

Brett and I cried many tears and I spent many nights on my knees hoping that God would lead us because I was afraid we did not have the courage to make this decision on our own. Well, the answer did come and it was through Jake. This was a turning point.

We have scheduled Jake's surgery for February 19, 2008. The surgery will be in St. Petersburg, Florida, at ACH. We anticipate Jake will spend 3-5 days in the hospital and it will be 4-6 weeks before he has his first limb. He will spend those days in a wheelchair or use crutches to ambulate. We are told it will be 6 months before he is walking comfortably again.

So, we are 99% sure this is the right thing to do ... the remaining 1%, I believe, is fear. Jake is not interested in the conservative route to wait and hope. He is brave and determined and willing to take this giant risk just for the opportunity to have a better quality of life. At 7 years old he is daring to dream and willing to take this unbelievable leap of faith to follow his heart. Something many of us will never do in our lifetime. His tenacity blows me away.

There is no doubt in my mind that the future for him will be without boundaries no matter what obstacles we encounter with this decision. Jake will never accept less.

One of the surgeons we saw said, "If I were Jake I would say yes ... set me free." I said, "You realize he's 7" ... he said, "Yes I do and I am confident he knows exactly what he is signing up for. He is wise beyond his years and he is focused on what could be ... so set him free."

So this is what we plan to do. You can imagine how we have agonized over this choice. And while amputation is a viable choice and there are many high functioning amputees ... we have seen it and met them and it is proven. It certainly does not make it easier. It does not make it easier to choose this for your own child. He will live with this choice for the rest of his life. He will carry it with him every day and as parents it is almost beyond our ability to grasp.

I know this is a season in our life and someday this will be just a memory. But, today we need your prayers. If for some reason this is not the path that God has planned for Jake something will stop us along the way. We will be praying every day until we watch him roll through those surgery doors on the day of the amputation hoping that we are making the right choice. Then, when we have him back in our arms a new day will begin. It will be different than anything we had ever dreamed for our family but I believe when the healing is done and Jake has adjusted we will finally have peace.

> *2 And we rejoice in the hope of the glory of God. 3 Not only so, but we also rejoice in our sufferings, because we know that suffering produces perseverance; 4 perseverance, character; and character, hope. 5 And hope does not disappoint us, because God has poured out his love into our hearts by the Holy Spirit, whom he has given us.*
>
> Romans 5:2-5 (New International Version)

This I pray.
Love,
Brett, Jodi and Jake

******

Within 24 hours, the e-mails and calls began rolling in. Just as I knew, God sends his angels to lift us up when we think we can no longer walk ourselves. The words of encouragement and more importantly words of validation on our choice propped me up and began to help us get our minds around February 19 and how our lives would be different.

******

From: <u>Fagan, Kelly</u> (Jake's physical therapist)
To: Jodi Bainter
Sent: Thursday, February 07, 2008 1:51 PM
Subject: RE: with love
Dearest Jodi,
Your letter took … takes my breath away.
I truly believe this is the best decision for Jake.
A world of adapted normalcy … sports … fun … is just around the corner. … I believe this with all my heart. Jake is really an incredible person. I can't believe he made the choice himself … that too leaves me speechless. …
Jodi, I admire you tremendously.

You, Jake, Brett, Pop ... and your entire family is in my prayers,

Miss Kelly

******

From: Matt Bishop (Uncle Matt/My brother)
Date: Monday, January 21, 2008 10:43 PM
To: Jodi Bainter
Subject: Re: letter
Jodi,
I love you so much I can't even begin to explain it!!!! Whatever you need, please let us know. Whenever, whatever, if I can give it, I will! I can't wait to be down there and be with you all.

With so much love
Matt~
Only with great will, will great things happen!

******

From: Neal, Beth A. (sweet friend)
Sent: Saturday, December 15, 2007 1:14 PM
To: Bainter, Jodi
Cc: 'DONALD NEAL JR'
Subject: RE: update
I can't even put into words what I want to say...
But I will say this ... Dr. Beck's encouragement & the fact that Dr. Novick has performed over 50 pediatric amputations is a solid foundation to move forward on. You have covered your ground, turned over every stone and are making this decision knowing so – and I can hear that through your words. This is an unimaginable undertaking...but know this ...**we will all be here for you** – **whatever is needed!**

We love you, Beth

CHAPTER 41

The preparation and the waiting

Monday, February 04, 2008 3:06 PM (journal entry) Jodi

On Friday, Brett and I had the opportunity to speak to Jake's first grade class. I was definitely feeling a little intimidated when I walked in and saw those little eyes staring at us waiting for an explanation. I kept thinking now, how do I get to the part about the amputation. But, the class was so warm and open, it all came quite easily.

While I was speaking the words, I just kept glancing over at Jake. Our sweet little boy, sitting on a stool in front of his entire first grade class listening to his mom talk about amputation with his teachers and principal listening. I could feel my heart race and my palms sweat. I just wonder what he is thinking. But, in true Jake form he handled it like a champ. He was quiet, calm and listening, hanging on my every word.

His trust is almost a little overwhelming. He listens to what Brett and I say and he believes our promise for what can be. So, I have to be careful to not over commit or paint a picture that could create disappointment. This is a hard balance to be optimistic yet ground him in reality.

He chimed in and answered a few questions. Like the one about "Will he be sleeping when they take his leg off?" I said, "Yes he will and he has done this before so it may not be as scary." Jake said, "Yeah, like 16 times I've done this." Pretty much confirming this was no big deal.

I felt the lump rise in my throat when I was explaining to the children that it is not about how many legs you have or how fast you can run, it is about what lives in your heart. And, when Jake returns to class, even though he will look differently on the outside he will be the same Jake on the inside. I thought courage; don't fail me now and save those tears for another day!

We had invited our amputee friend Ricky who we met at Stan's. So, the kids were able to see firsthand what a prosthetic leg looks like, how it works and what to expect when Jake returns, leg on or off! Ricky was awesome; he was so open with the children and truly made this whole thing look easy. We are so blessed to have met Ricky; he is a neat guy and awesome inspiration for us all! And Jake adores him!

In the end, I asked the children what they thought and the unanimous response was "Cool." I had to smile. I'll take that. My goal was to educate the kids, because with knowledge comes acceptance. And, cool was pretty good validation.

Thank you, thank you, thank you for sending us messages and quietly lifting us in prayer. Love, Jodi

Wednesday, February 06, 2008 12:05 PM (journal entry) Jodi - inspiration:

Recently a wise friend sent me this message; I found it so profound and powerful in relation to Jake and his courage through this decision. I decided I would share, he said this; "Obstacles are those frightful things you see when you take your eyes off your goals. Jake is focused on his goals in all their simplicity, such as running and bike riding. And his courage is not the absence of fear, but rather the judgment that something else is more important than fear."

Isn't that amazing? If we all could write this down and remind ourselves, it may help you think more clearly in those difficult situations.

Jake and I briefly talked last night about what lies ahead. I just wish I could truly understand what he is thinking. My biggest fear is whether we have really prepared him. I asked him how he will feel when he first sees his leg, he just shrugged his shoulders. We talked a little about how it is going to take a while to learn to use this new leg and that it might not be easy right away. He said, "I know." I said, "Well, the goal is that this leg will eventually work better than the leg you have today." He just looked at me and said, "I hope so mom."

Praying, Jodi

Wednesday, February 13, 2008 11:12 PM (journal entry) Jodi – what happens if I don't like my new leg?

Tonight at bedtime after we finished reading, I turned out the lights and I was lying in Jake's bed. He snuggled up close to me and said "Mom, if I don't like my new leg can they sew my old leg back on?" My heart sunk to my feet. I sat up and turned on the light, I knew I had to see his face when we had this conversation. I needed him to understand this would be forever. I looked into his little blue eyes filled with fear, curiosity, and hope. I told him that once his leg was gone we could not put it back on.

Without any tears or apprehension, he said "could they give me another little boy's leg?" I said, "Oh Jake sweetie, once they take your leg, we won't have any option to put another "real leg" on yours." That Stan will make him an artificial leg. He sat there thinking about this for a few minutes then he said, "OK." I think that will work OK. I didn't want to exhaust him but I so wanted to make sure he understood. I asked him if he had any other questions. He said no, he lay back down and just stared at the wall. I snuggled up next to him and said "do you think a new leg like the one Stan makes will work?" He said, "Yes, I think so."

I turned the light off. We laid there in the dark, I am sure our eyes were both open and we were just staring into the darkness both of us running it through our heads.

With love, Jodi

Friday, February 15, 2008 9:52 AM (journal entry) Jodi

Last night I reminded Jake that next week by this time the surgery will be over and the recovery will begin. He just laid there looking at me thinking, and then he smiled :)

Brett and I have been trying to manage Jake's expectations telling him that it will take a while to learn to walk and run again. We want him to completely understand his recovery will not be immediate. In true Jake fashion he has been listening and processing. This week we were playing catch in the yard and Jake asked me if I thought he would be running by next year at this time. I told him I thought for sure he would be running by then, why? He said his friends from school were playing baseball this year and it begins this month. He thought he might want to play baseball next year. Our cool son is already thinking beyond next week.

We are beginning to look forward to Tuesday. I think the whole family is ready to be on the other side. There is no turning back and each day I spend less time praying about whether we are doing the right thing and more about all the hopes and dreams we have for Jake. I am praying specifically for no complications, minimal pain and a speedy recovery. Once the healing begins I know Jake will lead the way. In fact, Brett and I may need our running shoes to keep up!

Today, our dear friend Tommy Kelly took Jake and Brett fishing. Tommy called and said "I don't know what to do but how about taking Jake fishing?" Well, you would have thought Jake won the lottery! Tommy's offer was the best gift.

As my brother Todd said, while other kids were playing t-ball, soccer and riding their bike, Jake was on our dock fishing. In fact, that is how we coined his trade mark phrase "Got One!" It didn't matter how many lines were in the water, or how many fisherman on the dock, it was common knowledge that you would be hearing "Got One" over and over before anyone else even had a bite!

Being outdoors, experiencing nature and being close to the water have been so healing for him. It is the one sport he felt completely equal. So, the blessing to go fishing prior to his surgery was truly fuel for his soul!

We were talking about what he will do during the weeks of healing prior to receiving his first limb. He responded. "Well, I think I will fish, I can crawl, scooch, hop all over the dock and the good news is I still have my arms!" Again, I had to smile, the good news is he still has his arms!

As I have always said, unfortunately our Jake has to do the heavy lifting, but there is no doubt in my mind, he has the will of a giant. Therefore, he will do this with strength and grace and a Christ filled heart. So, smile for us—and get ready for Operation Jake—the new and improved version. Is that possible?

[12] I know what it is to be in need, and I know what it is to have plenty. I have learned the secret of being content in any and every situation, whether well fed or hungry, whether living in plenty or in want. [13] I can do all this through him who gives me strength.
— *Philippians 4:12-13 (New International Version)*

This bible verse has been powerful for me. Letting go of hurt and choosing not to be remorseful even in the most trying situations, choosing to surrender and accept God's plan can be the most difficult yet gratifying act. I have learned we have the freedom to choose, in plenty or in little we can still choose joy and through this everything becomes more beautiful and you become grateful.

This has been a long walk filled with disappointment and trying times. But, when I truly surrendered all my personal quests and chose joy no matter the situation, I found peace. And through the grace of God, I have been able to share this with my sweet son and my special husband. In him, Jodi

My girlfriends: Beth Neal, Kerry Gross, Barbara Wilhelm, Jill Thomas, Kim LeFauve, Melissa Moore, Staci Ray and Dawn DeStefano came to the rescue the weekend before Jake's surgery to lighten the mood. They showed up Sunday afternoon with pizza and spirits and plenty of surprises for all three of us to include a journal filled with letters of love and encouragement from all of our friends and family. This was such a treasure and we were feeling so blessed and loved. The countdown was on and we were grateful for all the support. I have been so lucky to have these amazing women in my life. Their friendship was my anchor (truly) and I will always be grateful.

A final blessing came that evening before Jake went to bed. Brett's cell phone rang and the person on the other end asked to speak to Jake Bainter. To our surprise it was Kevin VanDam, one of the best bass fishermen in the country. Jake is a huge fan and was thrilled by the call! Kevin proceeded to tell Jake he had learned about his courageous decision and his passion for fishing and just wanted to call and wish him the best. When Jake got off the phone we were probing him for details of the conversation. He told us they talked about fishing tips and techniques; but, unfortunately the information was confidential. The call from Kevin was pretty remarkable, and allowed Jake for just a moment to forget about what lay ahead.

CHAPTER 41

We're Ready

Monday, February 18, 2008 6:19 PM (journal entry) Jodi – JAKE'S OFFER

The grandparents (my mom, Grandpa Mike, Grammie and Pop) waited while we did pre-registration and Jake's physical. When the pain management coordinator asked him why he was here he said "To remove my leg." She said, "Why do you want to remove your leg." He shrugged his shoulders and said "So I can walk better." Simple as that!

The last four years have been an unbelievable journey for our family, but there was a moment today, that I really saw God's grace emerging in Jake's heart, and how life can come full circle.

A few weeks before the surgery Jake had asked me if I thought we should contact "Miss Dee Woolford" our dear friend from TransLife to ask her if he could donate his leg once it was removed. He said it would no longer be of value to him but could quite possibly help someone else. I wasn't sure of the logistics but we were compelled to share his request with the team at ACH. So after we were done with the pain management team we asked if could speak to the lifeworks team.

We explained to them what Jake had asked me, we told them that he thought maybe they could use his leg for tissue donation. You can imagine the impact this request had on the lifeworks team and the pastor at All Children's. They couldn't believe a seven year old was making such an offer. How could he even have the capacity to think of something like this?

They immediately started their investigation about whether this was even possible. About an hour later the pastor and team came to see Jake in pre-op, with tears in his eyes; the pastor got down on one knee and explained to Jake that unfortunately he wouldn't be able to donate his leg as he had hoped, that only adults can make that kind of decision. But never in the history of the hospital had a child suggested such a generous and brave donation.

It was a pretty powerful moment. Jake was OK with the idea, he still felt he had no further purpose for his leg so it would have been better to give it to someone else. But in the end he was OK with the answer. He then wondered what they would do with his leg and we later learned it would be cremated. Jake, again, was fine with the idea, he was already beyond that damaged leg and ready for something new and improved.

Now that we are finished with our surgery prep work we are going to have a bite to eat and then hopefully an early bedtime.

While we feel ready, I am not sure you can ever fully prepare yourself for something like this. We are nervous, excited, anxious and every emotion in between. This is like nothing we have ever experienced before. Jake is calm and beautiful.

Pray for a restful sleep, to be continued tomorrow. Love, Jodi

Tuesday, February 19, 2008 10:24 AM (journal entry) Jodi – DIVINE APPOINTMENT WITH BOSTON BILL

We headed to the condo to meet up with the grandparents around 9 a.m. On the way we passed three men on the side of the road, bike riders. They had stopped and were working on something. We had to do a double take because Jake said that guy has a prosthetic leg. We couldn't believe it. So, we turned around and pulled up to them. We hopped out of the car and introduced ourselves. We learned the man's name is Boston Bill, that is how he is universally known, and his real name is Bill Hansbury. He is a below the knee amputee and well known in the biking and running community. We went on to tell him and his friends that at 1 p.m. today Jake would become an above the knee amputee.

Bill immediately engaged in a conversation with Jake. He said, "Was this your choice young man?" Jake said, "Yes."

He went on to tell Jake a story about a friend of his who was in a car accident years ago and just like Jake had lots of surgeries and in the end made the choice for amputation. He told Jake this was a brave decision and how he would have no regrets.

He went on to tell us he was about to ride 25-30 miles today. Jake was amazed and grinning from ear to ear. Brett told the men that Jake hasn't rode a bike in four years, and the man said, "Well, Jake that is all about to change." It was such a God thing; Boston Bill just gave us final confirmation that the sky is the limit for our young Jake! Even Jake felt inspired. Only our heavenly father who loves us so much would place this gift of validation in our path on such an emotionally charged day.

Boston Bill said, nothing is by chance and I am happy I was here on the side of the road today. This is surely a divine appointment. He gave us his phone number and said call anytime. We took a picture of Bill and Jake and he then kissed Jake on the head and said you are a courageous young man. You will never regret this decision.

We will be leaving for the hospital in about 40 minutes. I am sure the mood will begin to become tenser as the hours progress. This is a big day. Brett is doing great and we are strong and ready as a family. Godspeed, Jodi

Wednesday, February 20, 2008 12:56 AM (journal entry) Jodi

I have been staring at the screen for about ten minutes now. Where to start?

The last 24 hours have been surreal in so many ways. We have been waiting for this day, planning, preparing and praying. But, when we found ourselves at the doorstep of ACH yesterday, it truly took our breath away. And quite honestly I don't think I have caught my breath yet.

I am sitting in room 463, the lights are dim and the room is quiet. I continue to try and process the little guy sitting next to me is an amputee. Today, he joined a whole new world of possibilities. Yet my mother's heart is still struggling. My emotions are mixed not with sadness or grief but angst over watching him lie helpless in the bed. I have pictured this over and over in my head and while it is exactly what I expected it is still hard to process. For now, he is in the hardest part so it is difficult to begin the forward motion. I need to continue to be quiet and still, because I know time will heal. In fact, earlier Jake was throwing up and I said, "buddy you know this is temporary." He shook his head and said "it's OK mom."

In all, Jake is completely exhausted. The combination of everything, including the anxiety of pre-op to the medication, has put him into a pretty good slumber. He is not yet experiencing any major pain, the epidural seems to be doing a good job of keeping the nerves at rest (or numb). Unfortunately, with all medications come side effects and therefore, you spend much of the time counteracting the effects of each. Two side effects of the narcotic in the epidural, is nausea and itchiness. Jake is experiencing both. He has had vomiting ever since post-op. They are treating him with non-nausea medicine, but like I mentioned, that brings new side effects. And the game goes on.

For the moment, we are choosing "no pain" over nausea and itchiness. Keeping him pain free is very important. It will be important for him mentally and physically in rehabilitation, to not let the pain creep in and control this recovery.

Earlier he was trying to get comfortable, but he kept itching his nose, then face, then tummy. I kept sort of guiding his hands to make sure he didn't pull any tubes or hurt himself unintentionally. A little later Brett was watching him do the same thing. I sat up and said "Brett just watch that he doesn't hurt anything." Jake then whispered so quietly "Daddy, tell mom I know where my cords are." Brett couldn't hear him so he said "Tell me again" Jake repeated with all the voice he could gather "I KNOW WHERE MY CORDS ARE." Meaning, could you two stop doting on me, I know where my cords are for Pete's sake! This is a good sign.

Before I end tonight, so much happened today that I wanted to take a minute to give thanks.

I am thankful for Dr. Beck and Dr. Novick. This was really Dr. Novick's show but to our request Dr. Beck took the time to scrub in and be with us on this day.

Dr. Beck has been Jake's orthopedic surgeon since July 2005. He has not only been Jake's surgeon but he has become a trusted support system for Brett and me. He continues to look beyond the mechanics of orthopedics and thinks of Jake as our son and a seven year old little boy.

After the nurses wheeled Jake away, Dr. Beck took a few minutes to walk us down the hall and give us that final re-assurance of our decision. We were having a fleeting moment of question and he did not allow that moment to linger.

When the surgery was almost complete he came to talk with us and tell us how the procedure went. He told us when they got inside the knee and could really look at the integrity of his knee joint, it was clear Jake's challenges were greater than we knew. And, after this surgery he was even more convinced this was the best option.

He went onto say that had we not chosen amputation that it was probable if not inevitable that Jake would be what they call "birthday kids." Every year he would have surgeries like others celebrate birthdays. Once again the confirmation we needed.

I thanked God time and time again today for the skilled work of Dr. Novick. It is my understanding that most surgeons do not like to do amputations and often they consider this work a failure. But, Dr. Novick has told us in the past and reminded us today that she is an advocate of amputation for the right kids in the right situations. Further, she has the uncanny ability to look beyond the sacrifice of the leg and think about the freedom and possibilities she is creating for the child. I know that she feels this way for Jake and I am so thankful for her tenacity and attitude to put aside medicine and believe in the child.

I am thankful once again the outpouring of love and prayers for the Bainter family. While Brett and I had our heads down today, all your messages and prayers were with us. This website alone is a testament of all the amazing people in our lives.

Thank you to Mom and Mike and Grammie and Pop who were here by our sides today quietly lifting us up.

Sending our child for surgery today for an elective amputation was beyond anything a parent can ever imagine. Yet Brett and I through our worry and our desire for

Jake to have minimal suffering we still remained peaceful with our choice. The tears we cried today were sort of a goodbye to many years of struggle, for heartache that Jake has had to experience, for the excitement of a new beginning. We have opened our hearts and surrendered our wants and needs and allowed our heavenly father wrap his arms around us, and continue to offer us peace.

We have come this far as a family and we are feeling stronger than ever. The days ahead will not be easy. But, there will be no turning back. The future is ours to capture.

We are blessed to be loved by so many! Even I, as the mom am amazed beyond my expectations for how Jake has handled this monumental hurdle. He went into the surgery today with focus and no fear. He is one special little boy. I praise God that he granted Brett and I this special privilege.

Jake, Brett and I can feel your hugs and love. Keep the messages coming! Love, Jodi

Wednesday, February 20, 2008 12:54 PM (journal entry) Jodi

One night down! Jake was a champ last night. He was up on and off through the night for vomiting. The epidural medication is just hard on his little body. He would sleep for a few hours and then he would wake up because he had to vomit. There was nothing left in his body but he continued to have the dry heaves.

So the plans for today, manage the pain, stay awake for portions throughout the day and try to eat some ice chips. They also started a breathing treatment every hour to avoid the chance for his lungs to collect any fluid for sitting still for so long. The goal is to find the perfect balance of no pain and no vomiting. Also, the epidural narcotics are making him very drowsy and sort of groggy. He is still whispering to talk almost as if talking is just too much work. In fact, he has hardly spoken, mostly eye blinks and pointing.

Really for the next 2-3 weeks Dr. Novick has ordered minimal activity. She is limiting him to bathroom transfers and maybe a wheelchair ride. But, mostly she wants him to remain as low key as possible to minimize swelling and encourage healing. It will be very important that the swelling is managed properly to not pull the stitches and create space for infection or delayed closure.

The last time I was up with Jake was around 3:20 a.m. When I woke up at 5 a.m., Brett was sitting in a chair next to me. The nurse later told me he arrived around 3:30 a.m. just after I had fallen asleep and he was sitting there ever since. He said he just felt too far away at the Ronald McDonald House.

Everyone is doing well. I have been hibernating in Jake's room. I just can't get myself to leave, we have come this far, I am not leaving now! Pop and I are juggling for who can wipe his forehead or jump first when he needs something!

We have not discussed his leg at all yet. This morning he did pick up the blanket and look. He didn't say a word. He just looked for a few seconds put the sheet back down and went back to sleep.

I wish I could pay tribute to how strong he has been. I know I said it in my last update but it is really unbelievable to me AND I know this kid so well. He is almost reassuring us. When he is sick he continues to tell me "mom, it's OK" When I tell him that he just needs to hang in there tomorrow it will be better, he nods. When I ask him if he is OK, he gives me the thumbs up.

For now, Jodi

Wednesday, February 20, 2008 10:18 PM (journal entry)
Jodi – IT IS GOING TO BE OK!

I could tell you many things about today. I could tell you how Jake finally ate his first popsicle at 6 p.m., or that we saw a little smile when Dr. Novick came by for a visit, or that we have managed to outsmart the nausea or even that we were able to move him enough to change his sheet today. All of these little details were marked milestones in his recovery today.

But, what I am going to share tonight supersedes everything else. Because when you understand this, all the details of his day to day recovery begin to blur and greater picture of his lifetime becomes bright. Today and tomorrow will pass quickly but Jake's new leg will be his for a lifetime.

After Grammie, Pop, Mom and Mike had left for the evening, Brett and I spent some time just hanging out with Jake. He was awake and more lucid than he has been in the last 24 hours. Shortly after Brett left to make a trip back over to the Ronald McDonald House I was sitting in the chair next to Jake's bed. He motioned me to come closer. I stood up and leaned in. He is still having a hard time with his voice so he was talking in a whisper so I had to listen closely to what he was trying to say.

He said, "Mom, do I still have a tube in my throat?" Of course I didn't know what he was talking about but I told him "No buddy you don't have a tube in your throat." He said, "Pop told me I had a tube in my throat." Well, then I realized that Pop had tried to explain to him why his throat was sore and it was hard for him to talk. So, I repeated what Pop had attempted to explain earlier about the tube.

That's when Jake stopped me. He said, "Mom did I have a surgery?" Well, at first I was surprised and thought he was teasing. But then it became clear to me that he had been very groggy over the last 24 hours and he was finally starting to put the pieces together.

I told him, "Yes you did have a surgery yesterday." Then like he was hit by a bolt of lightning, he looked me straight in the eyes and said "Mom is my leg gone?"

It seriously took my breath away because I knew that he was aware of exactly what he was asking and that he honestly did not know the answer.

I told him, "Yes Jake, your leg is gone." His first response was the biggest grin I have seen in the last 24 hours, with tubes hanging off his right arm, he made a fist and pulled his arm down quickly and said "YES." Like he had just won the lottery!

I was almost giddy I was so tickled. And quite honestly his response was so unexpected I sort of got caught up in the moment and went on to say, "Jake, the surgery is over, we are on the other side, now it's all downhill." His dimples were beaming. He just kept looking at me and smiling. I said are you excited and he shook his head his smile never leaving his face.

Quite honestly it was all in his eyes, Jake was already celebrating his new found freedom and we don't even have the stitches out yet! Imagine when he actually gets to put on his new leg. Hold on my friends is all I can say!

To some it may seem we are carrying the most difficult burden but for me, tonight confirmed that we are living in God's abundant grace.

I realize this is not a free pass and I would be naïve to think there are not challenging times ahead. But, in this moment my heart is full. For our child to be filled with joy no matter the situation is more grace than any parent could ever ask for.

I called Brett because I was so sorry he missed this conversation. But, I was tickled to hear him on the other end of the phone. I didn't even need to see his face to know he was smiling too! May your hearts be lifted and your faith refreshed by tonight's update.

We may need to pull out the marching band for Jake's return to Orlando! This kid just continues to amaze! Goodnight and God Bless, Jodi

P.S. By the way, I reserve the right to take all this back when they take the epidural out in the next 24 hours and transition to oral pain medicines, and Jake hates all of us!

Thursday, February 21, 2008 11:54 PM (journal entry) Jodi – BOSTON BILL'S HOSPITAL VISIT

We should have known the Boston Bill story was not yet complete.

Today around 11am Bill showed up in Jake's hospital room and spent about 45 minutes visiting with us, he even brought Jake a pair of special Boston Bill sunglasses for his bike riding in the future!

We had an opportunity to sit down and visit for a while and tell him how seeing and meeting him on the day of Jake's surgery was such a "God wink" for us. We knew that Bill had been placed in our path not by chance but rather to offer us final confirmation that we were making the right choice. More importantly to give Jake that final dose of encouragement. Jake is so hands on and Bill was clearly a hands on example of what is possible!

We told Bill that we hope he didn't mind but we went onto share our chance encounter with a few of our closest friends.

He said, "Well, let me tell you the part of the story that you don't know." We thought—there's more? Well, sure enough the story grew more amazing.

Here's the story from Bill's point of view.

In October of 2007, Bill lost his leg to the MRSA (staph) infection. He had a hard recovery from the infection but a quick bounce back in adapting to amputation and rehabilitation.

In fact, he began cycling with a hand cycle right away but just began cycling again with his prosthesis six weeks ago. Now, let me remind you that he is 70 years old and intended on riding 35-40 miles the day we met him and has continued to do so each day since!

On Tuesday morning Bill was going on a ride with about 30 other cyclists, so about 15 minutes before we saw Bill the ride had started.

The night before the ride Bill decided to change the cleats on his shoes. Apparently the cleats he had been using were getting worn and he was worried they could become problematic during the ride. Since it was the first day he was using the new cleats he had arrived early at the ride site to take a few practice runs. The trick with the cleats is that they snap into the pedals of your bike. Then you slightly twist your foot to easily release the cleat as needed. It is very important that the cleat release works properly to avoid falling.

Tuesday morning Bill spent about 20-30 minutes prior to the ride testing his cleats. He said he would ride a little then twist his foot and the cleat would release. Feeling confident he started the ride with the rest of the pack. A few minutes in on the first turn, where we saw Bill, his cleat would not release. He tried again, but no luck. He knew this was a problem so he would need to stop to try to see if he could fix the cleat.

Since he was biking alone he asked two of the cyclists to help him out. He asked them to ride ahead and stop, he would begin to slow down and as he reached them they would grab his arms and bring him to a stop. All the while we were preparing to leave the Ronald McDonald House. The place where we saw Bill is about five minutes from the Ronald McDonald House. With the help of the cyclists Bill came to a stop. He sat down on the side of the road and the two bikers waited to see if he would need any further assistance.

By that time the cyclist pack had rode on and the street was empty. Right about then, we turned the corner and began down the street headed straight toward Bill. You already know this part of the story; we pulled over and met Bill. Well, here is where the story really becomes divine. First the timing was impeccable. Bill rounded the corner, flagged these men and came to a stop; the congestion of all the other cyclists had passed making the road clear for us. Then, after meeting us, Bill fixed his cleat, hopped on his bike and finished the ride. He said the amazing part is he has not had a problem with his cleat since! The only cleat problem had been in that five minute window of time just when we were driving down the street! His cleats have worked impeccably since. He went on to tell us he has repeated this story 100 times in the last 24 hours and that we had equally impacted him. We really enjoyed reliving the story with Bill today and relishing in the glory of the timing for both. Bill of course is a new friend and I won't be surprised if we see him again before we head back to Orlando. God missing nothing.

Sweet dreams, Jodi

Friday, February 22, 2008 8:17 PM (journal entry) Jodi

Today was a big day. As grandma said we had a lot to accomplish. In fact, I think this is the first time I sat down all day!

We started the day with a wheelchair ride. Jake was so worried about this because after surgeries in the past the wheelchair transfers have always been so painful. He was cooperative but so anxious that he was sweating and chattering his teeth. It was a family production, one nurse was holding his head and back, the other holding his hip and leg, dad and I on the other side holding his left side, Pop holding the catheter bag, the grandma's getting the wheelchair ready. We did a one, two, three lift and transfer. We sat him down on the wheelchair without his body even moving. He said "Aaahhhh, OK, I am good." It was an excellent example of teamwork and secretly we all had a lump in our throat, another small detail in the day yet giant step in Jake's world.

We turned the epidural off sometime around 12 p.m. Then he began oral pain medicine, the concern was that the oral medication doesn't have the same numbing agent as the epidural and there was potential that when the epidural wore off he would have unexpected nerve pain. The good news is, it is 8 p.m. and no nerve pain yet!

Each day I see the sparkle return in his eyes, he is getting eager to go home and see his friends. Thank you for all the surprises that are beginning to arrive. That certainly puts a twinkle in his eyes!

I am hopeful that tomorrow will be our last day here. We are all tired of cafeteria food and I in particular look forward to a bed and no beeping throughout the night.

Every step continues to be graceful and planned. I am getting eager to roll him out the front doors of this hospital, and watch as he captures his new sense of identity and freedom. In some ways, I feel like I am taking home our new baby, I can't wait for him to experience this big new world with the freedom of his new leg.

Did I mention we love every message? We are far away but we feel your arms around us and surrounded by love. More tomorrow. Jodi

CHAPTER 42

Going home

**Saturday, February 23, 2008 9:59 PM (journal entry) Jodi –
Home**
The Physicians Assistant (PA) came by around 9 a.m.
this morning and after a few questions and a quick look at
Jake she said "Are you guys ready to go home?" There was
a unanimous "YES" in the room! After she left we were all
celebrating, Grandma Bergen, Grammie, Pop, Daddy and
most of all Jake!

Jake quickly sat up in his bed and pretty much had the
attitude of bring it on. He took the lead guiding his new leg
into his shorts no problem. Soon he was dressed and sitting
up on his hospital bed looking very liberated!

We moved him to his wheelchair and as I started packing with mom he started to wheel out of the room. He
called to me, "Mom I am headed out to the nurse's station"
and off he went. I just could not get the smile off my face.
It was almost like he wasn't sure how he was going to feel
and when he realized he was OK he was empowered almost
proud to be showing off his new leg. Sure enough he
wheeled down the hall past the nurse's station and around
the circle, mom trailing behind. Jake was smiling and giggling the whole way. He was saying Bye Bye Hospital, Bye
Bye Catheters, Bye Bye tubes!

Pop and Grammie were waiting out front and Jake
came wheeling out. We were all standing there getting
ready to go and he said "Well, that's it; I don't have my leg
anymore." Everyone agreed. I guess he just wanted to state
it one more time. We loaded up and headed home, smiles
on our faces.

We will always be grateful for Dr. Novick and Dr. Beck who dared to think amputation is not failure yet liberation for Jake. I am not sure they will ever fully understand the way they have impacted this family. Dr. Novick came by Wednesday, Dr. Beck came by Thursday, Dr. Novick came by Friday. By the way, they had physician assistants there for that exact purpose, to tend to patients during their rounds. But these doctors came by for no other reason than they felt compelled to personally check on Jake. I could never ask for more.

I must say it is good to be home. I am sitting in Jake's room right now. We moved his mattress from his bunk to the floor and he is watching his TV. His leg is propped and he is resting comfortable. We are five days into this new chapter of our lives and it is still a little unbelievable. I can't wait to see what's next! So far, no infection, minimal pain, great attitude, 5,000 hits to Jake's website in 5 days and home.

Well, my friends, God is Good. Love, Jodi

CHAPTER 43

Let the healing begin!

It wasn't long after we got home that we had our first official bump in the road: a pain management problem.

I knew this part would come, but I never predicted it to be as extreme as it was. The nights were almost unbearable. He was definitely experiencing phantom pain, charley horses, muscle spasms, and just ongoing residual limb pain.

He would wake up out of a dead sleep, completely startled in the night with a scream. He would say it felt like someone was pulling his pinky toe to the side as hard as he could. This would go on for at least 30 minutes, and then the pain would subside. He would always say, Mom, make it stop. He would beg me to make it stop. I was so helpless. We were trying everything, but nothing worked.

When the pain would strike, he would clench his teeth and grip my hand and just close his eyes. When he wasn't having these moments of sharp pain, he would complain of sort of a gnawing and continuous pain. He also was experiencing what is called restless leg syndrome with his left leg. Since he was confined to no movement or minimal movement, his sound leg would get restless at night. So frequently, we spent the nights doing "pedal the bike" and leg lifts to help him make the restless leg go away.

Night after night for weeks and even months to come, he would toss and turn and then find a break from the pain in a comfortable spot. He would drift off to sleep and then wake up again. This continued through the night. He would wake, we would "battle" the discomfort and pain, find comfort, and go back to sleep.

This was so familiar to past surgeries, yet such a disappointment at the same time. We were so hoping that this surgery recovery would have been minimal pain. Dr. Novick had told us several times that

Jake's knee joint was not a pristine environment and therefore, the surgery was sort of unearthing an old injury. He had undergone 17 surgeries in four short years on that small knee joint, not to mention the trauma of the initial injury, so it stands to reason that extended healing time would be needed.

Jake would get so irritable, with good reason, and beg me to make it stop. I sat there calmly trying to talk him through it, feeling completely helpless. This was the hard part, for sure. It was so hard to see him suffer. We were just sick that he had to experience all these side effects to get to his final result.

Jake had described his pain as a tornado in his leg with a giant lightning storm. Nerve activity during the healing process is common in the days, weeks, and sometimes months following surgery or trauma. For the next four months, I spent most of my nights in Jake's room, sleeping wherever I could. You will see in my journal entries that we definitely went on a "stop pain pursuit" and tried many approaches, some that worked others not so much. In the end, we were able to stabilize his chronic pain with medication. As difficult as it was to give him more medicine, he couldn't live with the pain.

We had wrestled with pain for the last four years, a kind of pain no child should ever experience. We dreaded the nights; they brought tears, discomfort, stress, and anxiety. Too many times to count, Jake and I were still up and I was tapping his leg gently as we watched the sun come up. In fact, I remember one night about 30 days into our battle with phantom pain. It was the middle of the night, and Jake was once again crying out in pain, begging me to make it go away. At one point I said, "Jake honey, what can I do?" He said, "Make it morning."

"Please mommy, make it morning" –if only I could.

Wednesday, February 27, 2008 7:46 PM (journal entry) Brett

It has finally happened, tonight for the first time in a long time I see the exhaustion in Jodi's face. And before I could mention to her about the website, she asked me to do her a favor. She said, "Would you write an update and let everyone know we are doing OK" So, for the first time, in a long while, here I go.

Today was another good day for Jacob. As always, Pop was here at 10 a.m., SHARP. He is always ready to offer his assistance in any way possible. And again today, both he and Jake were on the front porch working on more sand art. I am not sure how many trips Grandma Bergen has made to the craft store for more sand! It certainly passes the time and it helps obey the doctor's orders of not moving around.

Overall the day was another success. However, I would be remiss not to mention that Grandma Bergen spent her last day here. She left to go back to Michigan at 6:00 p.m. tonight. I just say "thank you" Laura for everything that you have done over the last nine days. It is nice to have an extra set of hands around and it was great to have you helping us. Thankfully Uncle Matt flies in Friday so additional reinforcements are on the way.

I hope that tonight is a pain free evening and both Jodi and Jake can get a good night's rest. Till tomorrow, sweet dreams! Brett

In many ways, Jake's entire recovery came down to one thing: his attitude. Once the doctors had done their part of mending him properly, the rest was up to Jake. And like I said, he woke up every day with a smile, regardless of how frustrated he was through the night. Even his disappointment over another missed spring break and other activities was brief, and he quickly diverted his mind to what lies ahead. Disappointment is a hard pill to swallow, and Jake had faced many disappointments in his short seven years.

I was so proud that he had not allowed this to swallow him. Pain and disappointment can often alter your spirit. But not Jake, instead, he just overlooked it and eagerly waited for the good things.

"For I know the plans I have for you," declares the LORD, "plans to prosper you and not to harm you, plans to give you hope and a future."
—Jeremiah 29:11 (New International Version)

I am reminded of all the good he has planned for us. Even in the toughest times, knowing he has plans for us is kind of exciting. His plans are great no matter who we are or what our journey. Our sweet Jake held onto this promise in the weeks and months ahead.

Tuesday, March 04, 2008 7:41 PM (journal entry) Jodi

Video games have been the new distraction. Thank God for the 21st century! It seems Uncle Matt has introduced Jake to a whole new world. And it is a great way to keep Jake's mind off pain and boredom. Uncle Corey also flew in to spend a few days with Jake and joined the boys on the air mattress for a full day of video game battling.

Jake did tell Uncle Matt today that he is having fun BUT the real fun will begin when he gets his new leg and they can fish and play outside. In true Jake form he is doing his best to pass the time but he certainly has his eye on the prize which has nothing to do with sitting around!

Thank you for all the messages, meals and surprises; we are overwhelmed by the outpouring of love. Friday will be a big day. It will be the first time we lay our eyes on Jake's new leg. I can feel my heart swell as I write, nervous, anxious, and excited and everything in between. Tonight I am feeling very grateful for:

Pop, tried and true and always here, quietly waiting to step in

PlayStation 2 (I can't believe this is on my gratitude list!)

Jake's pain medicine

God's word – which walks me through

Brett's smile – its back!

Uncle Matt – just because he rocks!

Uncle Corey – For the surprise visit!

Love, Jodi

CHAPTER 44

I need a drink!

Thursday, March 06, 2008 8:26 PM (journal entry) Jodi

The fire drill began yesterday around 2pm when Jake started shouting my name and then progressed into panic. When I got to him I realized his dressing/cast had rotated about 45 degrees around his leg and was sliding off. It had slid halfway down his leg.

He was freaking out because he thought it was going to slide right off. We pushed it back on as far as we could but it was in an awkward position.

I called Dr. Novick to see if we should come to see her, worried that the shift could affect the incision. She said, definitely come now, better to be safe than sorry.

We arrived at ACH (in St. Petersburg) Emergency Room (ER) around 5:45 p.m. Brett met us there as he had been in a meeting in Sarasota earlier that day. Within 10 minutes Cara Cimilluca, the PA on call and Dr. Novick met us in the patient room.

The plan was a quick dressing change and we would be on our way. We had a little chat with Dr. Novick as she explained to Jake what she was going to do. Instantly he made it clear he wasn't on board with the plan.

I soon learned his response was way more intense than situations gone by. He was completely desperate and so frightened that he was working himself into a complete panic begging us not to continue. At that point, Dr. Novick paused, she had taken off a couple layers of gauze and we were down to the soft cast, she was more than halfway there. But Jake was getting so distressed she decided to stop.

Dr. Novick pulled out all her tricks to try and distract him. She even had the nurses get bubbles and play-dough to see if we could get his mind on something else. He was relentless, his eyes were on his leg, his body was tense and he was non-negotiable. I mentioned to Uncle Matt that I didn't think we were going to be able to find a distraction great enough to take his mind off what was happening. Uncle Matt said "short of backing in an 800 lb lion in the room we are probably out of luck!"

Dr. Novick suggested we consider a mild sedative to ease his tension, get him in a better frame of mind and then proceed with the change.

Well, like all things in life, this sounded good in theory but was a little more challenging than we anticipated. The ER was packed; they had two trauma cases in surgery and two in waiting. It was literally standing room only. Therefore we were waiting our turn for a nurse to do the sedation. It took about 1½ hours for everything to come together.

So at that point there was nothing to do but wait. Dr. Novick and Cara were awesome, Cara found a comfortable seat on the floor, Dr. Novick on Jake's bed and there we sat. Dr. Novick, Cara, Uncle Matt, Brett, Jake and I. We felt awful because Dr. Novick wasn't even working and Cara's shift had ended hours earlier. But there they sat committed to doing this the right way for Jake.

Dr. Novick kept saying I will sit here all night if that is what it takes to make this easy for Jake. She was unwavering and patient with the whole process. Love that girl!

Finally, it was time for the medicine. Rather than to use an IV, we agreed to administer it nasally. We were a little unclear about the process but we knew it was inhaled. Well, we quickly learned it is a liquid administered through a syringe up his nose and just for the record Jake is not keen on this type of sedation.

Needless to say, Jake FLIPPED!

I mean, flipped like I have never seen him flip before. He was screaming at the top of his lungs. He was lying on his back and we had to keep him still because his bandages were half off. He was kicking and hitting and screaming. He said he could taste the medicine in the back of his throat and he started screaming, I need a drink! Well, he couldn't have anything to drink at risk of aspirating. So, he had to just cooperate.

He was so angry, he grabbed me by the shirt collar and pulled me close and in his loudest, deepest, angriest scream said "MOM ... I NEED A DRINK." Well, at that point I looked at Dr. Novick thinking this is out of control; she had a big smile on her face, which was comforting that she wasn't frustrated or angry. She said incredibly coyly, "Actually, Dr. Novick needs a drink!" A good chuckle was had by all.

Well, within minutes, Brett's claims about three minutes not that anyone was counting. He stopped, laid his head back and asked if she was done yet. Dr. Novick was almost done. She was so quick and steady she had removed the bandages. The incision site was really beautiful. Clean with no dried blood or drainage, just smooth soft skin. His little leg is so tiny and small. The incision runs from the inside of his leg/knee area, around the back of the limb and to the other side. There were a few strips of tape covering the stitches but it was beautifully done. Dr. Novick even commented that this was the best looking limb she has ever seen in a two week check up. A testament to her work! We were all smiles.

For the next 20 minutes we had a great time. Jake had the biggest smile and was so happy about how great his leg looked. After our goodbyes and thank you we finally walked out of the hospital with Dr. Novick around 10 p.m. It was a long night and we were relieved, grateful and exhausted. Dr. Novick's ears must have been burning all night; we re-lived the evening over and over on the car ride home and today. We just kept talking about how everything, although chaotic, seemed so planned.

Having my brother there with us was a special treat as well. Had we kept the Friday appointment he would have already flown home. Jake loves Uncle Matt so much and he was quick to offer some comic relief, which was invaluable last night.

Brett was in full family protection mode. He was right there helping and taking the lead when he knew I was getting tired. We were really a team again and it felt nice.

The dedication of Dr. Novick last night was a perfect example. I am not sure if she will ever understand my gratitude. This brings us to today. Jake's leg is now wrapped in a small ace bandage. It looks different, so small and fragile. Per the doctor's orders he has begun moving around; in fact he tested out scooching today. Pop even took him to the dock for a little fishing and of course he landed a big bass wheelchair and all!

All in all, last night was another giant milestone. We are going back to St. Pete on Tuesday or Thursday to remove the stitches. We are already strategizing about the procedure. Tonight I plan to snuggle up next to this little guy and count my blessings. Love, Jodi

Within a week we were headed back to St. Petersburg for Jake's stitch removal. I must admit, that day was an all-time low for us. How many times you can hold your child down, I mean, physically a team of people hold him down, while he is screaming and crying and begging you to stop? Desperately begging, "Mommy, I don't want to do this." Well, for us, we have done this one too many times to count. And, that day really hit me hard; I remember feeling so sad for what he had been through and what still lies ahead.

The entire staff at Children's Ortho was awesome; every single one of them treated us with such support and compassion. They did everything right. The fact of the matter was the area around his incision and the end of his limb had not been touched or exposed (painful), but the steri-strips had to be removed (painful), the stitches had to be removed (painful) and the incision had a little area that still was not healed and needed to be cleaned (again painful),

All of this had to happen, and everyone tried to make it as smooth as possible. But no one can take away what Jake had endured to bring him to this point. Rewind to Good Friday 2004, Jake was running and riding his bike, and here we are four years later, after 17 surgeries, endless nights of tears and pain, years of trying to keep his life "normal."

I guess a family cannot go through heartache and disappointment like we had without having days when it catches up with you, and stitch removal was one of those days. I remember just feeling a little defeated. I wanted the pain to be gone once and for all. We just wanted to be normal again.

While we survived the stitch removal, other issues were brewing. In short order, I was becoming a nerve pain expert. I had spent an extended amount of time talking with Dr. Novick at the stitch removal appointment. I just had to understand why all the pain was occurring and how to get it to stop.

As usual, there were no easy answers. In fact, the veteran's hospitals had been trying to solve the mysteries of nerve pain for years as this was a common occurrence for amputee servicemen and women.

There was a point where I felt the pain was beginning to take over and that we were losing focus. I was weary, and Jake was growing frustrated. As I had in years past, I knew it was time to find my people. I once again started casting a wide net through phone calls, Internet search, websites and support groups. I was in hot pursuit of any and every resource I had available.

I made some great connections along the way, like a conversation with Kevin Carroll, a well-respected prosthetist. Boston Bill became an incredible resource, with weekly phone calls and healthy holistic ways to get Jake's body back in order. I reached out to all of the amputee moms I had met over the last year, and each gave me new insights. I was leaving absolutely no stone unturned. People sent me e-mails about mirror therapy being used at Walter Reed Medical Center. Others sent me notes about rhythm therapy, tapping, stroking, squeezing, which by the way worked and is a method we still use today. I began to be flooded with ideas. Sadly, though, no solution provided a consistent fix.

We got into a routine of just trying everything until something worked and Jake could get to sleep.

I was learning that the nerves must be stimulated. The nervous system is pretty miraculous and sort of dumb at the same time. The nerves fire signals of distress and pain for a limb that is no longer there. They will continue to do so until they are settled (through pressure, massage, desensitization, touch and/or medication). Eventually they will heal but they are sort of hard-wired and will record messages that have been sent over and over. It is important to stop the negative signals ASAP and reprogram the body to no longer send messages to the foot or vice versa.

As I learned more, it was becoming clearer at times I could actually see Jake's nerves firing because his leg twitches and you can see his skin retract. Each time this happens, it leaves him clenching his teeth. In fact, one of the doctors I spoke to said, "The nerves are just plain pissed off." I thought that summed it up well.

My conversation reinforced what we were already doing—massage compression, tapping, rubbing and just constant desensitization—was critical to the long-term success for his prosthesis to be pain-free.

Regrettably, there are no "cures" for phantom pain. The consensus was that the pain was temporary, but I am sure you will agree that "temporary" is a relative term when you are not the one experiencing the pain!

As we walked through this stage of our journey I kept trying to find my peaceful heart.

> *17 The LORD hears his people when they call to him for help.*
> *He rescues them from all their troubles.*
> *18 The LORD is close to the brokenhearted;*
> *he rescues those whose spirits are crushed.*
> *– Psalm 34:17-18 (New Living Translation)*

I was thinking, he has already heard our cries and he has lifted our spirits and saved us from brokenness. He helped us make the decision about Jake's amputation, he brought us Boston Bill, and he has surrounded us with more love and fellowship than any family could hope. Had we not had these gifts we may have lived in our brokenness for years to come. So, in a sense we are freed.

Then I was thinking, but I am still crying, have I not been given enough? Is it possible to keep asking for more? So, I humbly prayed for more.

CHAPTER 45

Officially crazy

Saturday, March 15, 2008 11:24 PM (journal entry) Brett

Tonight's update is me. Jake and Jodi are fighting through the nighttime ritual and Jodi asked if I could do an update. I think once Jake finally gets to sleep there will be no energy left!

This morning we were off to the B.A.S.S. Master weigh in. Jake was excited, and his Dad too! I have one word, AWESOME! It was an unbelievable experience, Jake was treated First Class. Or should I say as a VIP. When we pulled in we were in the middle of about 1,000 people all gathered around waiting for the anglers to show off their fish. We wheeled down to the stage and found our friend, Stacy Twiggs. He met us with VIP badges and ushered Jake behind stage. Jake was in the prime spot to meet every fishing pro on the circuit. And that he did! We watched the anglers come off their boats and then go up on stage. As they exited the stage, Jake was positioned to see each one passing by. Stacy would introduce each angler to Jake. They all were so nice. So many people stopped to talk to Jake, not to mention each one signed his hat which is now full of autographs. We took pictures and Jake shook hands. It was a great moment—he was all smiles.

There were so many highlights during those several hours, but one moment I need to mention is the meeting of Kevin VanDam. Jake has been a fan of Kevin for years, in fact, I think he aspires to be just like Kevin when he grows up, traveling the country fishing and winning lots of tournaments!

Kevin had called Jacob at home the Sunday before his surgery. Well needless to say, the meeting between Jake and Kevin was special. And by the way, Kevin won the tournament this weekend. Congratulations Kevin!

These men had no idea what Jake had been through over the last four years, let alone the last four weeks, all I can say is that day was one of his highlights. As sick as he was, he just sat there wide eyed with everyone he met. They had no idea but they gave him a distraction from all the pain he had been experiencing and for just a short while I think he enjoyed himself.

By the day's end, Jake had met so many anglers. They all were so nice. Did I mention that Jake ended up with enough tackle to fill two new tackle boxes and three autographed rod and reels? He had a great day!

I wanted to say special thank you for Stacy Twiggs. His time and commitment to provide Jake such an awesome experience goes beyond words. Thank you Stacy!

For now, good night and sleep well.

Please place Jake and Jodi in your prayers for a pain free and restful night.

Good Night, Brett

The week had gotten away from us. We had been keeping a methodical medicine chart tracking what medicines Jake took at what time. I was also monitoring his food and liquid intake. We had lists and charts and so many processes we were tracking. To top everything, we were running on little sleep and even less patience.

On Saturday, neither Brett nor I realized that by the end of the nighttime round of medicine, the Lortab prescription (pain medicine) would be all used up. Couple this with having spent the entire day at the B.A.S.S. Bassmasters tournament. Everyone was exhausted, especially Jake.

We got home from the tournament after dinnertime, much later than we expected. In fact, this was one of the first and only times Jake had left the house and we had pushed him to his limit. When we left the event, he was lying in the backseat, sort of tapping and moving around just trying to find some relief as his nerve pain started to ignite again.

Midway into the drive home, to our surprise Jake fell asleep. It was probably around 8 p.m., it was definitely getting dark, and so we were thrilled with the idea that maybe he would get some rest. He was due for his next round of medicine, but we decided to let him sleep and hope for the best. He was so exhausted; we just hated to wake him.

When we got home, Brett gently lifted him out of the backseat and maneuvered him upstairs and into his bed. He tiptoed in, laid Jake down, and slipped back out without waking him up. We were so happy but too tired to even celebrate. We headed downstairs to grab some dinner. Thankfully, a meal had been dropped by, so we were feeling so incredibly grateful for the moment of food and quiet.

Around 10:30 p.m. Brett and I were in a sound sleep and Jake started calling me. I immediately jumped up and headed to his room. He was sitting up on his bed, and he was upset. He told me his leg was aching and that is what woke him. I told him not to worry, it was time for medicine. I told him I would go down and get his medicine and then help him get back to sleep.

I trotted downstairs, grabbed the medicine jar, opened the top, and, to my shock, realized it was empty! We had given Jake the last Lortab that morning, and the plan was to pick up his refill on the way home from the tournament. We got so sidetracked and exhausted during the day that we completely forgot to pick up the refill.

I darted upstairs to Brett, I told him I needed him to quickly run to CVS and pick up Jake's medicine. Like me, he couldn't believe we had forgotten to pick up the prescription. He immediately got out of bed and started getting dressed. By now, it was about 10:45 p.m. Jake was in the other room beginning to call me over and over.

Brett headed down the stairs and out the door, and I went back and crawled in bed with Jake. Things started to heat up pretty quickly. He was really in pain and beginning to cry in frustration. I suggested we go into mommy and daddy's bed, sometimes just the change of environment helped.

He wanted to know if I had his medicine, and I explained to him Daddy went to pick it up. We moved into our room, I stacked the pillows around, propping his leg and getting him comfortable. That didn't last for long as the pain was increasing. We needed medicine! About 15 minutes later, I heard the door open. I was so relieved Brett was back and we could get the medicine working. As soon as Brett walked in, he headed to our room; Jake looked up and said, "Daddy, I need my medicine." Brett said "OK, buddy" "Honey, can you come out here for a minute." Jake was saying, "Mom, don't leave"—"I'll be just a minute, buddy, let me see what Daddy needs." "OK, mom, hurry!"

I step into the hallway, and Brett says "OK, stay calm, CVS is closed." I stood there just staring at him. "What?" He repeated "CVS is closed." "I know that," I said, "I mean, what are we going to do?"

In the meantime, Jake's cries are growing, and he is calling me over and over, "Mommy, come make it stop," "Mommy, come make it stop."

Maybe we can get through the night. Brett said. I just stared at him. "Brett, he has been on a steady stream of medicine since February 19th, and his pain is unbearable. Do you think tonight it is going to be different?" Well, we don't have a lot of options, he said.

I could feel my blood pressure welling up inside me. I was suddenly sweating simply because I knew Jake was suffering, and there we stood no solutions in sight! I immediately pulled out the heating pad and all of our other "tricks" and pain management tools. In the meantime, Brett Googled the closest 24-hour CVS Pharmacy. Jake was absolutely miserable and now crying and rolling around on the bed, which made it really difficult for us to focus on a backup plan. We were trying to talk, and he was crying so loud we couldn't even hear ourselves. He had no idea about the medicine dilemma; he was just in too much pain to focus on anything.

Brett found a CVS open 24 hours about 30 minutes from our house. He grabbed the empty medicine jar and headed out. I turned around and went back upstairs to see how I could help Jake feel better. The time between when Brett left on his adventure and returned are hours I want to forget. Jake was absolutely out of his mind with pain. He just rolled and cried, rolled and cried. I would get moments of quiet and we would try a new technique heat—then tapping—then pressure. We tried movies, books, and music. Each would find us a few minutes of distraction, but then the anguish would return.

When I heard the door beep and Brett walked back in, I looked at the clock: It was around 12:30 a.m. I was at my wit's end, feeling completely stressed and helpless. Brett came upstairs, racing into the room like a knight in shining armor, Jake and I were both so happy to see him. He told us he was able to get one pill!

Later, I learned that (at the time) the CVS prescriptions were not all electronically connected by store. So the pharmacist was not able to access our prescription and just refill it. He had no prescription, no doctor's script—nothing—to grant him the ability to fill the order.

The only thing he had was a desperate dad who had frustration in his voice and, I am guessing, a little bit of crazy in the eyes. So the pharmacist knew he had to try to do something. Hence the compromise: one pill to get us through the night.

So there we were. Brett saved the day with the one lone pill that he had traveled an hour round trip to obtain. Brett handed me the pill, with a glass of water and just the most hopeful look in his eyes. I took the pill from him, but when I looked at it, it suddenly looked like the wrong pill to me!

I looked at Brett and said, uh oh, this pill doesn't look the same. "What?" he said. "There's no way, the pharmacist took the script directly from the bottle." I said, "Hmmm, it just looks different." I was cringing as I said it. The tension and drama were so high that Jake was actually distracted from his pain for a minute, and he, too, was silent.

I jumped out of bed and headed to the hallway. Brett followed, closing the door to Jake's room. The tears welled up in my eyes. I was on the verge of completely losing it. I looked at him again. "This is the wrong pill." Brett just kept saying there's no way. But I had been looking at the pill for three weeks, multiple times a day. This pill was different.

We jumped on the Internet and Googled the pill looking for a photo, but we couldn't find anything, I was really feeling crazy, I had that racing feeling in my heart, and I wanted to just scream at the top of my lungs. I felt totally at my breaking point. I'm not sure what that looks like, but if you picture two parents, standing in the hall holding one pill, the mother crying, in old faded pajama bottoms and a T-shirt, messy hair, mascara smeared, sleep deprived, emotionally wrecked, just staring at a guy who was confident it was the right pill and a little boy crying in pain, calling, "Mom, I need my pill." That just may be a picture of crazy!

I said, "I can't do it." Brett patiently said, "Honey, are you sure?" "I can't do it," I repeated. If this is the wrong pill, we could change Jake's life forever, maybe even kill him. "I can't do it." I was sobbing by now. Brett just came and hugged me. "OK," he said, "we will get him through the night." It was now past 1 a.m. When I finally collected myself, I took a deep breath. Things had suddenly become quiet behind the bedroom door. We cracked the door slowly, and Jake was sound asleep.

I sat down right where I was standing, put my head in my hand, and cried. You would think I would have been out of tears, but no, I cried just an agonizing cry of relief. I didn't know if my mind was playing tricks on me or if I was just so tired, I was losing the ability to even think clearly. In the end we just couldn't risk it. The next morning, Brett got up early and headed to CVS to greet the pharmacist as the store opened. He brought the pill with him, handed it to the pharmacist, and told him our story. Are you ready? It was the right pill. Because it was a generic version, the numbers stamped on the front were different. So it did indeed look different, yet it was the right pill. We chalked the whole evening up to what happens with extreme sleep deprivation. You just stop losing the ability to be rational. The stress of keeping Jake comfortable had reached an all time high.

Thankfully, Jake slept through the night. When morning came, it was time to take on another day.

CHAPTER 46

The war against phantom pain

Wednesday, March 19, 2008 12:57 AM (journal entry) Jodi – Another trip to the ER

Today after much deliberation we ended up in the ER at APH. We spent last night once again fighting the phantom pain until the early hours in the morning. Jake was soooo tired he would actually close his eyes and begin to fall asleep and his leg would shoot up, and startle him. We did this for five or six times over the course of 30 minutes until finally he fell back asleep and I pinned his leg down under a bunch of pillows. Under the pillow stack his leg was kind of immobilized and it wouldn't wake him up when the nerve fired.

When we woke up this morning Brett and I agreed another day could not pass without resolution. When I received the call from the pediatric neurologist who informed us their earliest appointment was next Tuesday, I finally lost it. I told her and everyone else I spoke to in the next 45 minutes that this was no longer a wait and see, something needed to change.

In the end, I called Dr. Coffman he said "Go to the ER." This was the one way we could get the attention we needed, consult with a pain specialist, get a holistic evaluation of Jake and his medication plan.

So, that is exactly what we did. We left around noon and unfortunately, Jake was in complete distress. He cried and kicked the whole way, poor Pop, he got the backseat position this time. We dragged him; literally Brett had to physically pull him out of the car and into the ER check-in area. He proceeded to throw a pretty good tantrum in the

ER waiting room. Usually Jake would never carry on in front of everyone he would be too embarrassed but this is how out of sorts he was—he just didn't care.

He was in such pain, lack of food and complete distress. It was without a doubt absolutely heartbreaking. He was rolling himself out of his wheelchair onto the floor and repeating I want to leave over and over. This is the type of mood swings he has been experiencing over the last couple weeks. I felt so bad for him but I knew we were in a place that could help. The tantrum just confirmed for me that we needed to do something. Of course, all the families in the waiting room were looking at us like our kid had gone mad. We didn't even make eye contact. Brett and I just stared at the floor. This was way too complicated for any explanations!

Once we were in a room, we got Jake comfortable. He had a TV and a heated blanket and I was able to massage his leg. He was almost lifeless; his body had just been through too much. I stood there looking at him, once again in the hospital, in my head I was screaming, "God, please help us now, we need help." Just give our sweet boy some peace. I just kept playing it over and over in my head. Inside I was dying; to Jake I was mom trying to save him.

He was able to pull it together for the nurses and the doctor and basically attempted to be a good sport. I think he was just emotionally spent, he had nothing left.

We spent the next three hours in the hospital room and he was just sort of out of it. He watched TV; he slept on and off and of course was entertained by Pop.

Once we finally got everyone to understand how we ended up in the ER—Accident in 2004, limb salvage procedures over four years, amputation four weeks earlier, pain medications for the last three weeks, no sleep, lost appetite, dramatic mood swings, temper and persistent pain. The biggest challenge of all, finding someone to modify his pain management plan and manage it going forward ... blah, blah, blah!!! Finally, things began to roll.

We went through the whole rundown, until the nurse practitioner finally said "I got it." And, I promise you we will get this sorted out. She and the nurse both assured us we wouldn't leave without a better plan for Jake. He has lost seven pounds, his eyes are red and his color pale and everyone agreed he was physically ill from what his body had endured.

As Dr. Novick had indicated to me, we knew the pre-existing nerve damage was going to be a challenge I just think we underestimated to what degree. Sometimes you just have to learn as you go.

To summarize our visit, we ended up meeting with Dr. Maggie Hood. She is the pain management doctor for APH. We had never met her in our previous stays, she is four months new but apparently, had been recruited to come and lead the pain management team at APH. We were just lucky she happened to be on call today and passing through the ER—timing is everything!

She was great; I immediately liked her style, concise and informative. She met Jake and then asked us to step into the hall, which I thought was a great idea. Her first question was "What do you want to happen here today?" She listened closely to our answer which led to a great dialogue. We brainstormed the best combination of medicine and how to address nerve pain. She was not opposed to Lortab which she said is a great pain medication. However, she agreed it was time to focus on managing neuropathic pain. And I believed the Lortab was part of our problem, I believed Jake's mood swings and loss of appetite was coming from that particular drug.

When we went back in the room she asked Jake "What can I do to help you today." He said, "Help me sleep, make my leg stop hurting and let the nights not be so scary." It was as simple as that. As we worked on a modified pain management program, she said sleep is our first goal. It is so critical to his healing. She felt much of his behavior and loss of appetite contributed to lack of sleep. She did say the Lortab was certainly responsible for some of his symptoms but lack of sleep is equally indicative of these types of symptoms. She asked us how we would act with severe sleep deprivation, Brett said, "Look at us"! Point made!

Tonight we started the neuropathic meds which have a progressive dose plan and we have a progressive plan to reduce Lortab and Valium. The new medications will not work immediately but should begin to provide relief and increase over time. Fortunately, I had done a lot of homework and research through my fellow child amputee moms and other resources. I was familiar with her suggestions, I had researched the drugs and aware of the impacts. She wasn't recommending anything I hadn't already researched but again, the process is still unnerving.

At that point, I felt we had no choices, this extreme situation called for extreme action.

We left feeling good, yet uneasy. It is never easy to give your child medication under any circumstances. But, leaving Jake on the path he was on will just continue to delay his recovery and cause more harm than good.

I got my confirmation tonight at bedtime that we are doing the right thing. Tonight was worse than ever. He had a really hard time falling asleep. He finally fell asleep just at midnight. But, his nerves were so fired up his leg was actually jerking up off the bed. He would be sleeping soundly and then his leg would jolt up. I held his leg for 45 minutes after he fell asleep, it continued to jerk and twitch in my hand. I had to apply pressure to keep it from shooting up in the air. It is by far one of the strangest things I have ever experienced. That leg has a mind of its own! And those nerves are certainly angry.

I was explaining to Jake the new nerve medicine is going to go to the end of his nerves and gently pet them and soothe them to calm them down. Just before he fell asleep he said "Mom, I think the medicine is working on one nerve, it is listening and calming down, the problem is there are 100 angry nerves so the medicine has 99 more to go!" So there you have it, another long day, looking forward to better days ahead.

Blessings and love, Jodi

CHAPTER 47

Sleep is overrated

Friday, March 21, 2008 1:49 AM (journal entry) Jodi

The stress that is wrapped into this nighttime ritual is just crazy. Finding that perfect position, massage, heat/cold, the magic combination when he finally closes his eyes and drifts off to sleep. It is a team effort, Jake will say, "Should we try some heat" or "Maybe mom you should massage my other foot, sometimes that distracts me." The pressure of helping this little guy work through is like a ton of weights on your shoulders, I can't describe it any other way. As mom's we try to offer our children comfort and to not have the ability to solve this for Jake just makes me crazy.

Unfortunately, there doesn't seem to be a magic formula. Just when I think I have mastered the perfect technique, it fails to be replicated!

Jake is doing his part and I know that God will do his. Love to you, Jodi

Sunday, March 23, 2008 11:58 PM (journal entry) Jodi – Another Easter

On this Easter Sunday, I am endlessly grateful for Jake's attitude despite the challenges of the last four years, he continues to remind us all that bright shiny days are just around the corner.

I am grateful for so many things, but today I am feeling most grateful for Brett. I was teasing him yesterday saying that we are maybe having a role reversal. As of late, when I felt like the burden was just getting too great to carry, Brett was there to catch me.

For so long he struggled with his own guilt and sadness but by the grace of God he is finally finding peace and feeling optimistic about the future. For us, this is by far one of God's greatest blessings. He is not only giving Jake a new lease on life, but he is giving Jake back his daddy, and me, my husband who I missed so much.

Blessed are those who seek him, we are learning that more every day, not just as individuals but as a family. The Easter season is a time of renewal and through Brett I can see Gods work.

I hope we will be able to someday talk to other families who are struggling through challenges like our own. A marriage is hard with normal day to day pressures add a crisis and most times the marriage will fail. Trust me we heard the statistics over and over following the accident. All I can say is that we have learned some hard lessons and I am confident the future will not be free of new struggles but today we get to celebrate together, hand in hand as a couple and watch our son embrace this new life.

I hope this is a powerful testimony of what can be.

Tonight before Jake fell asleep he a got a jolt and flinched pretty good. I said "are you OK buddy?" He said, "Have you ever dropped a hammer on your toe and then got struck by lightning?" I tried not to smile because he was dead serious, I said, "No" he said "Well then you wouldn't understand what that just felt like." The interesting part, is either it is hurting less or he is adapting because he expressed the pain, but nothing like he has done in weeks past. He is no longer, hitting and kicking, there is no doubt in my mind that the medication is really giving him the relief he needed. But as I have said before there is no tried and true method for managing this crazy thing called phantom pain. Time will be the greatest healer.

As I reflected on Easter four years ago, I was reminded how quickly things can change. We got another chance with Jake but I no longer take life for granted. Give an extra kiss tonight to those you love, if I have learned anything it is that life is unpredictable. Every day is a gift and sometimes you don't really understand that until the things you love most are altered.

Who knew Jake would be an amputee, had you asked me that question five years ago, never in my wildest dreams would I have imagined. But, life changes and so have we. Pass on some love to those who are on your mind. Don't wait till tomorrow.

Love and Blessings tonight from our home to yours!
Jodi

CHAPTER 48

Stay the course

Tuesday, March 25, 2008 6:48 PM (journal entry) Jodi

We may be turning a corner. Jake is finally feeling a little better physically but he has established patterns and routines that have to slowly transform. Homework, re-immersing him back into school, proper bedtime, picking up, resuming the responsibilities and manners, all are going to need a bit of reprogramming and time.

Right after visiting Stan today we headed to school. He participated in music which was fun then to the classroom. I left him at the door and told him I would see him in an hour. I could tell he was tired and not completely convinced about school today but we need to start somewhere.

I came home and within 15 minutes the phone rang. It was Jake and he said "Mommy, my leg hurts." Well, I knew his leg probably didn't hurt but I also knew this transition was not going to be perfect or easy. So, I headed back to school. I watched him through the classroom door for about 10-15 minutes. He was fidgeting in his wheelchair, trying to work but being pretty distracted. Soon he saw me and wheeled out. When he came in the hallway he immediately got into my lap. He just needed a little comfort I think.

It is so hard because you struggle to find the balance between pushing him yet understanding what he has just been through and giving him the time to ease back into his routine. I just need to be patient with the process.

I apologized to Mrs. Baucom for disrupting the class-room. It is such a distraction when Jake is wheeling in and out. I just so want him to slip back into class and pick up where he left off. I am feeling so anxious about catching up his work and re-introducing him to the world of just being seven again. I know it will happen in due time but five plus weeks have already passed.

So, when I was feeling vulnerable and weary, Mrs. Bau-com gave me just what I needed. She was awesome. She told me "We knew this wasn't going to be easy and its o.k." What a gift to give me "Its o.k." What more could I ask for. I am such a "doer" and I like things to happen in an orderly and timely fashion but these life things there are no rules or guidelines. It is such a personal and individual journey and I need to allow Jake to move at his own pace.

I had to chuckle to myself. The battles are typical from what to eat for breakfast to brushing his teeth. He just has an added complication of being out of sync and kind of not in any hurry to get back into the process of these daily rit-uals. In fact, the uniform became a stumbling block this morning. I said, "Jake, can you put your uniform on?" Of course he said "What, why do I need to wear my uniform?" "Because you're going to school and that is school policy" (ARGH). Well, he negotiated a million reasons why he shouldn't have to wear his uniform. Again, Jake was strug-gling for control and independence. I was thinking, come on kid; throw me a bone here, but no chance!

Jake and I had a conversation when we left school today about when he calls me he doesn't need to say his leg hurts, he can be honest and say he is just not ready. It's OK to not be completely ready; I just want him to feel com-fortable to tell us that.

He said, "OK mom, I will do that." Then he said, "But I have to tell you as soon as I rolled into the classroom my nerves in my leg were like, Oh boy, we do not want to be here, we don't feel like doing any reading or math!" "Then, just when we left, they were like, that's better we feel good now that we are going home."

I had to smile.

I think Jake may have been using his nerves to talk in third person but I got the point. The good news is the med-icine has not affected his ability to be clever Jake! And who can blame him for not being in any hurry to get back to reading and math.

How exciting. Much love, Jodi

Saturday, March 29, 2008 4:17 PM (journal entry) Jodi:

We left St. Petersburg smiling yesterday.

At last a visit when Jake was in a great mood, his leg is healing beautifully and we had nothing but good things to celebrate.

We were all quiet on the way over, not because we were nervous or worried, just kind of tired of the process. At this stage we are in waiting mode. We are through some of the really hard stuff; kind of getting our footing again and anxiously waiting for the next move, so quiet was OK and quite honestly welcomed.

From the moment we arrived at Dr. Novick's office Jake was a chatter box. We of course took Tweek (Jake's new Guinea Pig) who is now becoming a celebrity in her own right at the Children's Ortho office. Everyone looks forward to seeing her, as much as Jake.

Jake did the big reveal for Dr. Beck and Dr. Novick. I am always anxious to see Dr. Novick's reaction. She has a pretty good poker face but a big smile is a dead giveaway. So I know this visit was good. She gave us the go ahead to start swimming; we can even go to the beach, just no lake swimming yet. I cannot tell you how good it feels to know how far we have come. Swimming will be such good exercise for him and hopefully a great way to wear him out for a better nighttime routine.

The visit yesterday was great. As I have said so many times, the hard times often feel unbearable, but the highs well they just make your heart soar! And yesterday was good. We are not exactly sure what the plan is for Monday, but we hope to hear from Stan to find out when we go for our next fitting.

Jake essentially got the final nod from Dr. Novick and Dr. Beck that his residual limb was healing to their satisfaction. We were essentially being released to get back with our lives!

When we left Brett said, "Is that it?" You go through all this together and then we are done?" I told Brett it doesn't matter when we see them or how often we will always be connected. It is hard to explain. But I have to agree it feels a little funny to be so intertwined and dependent on their advice and guidance and then set on our own. The good news is that we have developed relationships that go far beyond doctor and patient. So, I know we will be in touch for years to come.

This week could be a BIG week. Walking by Friday, is that even possible?

Homework, PT, working toward no bedtime pain and A NEW LEG! I am frustrated, excited, weepy, antsy, CRAZY, super happy and a little tired just thinking about it. But there is no time like the present so let's get this show on the road.

Stay tuned ... Love, Jodi

CHAPTER 49

Prosthetics 101

**Monday, March 31, 2008 11:54 PM (journal entry) Jodi -
Starting the prosthetic process**

Drum roll please, this could be the week. Is it possible
that Jake will be walking by the end of the week? In one
respect I feel like I have pictured it in my head a thousand
times yet tonight I can't picture it at all!

Stan used the mold from Thursday to create the liner
for Jake's socket and leg. The liner is a silicone material
that is made specifically to fit Jake's leg.

We arrived at Stan's around 3:30 p.m., the really cool
thing about Stan's office is that all the patient doors stay
open and the patients kind of wander around and chat
with other amputees. Every time we are there we meet
someone new, people from all over the country. Today was
a real treat because Jake was able to meet a military solider
who lost his leg in 2005 in combat in Iraq. He spent an
extended period of time at Walter Reed Hospital for pain
management. He was an awesome guy, a true war hero who
continues to serve his country in the Army even as an
amputee.

When Stan rolled Jake's liner on the first time he got
a little emotional because he said it was hurting his leg. But
I think he was just nervous and it felt like more pressure
than he was used to. Once he gave it a chance he was fine.
Inside the liner Jake will wear a lotion that allows for the
liner to fit perfectly with no rubbing or sore spots. The
liner is a very important part of the prosthesis. It will fit perfectly inside the prosthetic socket for Jake's new leg.

While Stan measured and evaluated the necessary changes to adjust the liner, Roger Underhill brought in a little box and handed it to Jake. He said, "Here is your knee"! Jake opened it and there was a little mechanical knee. Then he walked in with a foot, "here is your foot!" He handed him a small metal foot with an artificial foot cover. Jake was very quiet. I think he was just taking it all in.

I can't describe how we felt when we were standing there holding his foot and knee. It was so cool to finally see the components of his leg knowing that in just a couple days they will be assembled and will be supporting Jake to once again walk on two feet!

Now THAT is something to get excited about!

Bedtime was good tonight, we are still definitely fighting nighttime pain but we have made a dramatic improvement. We are headed back to Stan's tomorrow morning for another fitting. We are a little beaten and battered but eager and excited. Love, Jodi

Wednesday, April 02, 2008 12:02 AM (journal entry) Jodi

We started the day with an appointment at POA. Jake was in a great mood and his new bright green liner was ready and fit perfectly. In a quick fashion, Stan and Roger casted Jake's leg overtop of his liner and then cut the cast off. The cast now gave them the mold they needed to create his "test socket."

There was a flurry of activity this morning; other patients were getting fittings, new liners and walking. Even Simba (Stan's border collie) sat close by and watched as Stan fitted Jake with his new liner.

We were there for about an hour maybe an hour/half in the morning. Then we returned in the afternoon. We spent the afternoon working on the details of the "test socket." By the time we came back in the afternoon the test socket was ready. Jake slid his leg into the socket for the first time as though he had been doing this for years. At first he flinched a little and showed Stan some areas of discomfort. Creating this leg is a combination of shop class and art. They shaved and adjusted ever so slightly until they achieved a form fitting socket. It was pretty impressive and Stan left no detail unattended.

Everything he asked Jake to do he did without question. After he felt comfortable with the test socket, Stan asked Jake to put pressure on his leg and test socket by leaning on a short stand/stool to see how his leg was going to tolerate weight or pressure. Jake leaned as hard as he could, he was very quiet and I could tell he was trying to decide whether it hurt or just felt uncomfortable. Not a word from him, no complaints, and no questions he just looked very intent. Not upset just focused. He was listening, following direction and processing it all. Once in a while Stan would make a comment and get a nervous smile out of him otherwise he was focused on the task at hand. It is still amazing to me how his maturity just sets in when he is faced with these adult situations.

I could tell he was apprehensive. Not necessarily nervous just cautious to go slowly. I know he was just so fearful of more pain. But Stan went at Jake's pace and talked him through every step. If Jake said pause that is exactly what Stan did.

Primarily the goal of today was to get a good fit between the socket and the liner, and make sure his leg was ready to tolerate pressure, that there were no pain points or areas of friction. A variety of times he had on the liner and the socket and he would be sitting in his wheelchair. He seemed to tolerate it well but there is no doubt it will take some getting used to. He would be sitting there and unconsciously fidgeting.

Again, another emotionally charged day, I was almost too tired to write.

Tomorrow our appointment with Stan is at 10 a.m. The plan is that Jake's leg will be ready for a trial run. So if everything goes well, Jake will not only stand on his new leg but quite possibly take a few steps. How's Jake? Well, he is very matter of fact. I think this is everything he imagined and he is just ready. He didn't have much to say but his eyes told the whole story. All he had to do was look at me after he slipped his leg into the test socket and I knew he was happy.

Literally and like everything Jake has done so far this too will not be easy or pain free. Fortunately, he is armed with confidence, determination, a strong dose of tenacity and faith. These character traits will get him through. He is a tough kid and showed me this once again today.

Can you imagine how intimidating it would be to put your newly amputated leg, fresh incision and still tender into a liner and hard, plastic test socket then to put all your weight onto that leg? I am positive I would not have been as brave. It makes me want to cry thinking about it.

I will leave you with this tonight. Today felt strangely normal. The idea that he will soon be mobile on two legs, one of them being mechanical just seems as if it was always the plan. I am going to savor this week; I want to always remember how grateful we are for this second chance. Rather than mourning what has happened over the last four years, this week is a chance for us to celebrate a new beginning.

Love and Blessings, Jodi

CHAPTER 50

Jake – back on two feet

Wednesday, April 02, 2008 5:52 PM (journal entry) Jodi - A day to remember:
Jake took his first steps today!

It has been two days filled with so many emotions but quite simply this is a day of freedom for sweet Jake. As tragic as the accident was in 2004, he is now restored and this is the beginning. I am not sure I could ever put words to how my heart felt today. I just don't think there are any.

Today I am especially grateful for the team at POA. Stan, Stephanie, Ricky, Roger, Greg Sarmiento, Brice Duba—and the list goes on and on. They gave Jake a space that felt comfortable and safe and for that he was able to thrive. These individuals are doing God's work, giving a child his leg again can only be classified as a miracle.

Love, Jodi

> *16 That is why we never give up. Though our bodies are dying, our spirits are being renewed every day. 17 For our present troubles are small and won't last very long. Yet they produce for us a glory that vastly outweighs them and will last forever! 18 So we don't look at the troubles we can see now; rather, we fix our gaze on things that cannot be seen. For the things we see now will soon be gone, but the things we cannot see will last forever.*
> *— 2 Corinthians 4:16-18 (New Living Translation)*

Thursday, April 03, 2008 9:37 AM (journal entry) Jodi - quick am update:

I have a strange combination of complete exhaustion and elation. We are still not caught up from the last 6 weeks and here we are soaring down a new mountain.

Thankfully Pop is already here this morning, when I looked out the window the blue truck was already in the driveway. He is now doing dishes and tidying up before Jake wakes up. I have kind of given up on the housekeeping for the moment. But if Pop is here and Jake is occupied, he generally has a towel over his shoulder and a laundry basket in his hand. There is no task too great or too small, Pop is there no matter the circumstances is willing and unconditional and I love him greatly!

We had another long night of nighttime pain. But, I know we will find a solution soon enough, the more he uses his leg in his new prosthesis in combination with PT I think the nighttime pain will subside. No complaints. We will take the nights in exchange for the freedom he is gaining.

In fact, he was telling me last night he wished his leg didn't hurt but it was OK. He also said "Mom what time are we going to Mr. Stan's tomorrow?" I said around 10 a.m., he said "perfect I want to do some more practicing in the morning."

Watching him yesterday the reality once again set in that things do not always happen as they do in the movies. That everything takes time and practice. And while Jake is very comfortable on the prosthesis and his balance is amazing. He has to learn and that will take time and hard work.

In reality he only spent about 15 minutes in total walking yesterday. The rest is adjusting to standing, finding your balance and just the feeling of the prosthetic on your leg. Imagine when we tack on a month of 15 minutes! It is so exciting.

We are headed to Stan's this morning and we will go back in the afternoon. I assume we will do the same tomorrow. Once Stan feels as if Jake has the basics down, we can go home with his new leg. I will write again tonight. Love, Jodi

Thursday, April 03, 2008 8:14 PM (journal entry) Jodi

Jake was amazing today. This morning he got right up and walking, we brought his leg home at lunch time and did a little practicing here. Then during our afternoon visit he was able to walk the length of the rails without using them for support.

Everyone was just smiling from ear to ear. He is so grown up during these sessions. Very quiet and very focused, then when it is time to leave he flies down the hall in his wheelchair yelling goodbye to everyone. Tonight he called "Bye Mr. Stan, see you tomorrow." We will go to Stan's everyday (twice a day) for the next week to ten days. He will be learning so quickly it is important we have frequent visits for gait training to make sure he is using the prosthesis properly. Not sure what that means for returning to school this week so once again I am reminding myself, day by day. I know keeping my patience is an important step.

I wish I could be more descriptive in the experience of watching him learn to use his new leg. I think it is just such joy because while we cannot see it today we know so much is going to be possible and more importantly things will be NORMAL.

How exciting is that, just to be a normal kid. Love, Jodi

Sunday, April 06, 2008 9:50 AM (journal entry) Jodi

Today, Jake was actually on his feet, standing and taking steps on his new prosthesis. He progressed away from the parallel bars and to using a crutch. When Brett, Jake and Pop came home I was floored when they called me to the front porch and around the corner came Jake. He was walking on his prosthesis with the help of a small child's crutch under his left arm. He walked all the way up the sidewalk. I was cheering and telling him how awesome he is doing, he just shrugged it off like what do I expect. He said it is nice to be able to stand up when you want to get somewhere, not hopping or scooching, what a luxury we take for granted, standing on two feet.

To walk, eyes straight forward when you can't even feel the contact of the ground has to be unnerving. Not to mention running or playing sports. So Jake continues to go slow and steady. I am confident he is going to master this just like all the other athletes before him. I have no doubt in his ability. We just need to remain patient in the process.

Like Stan said, we will have great days and some days will be hard. But in the end, we are working toward a goal that Jake WILL achieve. Today is a new day and we are eager to get started. Just think what this week will hold! Feeling the blessings. Love, Jodi

Wednesday, April 09, 2008 12:12 AM (journal entry) Jodi

Monday morning we chatted with Stan about Jake's inconsistency in wearing his leg over the weekend. Stan wasn't fazed at all in fact by the time we left Jake was walking without the crutch!

Stan was so tickled by his performance he said he didn't care how often Jake wore the leg. With this kind of progress soon he won't want to take it off. Walking on a prosthesis comes very naturally to Jake. Don't get me wrong, there is no doubt he is awkward and learning, but the idea seems quite normal to him. He has embraced this prosthesis almost as if this is the way he was born to walk.

Today, Stan decided to create the final socket. It is lighter and will give Jake a little more comfort and freedom. Hopefully it will make the prosthesis easier to control and allow Jake to better manage his gait. Tomorrow morning we go to try out the new socket.

Our appointments with Stan will continue, twice a day until further notice. It all depends on how Jake is progressing. I am hopeful within the next two weeks we will eliminate the wheelchair altogether.

Jake is a work in progress on many levels. We are working hard to put him back on a normal schedule—sleep, food, liquids, school—this surgery was a giant disruption for the last seven weeks and now we are trying to "reset" the program. I am sure all parents can appreciate this is no easy task with a stubborn seven year old. But we are being consistent, drawing some strong boundaries and holding Jake accountable. Just in the last week, we see him responding, so I am very pleased.

We are slowly blending all the old responsibilities of Jake's world, like school, bedtime, and good manners with this whole new world of learning to live as an amputee. This would be monumental for any kid to absorb and adapt, but I am confident Jake can do it. He proves this to me every day. Love, Jodi

CHAPTER 51

Absolutely divine

Wednesday, April 09, 2008 11:16 PM (journal entry) Jodi

Ironically (or not) today, April 9th 2008 Jake received his new and final leg, exactly for years from the day of his original injury.

I suppose you could find it ironic that on the anniversary of a day that symbolized such sorrow and hurt for our family, Jake would receive this beautifully crafted and perfectly designed new leg. A gift so authentic it will fit no one else but Jake Bainter.

I call this divine. We have prayed for four years straight along with thousands who have followed our story and only a power greater than us could arrange a day of such renewal.

I remember a few years ago as I reflected on April 9th the day of the accident. I had learned through medical records that the 911 call from Brett was received around 3:30 p.m. I have anguished so many times over what horror that moment must have been for my husband and my son.

My tears are falling as I write.

I glanced at my watch today around 3:30 p.m. just out of curiosity.

I was standing in the therapy room of POA. Jake was on the treadmill with his beautiful new leg, Brett was standing right behind him waiting to catch him if he falls. Stan started the treadmill Jake was walking at a slow pace and slowly Stan increased the speed. Brett was smiling from ear to ear watching proudly as Jake conquered this new task Stan had set before him. Within seconds, Jake had progressed into a small jog. We were all cheering him on.

As quickly as it started Jake's little legs were tired, just as his legs began to stumble, Brett scooped him up and planted his feet back onto the side of the treadmill. Brett was hugging him and telling him how proud he was, and Jake said "Thanks dad for catching me."

All I can say, is God is Good. He gave me that moment today; no one in the room could understand how far we have come. But, it felt like such a testimony of what is possible. We were so broken, but we had faith and we kept going.

Another blessing that has really become clear over the last few weeks is how incredibly important Jake's allograft (cadaver bone) was and is to his function as an amputee. As plans came together for the amputation we had realized that without the bone transplant in 2005, a higher amputation (up his thigh) would have been unavoidable. And as you may know, the shorter the residual limb the more complicated and less functional the prosthetic fit.

So, here we are, four years into this walk and we are already beginning to find blessings in the limb salvage process, which allowed for a "through the knee" amputation and ultimately a longer residual limb. Even today as an amputee, the small valuable piece of tissue he received from a donor in 2005—remains a very important part of Jake's body.

I have learned that when challenges come, sometimes you cannot see the solution, but if you just start walking, those steps will often lead to places you never imagined. For us, it was a tissue transplant and amputation—who ever thought those two hurdles would lead us to such a place of gratitude. Oh what a day. In him, Jodi

Sunday, April 13, 2008 2:58 PM (journal entry) Jodi – A quantum leap:

Well, I knew we would suddenly turn the corner but I didn't know it would be a quantum leap. The only way I can describe the last four days is unbelievable. Jake seems to be improving by the minute.

Let me see if I can elaborate. Wednesday—great day, Jake started walking on his leg in a more consistently. We saw Stan twice that day, walking nicely during both visits. In fact, Ricky took him outside and they walked around the entire building (¼ of a mile!). From that point on, the last four days he has worn his leg almost continuously.

He wore his leg when we went to the dentist Thursday afternoon (the nurses were all waiting to see him when we arrived!). He wore it when we went to Stan's Friday morning. Then, drum roll once again, he wore his leg to school on Friday afternoon. He was greeted with a hero's welcome by his class. Mrs. Baucom had the children gathered around the carpet for story time so she could let Jake come straight to the front and do the unveiling of his new mode of transportation. The kids were fascinated and so proud of Jake. It was pretty special. When I picked him up, he had taken his leg and liner off and was putting it back on. The kids were gathered around, handing him his ointment, holding his leg, helping with his liner. They were so eager to help him. Again, how humbled can one mom feel? Such an unbelievable welcome back, Jake was beaming and I know his heart was full.

Strangely, watching him walk down the hall felt very normal, it was just as I had pictured in my head so many times. I could feel the butterflies knowing that we are actually here, reaching these milestones we had spent so many days praying for.

I LOVE watching Jake walk on his new leg. I love watching his smile and his new sense of freedom. I like watching him sit Indian style with a knee that bends or squatting down with two bended knees. One thing I really relish is when he just stands straight up, two feet firmly planted on the ground his weight evenly distributed.

The goal is to visit Stan in the morning and go to school in the afternoon; it will be lovely if he could do this with cooperation and a pleasant attitude! Am I asking too much? I hope you find this Sunday restful and blessed.

Love from our house to yours, Jodi

Monday, May 05, 2008 12:13 AM (journal entry) Jodi
First, each day Jake's walking improves. He wakes up, puts his leg on and that's it, he keeps it on all day. He kneels, climbs stairs, stands on one leg, and walks smoother than he has in years. I love to see Stan's smile on Monday's, when he checks out the progress Jake has made over the

weekend. He just smiles and shakes his head telling Jake how unbelievable he is doing!

Today I feel this new sense of peace and a little excitement watching him walk on his new prosthetic. He still struggles to walk through the grass and even more with tackle box and fishing pole in hand. And even thought we still wrestle with nighttime pain and we've even gained some new and different challenges, there is no doubt; my heart rests more peacefully because I KNOW his days are filled with improvements rather than deterioration. It just lightens my heart to know this is only the beginning.

He spends time every week, every day working on his gait training. Stan is constantly teaching him new things. He wants to run badly, but we are learning it is harder than you think. So, every day when we go to Stan's he wants to run on the treadmill, in fact he ran for 10 minutes on Thursday. When he gets off the treadmill, he then tries to run using the same gait, but it just doesn't flow as easy. I can tell he is disappointed but he shrugs it off. I keep reminding him, he has only had his leg for a month! But, when it comes to running patience is not in the cards for Jake.

The transition back to socialization with friends is taking time. Interestingly the place he seems most adjusted and "the old Jake" is at Stan's office. He loves talking to the other amputees and the guys who design the prosthetics. I can only speculate, but I think he finds real fellowship in these people who understand what he has gone through. I think we can all appreciate finding places where we feel accepted and not different. There is something very comforting about those environments and for Jake it seems to be his safe place at the moment. Much love and thank you for continuing to check on us!

All I can say is, day by day! Jodi

CHAPTER 52

Coming up for air

July through December 2008

By July of 2008, I think we were finally coming up for air.

Stan built Jake a leg that fit like the proverbial golden slipper. Only two months into wearing a prosthesis he was moving with fluidity that I suspect is a privilege for most above-the-knee amputees. Jake simply embodied his prosthesis, almost as if the nerves flowed all the way to his foot. Somehow he makes the weighty and mechanical function of the prosthesis disappear in his stride. Even today, watching him can make your heart soar. And while it may not be what we hoped and dreamed for our son, the obvious problem is solved with the best possible solution we had available.

Our story was not yet over, but we had clearly begun a new chapter.

Throughout our journey, my pursuit of "finding our people" continued. As we began to enter the world of disabilities, I wanted to expose Jake to all the opportunities available to him.

With that, in June, just five months after Jake's amputation, we along with 400 amputees and their families attended the annual Amputee Coalition of America (ACA) conference.

It was held that year in Atlanta. We drove to Georgia not knowing what to expect. Stan and the POA crew were attending the conference as well and had invited us to join them. So we knew we would see familiar faces and were comforted knowing they would be there with us.

When we first arrived at the hotel, I remember getting out of the car feeling a little nervous. I just didn't know what to expect, and here we were. Once again I had dragged my family a few hundred miles from home in hope of what? I am not sure I knew!

As we walked through the hotel doors, I remember the experience like it was yesterday. I stopped in my tracks as the lobby was filled with amputees of all ages. I couldn't believe my eyes. Within minutes, Jake said, "Mom, look at that guy; he is an amputee," "Mom, look at that lady; she is an amputee," and on and on. I was nervous and Jake was lit up like a Christmas tree. In that moment I realized, these were his people, finally a world where everyone looked like him!

People who understood what it was like to have to hop to the bathroom in the middle of the night, or put a prosthetic on every day in order to have mobility, or had experienced phantom pain, or understood being stared at all the time. These were Jake's people, and it was amazing to see them all.

It was the first time in a long time that we felt like part of something. He was no longer the kid with the unfixable hurt leg. He was a strong and vibrant eight-year-old who found comfort and empowerment around these fellow amputees (kids and adults) who understood the implications of Jake's circumstances.

I felt a lump in my throat all weekend. We talked freely and openly about amputation, phantom pain, residual limb pain, limb care, prosthetic components, disappointment, hope, frustration, how to find a good fit, the implications of hopping, how to save and preserve the "sound knee."

We were in a community of people who live with limb loss every day, and we had the giant support group at our disposal. I don't think I have cried, laughed, talked, and just put all my protective barriers down in years. It was so healing and comforting for us all.

I have said many times, Brett and I cried our way through the entire weekend, hugging more strangers than we had in a lifetime. But we left with new friends, new confidence, and further peace that we had made the right choice for Jake.

During the conference, vendors in the exhibit hall renamed Jake the mayor. He zipped around to all the vendor booths, sometimes dragging Brett and me along, saying, "I want you to meet someone." We would walk over and there would be a man or woman amputee. He would say, "Mr. So and So is an above-the-knee amputee and he has a power knee." Or, "Look at his foot; he has the carbon graphite performance foot." He was truly taking all this in, listening and already processing what his life will look like as an adult. In Jake's eight years, I have not seen him this open and venerable in a group setting. Again, with every conversation and every moment, I just fought back my tears of happiness and relief.

Brett was soaking it all in as well. We would return to the room at night and compare notes and stories of all the people we had met. We could not wipe the smile off our face as we watched Jake and these other amazing amputee kids fly around the conference. They were playing ball, swimming and participating in tennis and run clinics. They dodged between the adult amputees at the run clinic like little skittles. We were so proud to be the parents of these happy and adjusted kids. What a privilege we had been given.

We have since attended the conference every year. This past August, we traveled to California to attend. The beauty is now when we arrive we are not filled with anticipation and fear, just excitement and gratitude. We said hello to old friends, we met new ones, and once again celebrated the gifts we have been given.

It always reminds me of how faithful God really is, the gifts have been so rich and greater than I could have ever expected. In fact, believe it or not, I was having a hard time remembering what it was like to live in the crisis until I re-read the pages of this book.

Jake has chosen Joy, and that is all there is to it.

If you have friends or you yourself are struggling through hard times, know this: Brighter days do come. They may not come in the perfect package you had hoped or in the timeline you are praying for—but they do come. This is God's promise to all of us. Just look at the Bainters!

We are renewed and feeling strong, but we could have never gotten to this place without the love and encouragement we received so generously over the years.

So as I write these final chapters, I smile knowing how far we have come. Slow and steady, one day at a time, keeping our eyes to the sky. That summer we were moving along swimmingly until December of 2008. Jake was once again living and playing wide open when I made the next journal entry.

Saturday, December 27, 2008 6:00 PM (journal entry) Jodi
Tis the Season!

Well, Friday December 19th, Jake broke his left arm just above the elbow. He fell in the yard while playing tag with the neighbor kids and just landed wrong.

I was at Nathaniel's Hope volunteering, it was our last Friday in Orlando and we were heading to Michigan for the Christmas Holiday. My cell phone rang at about 4 p.m.

and it was Brett. He had the tone in his voice, so I immediately felt my heart begin to race. Oh no, what now? Brett said, "It's not an emergency but Jake fell while playing with neighborhood friends and he hurt his arm." "How bad, is it broken?" "Well," Brett responded, I'm not sure but he is lying on his back in the grass and he doesn't want to move.

I said, "Can he talk to me?" I was trying to feel out whether this was a real emergency or whether Jake just needed to work through the fall. Brett handed the phone to Jake laying there in the yard and I heard, in the tiniest most tearful voice, "Mom, I need you to come home." I said "Honey, did you break your arm?"—"I think so." That was it; I was in my car and headed home. As soon as I saw him, I was concerned he indeed had broken his arm. It was swollen all around the elbow and he could not move it at all.

Brett had gotten him in the house and onto the couch; I sat down next to him and explained that we needed to go to the hospital. "No mom, please no" tears rolling down his cheeks. I said "Jake, honey, this is no big deal, if it is broken they will put it in a cast and you will feel better." Brett said, "You can do this buddy." He just laid there with tears rolling down his cheeks; the look on his face was one of "Why? This is so unfair!"

Brett had gotten some ice and wrapped his arm with an ace bandage to give it some support and relief. We all sat there for a few minutes, and then Jake said, "OK let's go." He was wise enough to know this was not going to fix itself and the longer we sat at home, the longer we delayed the inevitable.

By now it was after 5 p.m., Brett and I knew it was going to be a long night. We arrived at the hospital ER and found our position in the waiting room. He had his leg off and he was in his wheelchair and his arm was beginning to throb. The nursing staff was awesome and very attentive to helping him get comfortable.

We made it to a room sometime after 6:30 p.m., and then came the first round of x-rays, tears and frustration. Before the doctor came, in we were sent for a second round of x-rays which almost tipped Jake over the edge. He was being incredibly patient considering his history and lack of tolerance for hospitals in general. We were in the room and thankfully had the little TV tuned into Sponge-Bob, Jake had slipped into a comfy spot. Grammie and Pop showed about an hour into the process. They were a welcomed relief because Brett and I were feeling deflated. We knew that this was just a broken arm, but we didn't know if he was going to need surgery or what. When the surgeon finally showed up, he confirmed it was broken, and that it would need to be set, meaning his arm had gotten very swollen and it was stuck in a slightly bent position, but for the cast it would need to be moved to a right angle position.

The nurse came in and gently started to re-position Jake's arm, and he about shot through the roof! He spiraled into a very hysterical cry once again begging us not to hurt him. The doctor called me into the hallway to talk about a plan of attack. He suggested we give Jake a dose of Tylenol with codeine. This would help him relax and help ease the pain to re-set his arm.

For whatever reason, I could feel my blood pressure raising. My heart was thumping so loud, I could hear it ringing in my ears. I stood at the nurses' station, Brett, I and Grammie on one side and the doctor and a handful of nurses standing on the other. In that moment, I could feel myself beginning to lose it. I could feel the tears welling up in my eyes. They started rolling down my cheeks and that was it, I could not stop. I had a complete meltdown right there at the nurse's station. I turned and walked down the hall and just could not stop. I had a good cry, like one I had not had in a long time.

I cried for everything, the leg we had given up, the years we had struggled, the pain we had all endured, the many, many doses of Tylenol with codeine he had already consumed over the last five years, and now the pain he was once again about to encounter. I was angry—sad—and incredibly emotional. Grammie and Brett were pacing in the hallway not sure what to do with me. I was expressing all of this angst as I continued to cry. Finally the nurse came over and said, "Mrs. Bainter is there anything I can do?" She was very sweet and trying to help. She said, maybe we can come up with another solution. She went on to say, "It's going to be OK, it's just a broken arm." "After everything you have been through, this is nothing."

I started to giggle.

That was the point of my whole meltdown! Here we were, once again, standing in a hospital talking about pain medication. Through my tears, I started laughing.

I must have looked like a madwoman. I am sure they were talking at the nurses' station "we got a ringer in room 10." The mom melting down, the Dad and Grandmother pacing the hall, kid throwing a tantrum in the room and the Pop trying to entertain the kid. Whoohoo, another lovely night in the ER.

I suddenly had a moment of clarity. I had been telling myself for the last four years, these are choices, we have to accept the circumstances we cannot change, and just push through.

I stood there, taking a few deep breaths, trying to pull myself together. I could feel the laughter welling up in me. I started giggling again and couldn't stop. Even though the tears continued to flow, they were now contradicted by uncontrollable laughter.

I was so happy it was just a broken arm, and in a few hours we would be home. I started thanking God and laughing, I was feeling liberated.

Once I pulled my crazy self together, the nurse was still standing there holding the small medicine cup of Jake's Tylenol with codeine. She was just staring at me like, lady what do you want to do?

I looked at Brett and said, "OK let's do it." Brett was said, "What?" but he knew I was pulling myself back together. He smiled and said "OK honey, let's get this done and take Jake home." Brett walked over and hugged me. I just melted in his arms. I felt safe, he was stable, and we were going to be OK.

When I "came to", we got back down to business. I went in the bathroom and cleaned my face to make myself presentable for Jake; I didn't want him to see my sadness.

I couldn't stop chuckling in the bathroom, that cry felt so damn good! I looked at myself in the mirror, mascara running, pink cheeks, and another pathetic pony tail. I was a mess I just couldn't stop giggling. I imagined the faces on the nurses and what they must have been thinking, it made me laugh even more.

After a few deep breaths, I went back to Jake's room. Brett had already begun to explain to Jake that we needed him to take the medicine. That it would make his arm feel better, so we could adjust it for the cast. By this time, Jake was so tired; he sat up and took the medicine with no arguments. Within about 20 minutes he was falling asleep (it was close to midnight!). Anyway, the orthopedic technician came in and without even waking Jake, moved his arm into the new position. When Jake woke up, they were putting his arm into a sling. The whole thing took about 15 minutes and Jake was calm as he could be.

I literally wanted to lay down on the cold tile floor and go to sleep. My adrenaline had been through the roof and back in a matter of hours. Now, I just wanted to sleep. Once again, I felt like I had swum the Nile and climbed Mt. Everest all in one day and I was exhausted!

The next morning, I opened my eyes; I lay there staring at the ceiling, trying to figure out whether the last 24 hours had really happened. For a few minutes, I thought, it was just a bad dream until Jake came scooching in the bedroom, leg off, sling on! It was not a dream.

I have to admit I was feeling a little invincible. I thought, bring it on, after my hospital meltdown I was ready for anything. That afternoon, we caught a flight to Michigan and spent Christmas with my family. We were welcomed with open arms and showered with love and encouragement through the holidays; our trip was amazing. Jake played in the snow, prosthetic leg, broken arm sling and all. He didn't miss a beat.

We flew home early to get a real cast from Dr. Birnbaum, then back to school. In true Jake form, it was a "dust yourself off and keep moving" moment.

Merry Christmas and many blessings during the holidays, if you are having a bad day, pick yourself up and keep moving. Just follow Jake Bainter's lead. That's what I do! Much Love, Jodi

CHAPTER 53

Back to school – a run leg at last

Fall 2009

The fall of 2009, Jake started 3rd grade and things started to come together. We had gone through a full year without any surgeries, physical therapy, or extra medical care (minus the broken arm at Christmas). Dare I say our life was returning to normal?

Probably Jake's greatest challenge was catching up academically. He worked hard with both classroom work and a tutor over the summer and after school. We were so happy to see him spending his days worrying about normal nine-year-old stuff.

We were experiencing things with Jake that were a first for us, milestones that other kids had already met. I will never forget when he finished his first chapter book. He had worked so hard to catch up on his reading, and he was incredibly frustrated along the way. It wasn't really his fault that he had fallen behind, but he was aware that the other kids were ahead of him and it bothered him. He had already been through so much, but sometimes, as we all know, there is no rest or breaks for the weary.

This was just another task that only Jake could solve. He started his Accelerated Reader program that fall and was reading books on the second-grade level. He said it was embarrassing when he would have to go to the section of books at his reading level. Thankfully, the kids were kind, and his teachers, Mrs. Heather Gaskin and Mrs. Danita Parker, were amazing. They always encouraged him and their patience and commitment to helping him catch up was beyond words.

When Jake finished his first chapter book, he was over the moon. I picked him up from school and he jumped in the backseat and said, "Mom, you are never going to believe this, I finished my first chapter book today, all ten chapters!" He was absolutely beaming. I was so happy for him. I sent Mrs. Gaskin a note and reminded her that the work she and Mrs. Parker were doing, was truly impacting lives. Had Mrs. Gaskin not taken the time to help Jake find books according to his ability and had she not encouraged him through the process, he may still be standing in the library feeling overwhelmed. Thank you Mrs. Gaskin!

In regard to Jake's reading, it is not as if I thought the day would never come; I just knew it would only happen with Jake's hard work and some really special teachers. Life moves quickly, and another lesson I have learned is to stop and just relish those "firsts".

It took Jake all of 2nd and 3rd grade for Jake to catch up. The distraction of pain and continuous medication over the years had taken its toll on his ability to learn and more importantly focus. The impact was great and the catch up was even greater! We were thrilled when he completed his academic testing at the end of his 4th grade year and we learned he had not only caught up but was achieving scores in certain subjects well beyond his 4th grade level. Once again, our pride was overflowing. After everything he had been dealt, he would not give up, Jake is a fighter!

During this timeframe he was also getting back into the groove of socialization with his friends. He spent the entire summer of 2009, with a close friend Alex Page, who allowed Jake the space to take things at his own pace. It was a summer of growing and healing, and Alex was such a sweet friend and gave Jake the space he needed. They swam and fished and explored all summer long, just as two little boys would do, the only difference being that one had a rubber foot. And, we were quickly learning all the things Jake could do with a prosthetic foot.

First, every time Jake jumped in the lake, when he returned to the dock, he would simply stand on one leg and raise his prosthetic leg straight in the air and pour the water out of his foot shell.

Also, if Jake was around and there was a bothersome bee or wasp, we would all be running around looking for a fly swatter and Jake would just step on it with his prosthetic foot.

There was really nothing that Jake could not do. While being an amputee is not always convenient and it certainly requires additional endurance, it was good. Jake needed mobility and to be pain-free, and that is exactly what his prosthesis provided.

The sun was shining on us for sure, and we were soaking it all up.

Following the ACA conference, we started to get involved with an organization called Challenged Athletes Foundation (CAF), a nonprofit that raises money to help disabled athletes participate in sports and activities. We had gotten involved in the organization in the summer of 2008 after meeting the director at the amputee coalition conference.

Subsequently, we became more involved throughout the year and still are today. Jake began to participate in some of the kid runs here in Florida, and we started to volunteer for CAF at local events.

In October of 2009, the CAF team invited us to attend the San Diego Triathletes Challenge. This is a weekend of fundraising for the organization in which able-bodied athletes and disabled athletes all compete in a triathlon. CAF also told us they would like to sponsor our family to attend and would like to present Jake with his first run leg, the kind of prosthetic where the foot looks like a giant hook.

So, humbly, that fall, we flew to San Diego and on Sunday, the last day of the event, Jake was presented with his first-ever brand-new run leg. The components of the leg had arrived in Orlando the week before. We had been back and forth to Stan's, and he crafted and assembled the leg. Stan donated the socket and his time to make the leg; CAF and Össur (a prosthetic manufacturer) donated the mechanical knee and Flex-Foot. Stan once again created a leg that fit Jake perfectly.

CAF had also flown Boston Bill to the event, so on Sunday in a very emotional presentation, CAF and Boston Bill presented Jake with the run leg. The setting, the presentation, and the expression on Jake's face were all priceless. Stan and crew had also flown out for the event that year as well. It was incredibly emotional and a beautiful occasion.

I remember standing there thinking about all the people who had stepped in to give this little boy a chance to be normal. They had rallied around us, and just made sure that he had every convenience that he would have had with his God-given leg.

Jake had talked about running for years, he just wanted to run. He laughed as we called him Forrest Gump and said, "Run, Jake, run," and that is exactly what he did. He started running and bouncing around that weekend and has been ever since. Thank you God, for science, titanium, and the brilliance of everyone involved who designs and crafts such amazing equipment for the world of amputees.

I still chuckle today, when I drop Jake off at school and out he jumps with his run leg sticking out the top of his backpack. He takes his leg to school for PE and recess. There is no stopping him. My, how far we have come.

A final milestone for Jake that year was PE. At the end of the year, Coach Jason Shave presented Jake with an award for best participation in PE. He said that he could always count on Jake to show up with the right attitude and always be 100 percent in the game no matter the task. I loved the irony of this award. It made me smile. I know firsthand, that time does heal, and that so much of life is about attitude.

I have learned, things can change quickly, and you don't want to wake up and realize you missed them. This is what life is all about— finishing a first chapter book, learning to run, making new friends— playing a great game of dodge ball in PE! It is those small moments that really add the texture and beauty to our lives. Don't forget to take the time, to stop and appreciate them. You just never know what tomorrow will bring.

When I hear Jake whistling in the morning before school, I cannot help but smile, because I know; this is one of those small moments. I am aware and I am grateful.

CHAPTER 54

You must just smile

February 2010

As Jake regained his strength and health, his physical growth began to sort of define our lives. In any given week, day, or month, we can inevitably spend some time at Stan's for anything from a broken prosthetic knee or foot or just a new socket to accommodate growth. Swinging in for an adjustment had become part of our daily lives.

In February of 2010, it was time for another fitting, so we were spending the day at Stan's. A new socket fitting can be a multiday event. We had been there all day, and Jake was getting cabin fever. We decided to make a run to the nearby convenience store for a soda and a snack. I had gotten used to Jake having his leg on or off, so I didn't realize that when we left Stan's he was hopping to the car without his leg.

As we drove to the store I told Jake that I had to get on a conference call for work in a few minutes, so when we got to the store I would have him run in, buy his snack, and come back to the car. He was fine with the plan.

I pulled into the lot and parked in the handicapped space right in front of the store. I put the car in park and dialed into my call. Jake followed the plan and jumped out of the backseat and headed into the store. I glanced up and watched him go through the door and listened for my call to begin.

You can imagine my shock when I looked up to see his little head popping up and down inside the store. It took a minute to register that Jake was not wearing his leg and he was hopping through the store on one foot with fountain drinks in both hands and snacks tucked under his arm. My jaw hit the floor. I instinctually hung up the phone—thankfully I was not leading the call—jumped out of the car, and went to his rescue. When I got inside, there was a lady already helping him who was probably thinking, "What kind of mom are you, sending your kid with one leg in to buy your fountain Diet Coke, while you sit on the phone in the car?" I was absolutely mortified. I said, "Jake, honey, I didn't know you didn't have your leg on." To which he said, "Hey, Mom, do you care if I get a Slurpee?" he shrugged his shoulders and went on about his business. I said, "Buddy, it's hard to hop and shop in a store." He once again, shrugged his shoulders as if to say, "Whatever mom." We collected the goods, finished checking out, and got back in the car, him hopping all the while, of course.

As I was driving back, I looked at Jake in the rearview mirror as he was opening his bag of Chex Mix, sipping on his Slurpee, looking out the window completely unfazed. I was thinking how far we had come and how grateful I was for this child to have adjusted so well to his new situation. It was a truly a gift to know that he was completely unaffected to go into a convenience store with only one leg, hop around, and not even realize this may be a bit strange!

I felt a hint of joy well up thinking how far we had come. Life is a moving target, and we are empowered to own the outcome.

We pulled back into Stan's and out hopped Jake, Slurpee in hand, Chex Mix tucked under his arm, a smile on his face. Every day is a learning experience, and on this day in February, was no exception.

I sat there in the driver's seat and watched him hop inside the building. I just settled into the moment. I thought, things as a mom you would never expect to say, "Jake, is your leg on?" Well, now I know, and in the future I will ask.

CHAPTER 55

The long walk back

I consider those weeks, months and even years following Jake's amputation the long walk back. Even considering everything we had already been through, those days proved to be some of our toughest trials.

A friend and cancer survivor told me the hardest part of her healing was returning to the world after years of doctors, counseling, and care. Picking up where you left off is liberating, yet a bit overwhelming. There doesn't seem to be any orientation or warming up period, suddenly one day you wake up, and you're back. But you're different, and while some of the differences are clear and visible, others lie just below the surface swirling in your heart, your mind, your being.

Time is a wonderful thing, because I knew February, March, April, and May of 2008 (post amputation) would someday be just a memory. Over time, I knew we would forget the tears, the sleepless nights and the phantom pain and begin to only remember what pushed us to make the decision to proceed with the amputation.

I know, so many of you reading our story and can relate to what I am talking about. Living in crisis was incredibly complicated and a never ending juggling act. Then, even when the crisis subsides, the transition back into mainstream living is an unexpected hardship, and it was especially difficult for Jake.

Between February 18, 2008 (the day of his amputation) and when I finished writing this book in the spring of 2011, Jake managed to break his arm twice, his good foot once, sprain his wrist and break his front tooth in half. With each injury came disappointment and frustration. We were learning that living as an amputee came with its own set of challenges and life for him continued to be an adjustment. Finding his balance literally, was another piece of the puzzle.

Jake never returned to the classroom full time to finish his first-grade school year following the amputation. But, he did visit enough to begin the immersion process back into normal living. Throughout this time, the milestones were profound and most times left me in tears.

When he first returned to school I would push him in a wheel-chair and then sit in the hall outside his classroom. He begged me not to leave, just in case he needed something. So there I would sit, in the hall, patiently waiting for our sweet boy to get through the day. The loving parents, teachers and faculty of PCCA would pass me in the hall; they would give me an encouraging glance, and sometimes sit down next to me. But no one ever questioned my actions, they understood, and there I sat.

Eventually, he went from using his wheelchair to walking and I went from sitting in the hall to just walking him to his classroom door. Frequently, I would suggest dropping him off at the entrance of the school, and he could walk to class himself. For weeks he was adamantly against the idea. But one day, in early May, I pulled in front of the school, parked, and walked him to the front door. He looked at me and bravely said, "Mom, I can walk from here." So, there I stood at the entrance of the school watching as he walked down the hall, one perfect God-made leg and the other shining in all its titanium glory, beautifully and wonderfully made.

I know that walking to class is common practice for a second grader, but for a little boy who was regaining his independence and courage—this was huge. I was so proud of him, I kept shouting (in a whisper, so as not to embarrass him), I love you Jake Bainter, you make me so proud! At the door he just turned, giving me the shy smile, like "OK, Mom, I got it," you can go home now.

I jumped in my car, with tears pouring down my cheeks. We were turning a corner. I couldn't help but feel tickled; I thought to myself "we can totally do this."

Thankfully, the long walk back was a journey we did not have to make alone. The entire time we were surrounded by "our people," Mrs. Baucom, Mrs. Goodman and Mrs. Gaskin (Jake's first, second and third-grade teachers) who gently nudged him along helping him regain his academic confidence and embrace learning. The whole PCCA community (families, students, and faculty), Stan and all of POA, Our Ducks Unlimited and Walt Disney Company "families", Dr. Novick, Dr. Beck, Dr. Letson, Dr. Coffman, Miss Kelly, our parents (our sweet and unconditional parents), our siblings (Todd, Sandy, Matt, Steph, Corey and Tammy) Boston Bill, our amazing friends and even people we didn't know, were right beside us, cheering us on.

I honestly have never met such a selfless and compassionate group of professionals as the team at POA. Every time we walked through the front door, Stan and his team made us feel like Jake was their only patient. The line between business and humanity does not get blurred for this group. Insurance coverage and financial gain doesn't matter; the only priority they have is making people walk, equipping amputees like Jake with the best and most functional prosthesis available.

And finally, we could have never made this journey without the talents of the amazing Dr. Novick, who had the courage to give Jake his newfound freedom. For this, she will always hold a very special place in our hearts.

The years of 2004-2011 were a very difficult time for us. I would be lying if I didn't say I still spend some days reflecting, wondering why this happened to my family. Even wishing we could "redo" those seven years of Jake's childhood. Take away all the pain and hurt. But, mostly, I find my moments of reflection to be those of gratitude. I prayed many nights for peace, whatever the future held I just wanted peace for all of us. When we finally found a way to manage the pain and were done with medicine, doctors, walkers, casts, therapy, and all the craziness our lives had become, Jake really did find freedom. And through that we have found a beautiful peacefulness I wasn't sure was possible.

And, as for Brett and me, I also knew the healing would come, and as Jake improved so did we.

Our hearts will never forget—Brett and I do not have the benefit of youth, the scars of those seven years are imprinted in our minds forever. Yet despite it all, Brett did not allow the guilt to destroy him or our family. Instead, he gave us this amazing gift to see what the future will hold for Jake, our marriage and our family. I believe this: when you reach a crossroad in life, you have a choice. You can choose to be sad and wallow, or you can choose to persevere.

Addendum

What I Know

On April 9, 2004, our lives forever changed how we see the world and probably how the world sees us. Over the course of the next seven years, our faith was tried in a way we never imagined. I decided to share our story because it affected us and those around us in such a powerful way, that to leave the words unsaid, felt as if our story was unfinished.

I am an avid reader, and throughout our experience, so many other writers opened their lives to me. On the days when I felt so alone, I would read. I would plunge myself into someone else's world and learn of that person's suffering and trials. It was so therapeutic to connect through someone else's experiences, and through the words I would find guidance and validation. This connection helped keep my mind sane.

This story was our chance to return the favor. Here is a little bit of what I have learned.

Medicine

My insight on medication is that it can be controversial; but often necessary. All treatments should be in moderation and properly managed. When medicine is necessary, if you are the caregiver or family member, please remember that side effects are real, so behaviors such as irritability, personality change, appetite loss—all real. Medicine is a powerful tool, and the implications can be great. If you are in a situation where someone is taking medication, make sure you understand the side effects and keep your patience and proper perspective on their behavior. I just encourage you as parents, friends, caregivers to think before you act, be compassionate, be empathetic, and gently guide.

Find "your people"

I encourage you to seek, find, and share. Query your doctors, hospitals, and caregivers to find resources for support. I promise there is someone out there experiencing a similar walk. The size or type of the crisis does not matter—divorce, an ill parent or family member, a house in foreclosure—it is all relative to your own life experiences. A crisis is a crisis, and in those times we all need encouragement and support. In today's world, you don't even need to leave your house! Use the Internet or an online support group. I just encourage you to look, when you find "your people," you won't believe the gifts you can uncover. They just may be the pillar you need to help you get through the day. The trick is you have to be open; you have to search and then be willing to go on the journey.

Be organized

Keep proper phone logs of conversations, track the name of who you spoke to, company and date. This comes in handy when disputing an insurance bill or just making follow-up calls to doctors. Keep all key phone numbers in one organized location. If you have something at home that needs to be addressed, you do not need to be scrambling at work trying to find e-mail and phone numbers. It is so important to be efficient in your use of time. So keep key phone numbers and e-mail addresses close.

Accept help

If I wrote a book of all the gracious gifts we were given over the last seven years, the pages would be infinite. I have learned that individuals help because they want to. At first, I would say, no, that's not necessary. But I needed the help, so why I was saying no? Often, people feel helpless watching others struggle, so their gesture to help is really as important to them as it is to you.

In the first days and weeks after Jake received his prosthesis; Mark Martin our neighbor sensed Jake's initial frustration with learning to walk again. Mark stopped by one morning and told Jake that he would pay him one dollar for every time he walked down to Mark's house, which was about four houses away. Jake was inspired. For the next couple weeks, Jake and Pop would walk down to Mark's every day, sometimes multiple times a day. In no time, Jake went from using a crutch to walking smoothly and comfortably on his new prosthesis. Many days Mark wasn't even home, but Jake would leave a note on the door saying; Hi Mr. Mark, I was here today! Over the course of a couple weeks I am sure Mark incurred a tab greater than he ever expected!

Years later, over dinner, Mark and I started talking about the kindness of his gesture. I thanked him for the beautiful gift he offered Jake, just when he needed an extra push. I will never forget; with tears in his eyes, Mark told me this gift was his. That being a part of watching Jake learning to walk again, filled his heart and he was so grateful to be a part of the process.

I share this story, because in this moment, I learned that the gift of giving is a special formula. The blessings are received by both those who give, and those who receive. My parting thoughts are; it is okay to accept the help; be grateful, and when your day comes pay it forward.

Prosthetics are expensive

Prosthetic components are incredibly expensive, and often insurance coverage is not adequate to provide the best possible option for individuals. Therefore in the spring of 2011, in collaboration with Stan Patterson and Stephanie Kingston (Stan's business manager), we started a 501c3 nonprofit organization, the A3 Foundation, Amputees Active Again. Our family has been incredibly blessed to have adequate insurance coverage and financial help through grants and other assistance. I believe everyone deserves this support. Certainly, there are existing nonprofits today supporting amputees; we just felt compelled to join the cause. Walking and running should not be a privilege. It should be a part of life for everyone.

Lawn mower safety is critical

Each year, children are severely injured by lawnmower accidents. The mowers are very dangerous and it can be difficult to see behind the machine or hear children around the mower. The safest approach, is to keep children inside while the lawn is being mowed. These accidents are preventable so please use caution and be smart when operating these types of machines.

We have the power to change lives

The need for organ and tissue donations is greater than the number of registered donors. Knowledge is the first step to action. You have the power to make a difference, just like a donor made a difference in Jake's life. Please, don't let the opportunity pass. Learn more today by visiting www.donatelife.net.

Remember it is a marathon, not a sprint

Whenever you are walking through a crisis or a challenging time, keep yourself grounded in knowing the journey is a marathon, not a sprint. When you sprint, you may miss the most important steps and details along the way. Slow and steady is my advice.

Be strong in faith

Some people have asked me, do you wonder where was God that day? My answer is this:

He was cradling Brett as he wept in the front yard, covered in grass and blood

He was riding in the ambulance with Jake so he was not alone

He was by my side night after night as I wondered how I could face another day

He was guiding the surgeon's hands

Whispering in the ears and hearts of those around us to send us encouragement with timing only God can orchestrate

He carried Brett month after month when the days were too dark to get out of bed

He continued to stir in my heart, leading me to seek answers

Sheltering us each month when bills were due, providing when we wondered how we would pay

He put Boston Bill on his bike on the morning of February 19th

And, he rejoiced with us as we watched Jake walk again on his new leg

He helped guide my fingers as I typed this book

Life can change instantly, so no, I don't wonder where he was that day. What I wonder is how we would have survived without him.

Resources

A3 Foundation, Amputees Active Again – www.a3foundation.org
Amputee Coalition of America – www.amputee-coalition.org
Boston Bill Foundation – www.bostonbill.org
Challenged Athletes Foundation – www.challengedathletes.org
Discovery Church, Orlando – www.discoverychurch.org
Donate Life America – www.donatelife.net
Nathaniel's Hope – www.nathanielshope.org
Prosthetic and Orthotic Associates – www.poacfl.com
Ronald McDonald House – www.rmhc.org
TransLife (Of Central Florida) – www.translife.org

CPSIA information can be obtained at www.ICGtesting.com
Printed in the USA
BVOW031603131212

308158BV00004B/271/P